Moorish Circle 7

The Rise of the Islamic Faith Among Blacks in America and it's masonic origins

by
Keith Moore 32º

authorHOUSE™

1663 LIBERTY DRIVE, SUITE 200
BLOOMINGTON, INDIANA 47403
(800) 839-8640
WWW.AUTHORHOUSE.COM

First published by AuthorHouse 04/25/05

ISBN: 1-4208-3671-4 (sc)

Printed in the United States of America
Bloomington, Indiana

This book is printed on acid-free paper.

This book is dedicated to all the members of the Moorish Divine Movement of North America. This book serves only as a guide through the workings of the movement from its beginnings to its current status in America.

May the will of God be placed in my heart as I write this book for the love and the study of this science. To the Prophet Noble Drew Ali for his wisdom and courage in trying to uplift a fallen nation and teaching us to live by love, truth, peace, freedom and justice.

Never before have I witnessed time wasted at the hands of those minds that continue to not utilize its full potential. A man's mind and his thoughts possess the ability to draw from the cosmos of pure thought and yet man has settled for the feeble boundaries that other men have bestowed upon him. This is mental bondage at its fullest and this mental bondage can only be manifested for the change of better, which in turn can be shaped to perfection.

As I write the various topics of this research book I can only find within my heart a sense of enlightenment and a new way to tap into my inner consciousness. For man there is hope, and this hope is further manifested into human physical flesh, and these extraordinary individuals are somehow called to perform the tasks that God has bestowed upon them. People such as the Moorish Prophet, Noble Drew Ali, are often shunned; they are afraid because, like the prophets of old, he is ridiculed when he speaks the word of God. To the listening ear it is a wake up call to salvation. This book entitled, Moorish Circle 7, serves only as a tool to better understand the various dogmas of the Moorish Science Temple. However, all this has a much deeper meaning and understanding; for a man such as Noble Drew Ali has a primary mission of restoring a sense of knowledge to the black man in America. This would allow him to elevate from his or her current status to a more advanced character. All this in the name of Allah. Keith Moore

Table of Contents

Preface

Among people of African descent, Islam is a well established system of culture and religious understanding and one of the worlds fastest growing religions. In the past decade, we have seen a definite increase in Islam conversion and in doing so many have begun referring to themselves as Asiatic people or descendants of the Asiatic race. Defining who an Asiatic person is brings to mind current Asiatics such as the Arabs, Indians, and all people of Mongoloid decent.

The prophet Noble Drew Ali acknowledges the presence of African origins in their blood stream, and yet Asiatics come in all shades of color and all sizes. The first Asiatics were people of dark pigmentation and this was proven in the history books. Now what comes into play are the theories and religious doctrines of Noble Drew Ali. Ali defines the Moorish Divine Movement as the uniting of Asia, and perhaps this is a way for Ali to unite African Americans in a relentless and undying struggle for equality. Ali rejected the doctrines of Christianity because it was forced upon the African slaves. However, those African Americans who would embrace the religion of Islam did so to rid themselves of the Christian Doctrines that were used to enslave their minds and alter their way of thinking. Perhaps this is what Noble Drew Ali thought of when he was preparing the religious doctrine of the Moorish Science Temple of America. Even in his writing he states that, "we as a clean and pure nation descended from the inhabitants of Africa do not desire to amalgamate or marry into families of the pale skin nations of Europe. Neither, serve the Gods of their religion because our forefathers are the true and divine founders of the first religious creed for the redemption and salvation of mankind on earth Therefore, we are returning the church and Christianity back to the European nations as it was prepared by their forefathers for their earthly

ix

salvation while we, the Moorish Americans (black people) are returning to Islam, which was founded by our forefathers. for our earthly and divine salvation.

In a true sense, neither Christianity nor Islam is the true religion of Africans. However, both religions can trace its origins to those of African religions. But why would Ali choose being an Asiatic instead of someone else of African origin? Perhaps the original Asiatic was an African who in ancient times left the continent of africa and settled in areas throughout Asia. Then, we find a mixing of races. The Hindus of India are a mixture of two distinct races; the Dravidians, a descendant of the nubians of Africa and the Aryans.

I must point out that not all people of negroid descent will have the same features with the exception of skin color. Dr. Cheikh Anta Diop, states that, "There are two well defined black races; one has a black skin and wooly hair while the other has black skin (often exceptionally black), straight hair, aquiline nose, thin lips, and an acute cheekbone angle." We find a prototype of this race in India called the Dravidians. It is also known that certain nubians likewise belong to the same negro type. Thus, it is inexact and anti-scientific to do anthropological research, encounter a Dravidian type, and then conclude that the negro type is absent. This is a prime example of African presence in Asia.

It is said that around 2500 b.c. a group of pale skin nomads, the Aryans, invaded India and disrupted the well established black civilization. The inter mating of the two groups produced the modern day people of India. This one invasion sprung forth the people of Asia.

On the Moorish American nationality and identification card, Drew Ali speaks of honoring all the divine prophets, Jesus, Muhammad, Buddha, and Confucius. All of these figures were Asiatic with the exception of Jesus. Though Ali's teachings may speak otherwise. Moorish Science not only serves as a religious doctrine but it serves as a tool to awake the mind from a dead conscious--a lack of understanding placed on the Moorish Divine Movement, which aims to uplift humanity or the humanity of all Asiatics and designed to educate black people of their origins. How often have we heard of non-asiatic historians speak of the so called black race as having no history or no point of origin. But, we are learning that their history is in fact the history of the continent of Africa. Africa is the birth place of all races and within Africa every man has an origin or point of existence. Dr. Yosef ben Jochanan and Dr, Diop writings tell of the birth of Asiatics from Africans. It is apparent that Drew Ali's main mission as a leader is to establish a spiritual reality for American Asiatics. This was the original design of the Moorish Divine Movement and it is still carried out by the various sects and branches of the movement.

In the beginning, I used to drive by the various temples and see the Moorish Americans standing outside wearing their fezes. I decided to sit in on one of their study sessions, and to my amazement, their teachings reflected various other fields of study. I was enlightened by the presentation and decided to further research these doctrines, and then eventually, to write this book.

The Moorish American Moslem reads from the Holy Koran Circle 7 whereas the Orthodox Muslim reads the Holy Quran, which is read by devout Muslims worldwide. There are similarities; all Muslims including Moorish Americans conduct religious services on Friday at 8:00 p.m. The Moorish Doctrine speaks of holding services on Friday because that was the day on which man was formed in flesh, and it was on a Friday when he departed out of flesh thus returning to the earth from where he came. I have studied countless religious doctrines, many of them concerning Islam.

Islam is a religion of peace and harmony but if we were to examine the world view, it appears that not everyone agrees with this. The current rash of terrorist attacks and suicide bombings have given Islam a bad reputation for violence worldwide. However, what religion is not burdened by a past of chaos and anarchy? It is not the religion that creates the violence, it is the people who use religion as a tool to promote their own personal greed and personal gain. The media portrays Islam as militant and extreme throughout the world, but Islam in America is portrayed as being racist and promoting segregation. This was the idea in the early twentieth century when blacks were struggling for equal rights. Some of their groups became militant but that was a result of violent acts against them by racist whites.

Islam is one of the fastest growing religions in the world numbering more than 1 billion people, or approximately a fifth of the worlds population. In the United States alone there are approximately 3 million Muslims and this number has increased dramatically in the last half century through immigration, procreation and conversion. A third of the Muslim community in the United States consists of African Americans who converted to Islam during the 20th century. Noble Drew Ali was one of the earlier converts to Islam and his focus was on uniting people of African descent. One of the basic beliefs of the Moorish American Doctrine is establishing a nationality which gives them a name of origin and a home land. The concept of identity is important in the Moorish beliefs because it establishes the right of all Moors to enjoy the spoils of America.

Unlike the nation of Islam which promotes racism and the separation of races, the Moorish Divine Movement does not promote militant acts of racism. The Moorish Science Temple of American acknowledges America and all its laws; it teaches men to live in unity with other races but to remain separate in keeping to his own. The aims of the Moorish Science Temple were to promote self-understanding among blacks as well as self-identity. Its writings and doctrines establish the values that were lost in the times of trouble. Our minds were stripped of the knowledge of self and yet deep within our most intimate thoughts there exists a sense of enlightenment and belonging. This is the point the prophet Noble Drew Ali expresses in his writings. As human beings we tend to ignore this calling by being programmed to accept what is given to us by someone else other than our own.

Personally, I remember my first exposure to Moorish Science and it served as a reality check for my mind and my soul. Throughout my life, I have felt a yearning for something else other than what was bestowed upon me. I struggled because I did not allow my mind to explore and one day I reached a boiling point. It was a hot summer night in 1992 and I was invited to my first Moorish Science meeting. It opened with a Moorish American prayer and then a lecture. As this man spoke, I became fascinated with the knowledge entering my brain and I craved more. It became my personal drug to learn all that is learnable. After the lecture, I was offered a membership and became a part of the Divine Movement. They gave me the Holy Koran Circle 7 and I spent my time reading its scriptures, which were filled with the teachings of an age old wisdom that was long forgotten. Since that day, I continued an endless search into the Divine Movement. The Moorish Science Temple of America is designed to bestow upon its members a sense of identity. In this day and age we are referred to as African Americans. In the past, they referred to us as colored, negro, black and nigger--all negative and offensive terms. If we were to reflect on the literature of the Moorish Science Temple there is one section that addresses the issue of name calling among people of African descent. Within the literature there is a section called, "What shall we call him" and it states: So often various journalists find trouble in selecting the proper name for Moorish Americans; some say negro, still another will brand him race man, still another will call him African American, and then came colored, Dark American, coon, shine, the brethren, and your folks. It is indeed a hard matter to find something suitable for the various occasions where a title is needed. Is it that these people have no proper name? Did they have a national name when they were first brought to these shores in the 17th century? If so, what was it? Did the land from where they came from have a name? It appears a good idea for those whose duty it is to write for the various journals to find out what the national name of the forefathers of these people was. Look into the history of the founders of civilization and see who they were and where they stood in the building of the present civilization. A few hours in an up-to-date library would serve to relieve the strain on our men of letters. When the occasion presented itself they gave a title to these 22 million people. With all colors of every race of the globe this name was an act of european psychology. They gave him a name and defined it as something inferior to white, a color of purity. They chose black, a color they say represents evil.

The negro, as they were called in this nation, have no nation to which they might upon with pride. Their history starts with the close of the civil war or more precisely, with being forced to sere someone else. Thus he is separated from the illustrious history of his forefathers who were founders of the first civilization of the old world. This matter should be looked into the hope of correcting it. To accept the theory that people of African descent have no known history is to accept the theory that there is no known history in the world what so ever. Sadly, a loss of identity can invoke a variety of mental, physical and social problems. All this can be a result of what is referred to as Eurocentric hegemony. African historian, Carter G. Woodsen was quoted as saying, "It took me to twenty years to learn the eurocentric way of education. However, it also took an additional twenty years to undo the damage that it had caused.

Numerous centuries of oppression, slavery and mind altering techniques have stopped African Americans from changing for the better. Much of African America's experiences have been self-deteriorating, a result of having endured the worst element of eurocentric hegemony. Historically, many European Americans questioned the very humanity of Africans in the interest of material gain and control, thus creating an entire socio-political structure designed to enforce and perpetuate the dehumanization of African people. An example of this is the draining and pillaging of Africa and all of her resources and the slave trade triangle of North America, Europe and Africa. All that I have mentioned thus far are major issues concerning African Americans within our sheltered communities. We face these issues head on while not understanding who we are as a people or as a race. But as Noble Drew Ali writes, "This is a new day and in this new day change must come for all asiatics to return to that old time religion." Noble Drew Ali had a vision for change and that vision effectively recognizes him as a prophet of Allah. Unlike other major religions, Moorish Science gives it members a more universal approach. One unknown author writes, "The Moorish faith is unitarian in nature in both the more commonly used western sense and the less commonly used and understood west asian sense. The west asian sense believes that Allah is anything and everything. Human beings, of course, share in this as we are emanations of Allah, not simply objects of Allah's. This is "our legacy and our responsibility." Moorish belief is also essentially unitarian in the modern western sense of the term. The Holy Koran of the Moorish Science Temple of America states that all faiths are valid and that they are the numerous facets of the same Father-God Allah.

All people worship Allah, the one; but all the people see him not Alike
- Circle 7 Koran, X:13

A man's ideal is God and so as man unfolds his God unfolds. Man's God today, tomorrow is not his God. The nations of the earth see Allah from different points of view and so he does not seem the same to everyone.
- Circle 7 Koran, X:16, 17

The primary purpose of the Moorish Science Temple of America is to restore that which was lost; both a nationality and an identity. Never again should any man of color question who he is an an individual. His history and his religious beliefs will never again be questioned as long as he himself possesses a lucrative knowledge of self and the environment. For the Moorish American we learn by instruction from the holy prophet when he speaks in character saying, "Know yourself and your father God-Allah that you may learn to love instead of hate. Every man needs to worship under his own vine and fig tree." Just the mere utterance of these words would shake the very life of a people who have no idea of the power of pure thought.

Dr. Jose Pimienta Bey writes in his book, Othello's Children, he states, "very few organizations in the history of the United States have sought to give African peoples in the Americas a historical reason to love and embrace their Africanism. This would be especially true if one refers to popular grass roots organizations. Few groups emphasized the need for so called blacks to look back at their pre U.S. origins in order to better understand their true selves and to ameliorate their oppressed condition. Historically, the tendency among U.S. blacks has been to retreat into Christianity and theologically Eurocentric Christian churches. This is most ironic, given the fact that for centuries American churches, more often than not, validated the oppressive conditions from which blacks sought refuge." Even during times of slavery, the slaves often worshipped separate from their masters in different environments and Christianity was given to the slaves in a watered down form. It was so watered down in fact that it did not include salvation because with salvation slaves would the have realized that what they were experiencing was wrong. However, like all races that have been conquered by an opposing race, new religions are forced upon them and they abandon their original identity.

If I were to focus upon the mind of the oppressed I would find hope and that hope would allow the mind to gain that which was lost. It is the pure awareness of self that wakes an individual from a dead consciousness. Nothing will last forever and every situation that we may face in life must change for the better. Prophet Noble Drew Ali understood this. After being divinely prepared both mentally and spiritually the prophet broke ground and began walking upon an endless path to salvation. At the same time he shed light on everything that is dark and began his movement in 1913 A.D. calling all asiatics to unite and reclaim their identity. The prophet says, "Know your self and your father God-Allah that you may learn to love instead of hate." That we may steadfast as a wall of bass and hold firm in the defense of everlasting gospel! Teaching us to be ourselves with the divine instructions as our meal and the divine constitution as our bread, the prophet has instilled in all of us a sense of pride. He has fed us spiritually, raising our higher selves and teaching us to be upright Moorish Americans.

Introduction

Time is the one source that can never depreciate. It is so valuable and so infinite that we may never run short of its endless trials. Our time is our life, and life is like the study of Geometry--each line connecting to a point of destination, and yet, like all things it has a beginning; a point of origin. The old saying that "time changes all things" is so true that there can be no argument. It is exemplified in so many different ways as to require no comment. Yet, when we hear the phrase used frequently and thoughtlessly, it is natural to wonder if the individual who uses it realizes what he is saying, or rather, if he understands what those few simple words mean.

I cannot describe the heartless situation that time has effected upon the people of African race or for the black man in America. Time has caused many centuries of pain and suffering, and yet time will be used to heal and allow us to experience true salvation. We must acknowledge the true reality within our inner selves to invoke that spiritual part of us that allows us to become enlightened of our current situation and make the necessary changes to both our lives and our environment. Nevertheless, the black man in America has endured the most harsh treatment of human nature and yet we continue to exist. Just as Moses inflicted the 10 plagues upon the Egyptians the reversal has taken the same effect upon black Americans by way of drugs, poverty, unstructured families, illiteracy and loss of identity. Such plagues can be reversed if we were to wake up and acknowledge who we once were and the potential of what we can become. This potential can only be harnessed by way of exploring within ourselves. That unlimited abundance of energy that is stored within us.

Within the African community, there is an undying quest for self-empowerment, and this self-empowerment can take on many different manifestations. The most commonly known form is religion and all of its doctrines. By religion we are bound by our faith and perhaps this can be displayed by looking at other faiths like Christianity, Judaism, and most importantly, Islam. There are many sects in Islam, and this book deals with only Moorish American Islam, but I would like to focus on one particular group, The Druze. The Druze are a small religious group that live on or near the banks of Lebanon near Jerusalem. Little is known of their beliefs but I admire them for their close knit community and their religious solitude. The Druze tend to disregard the mainstream portion of Islam and settle for one that is less political and less extreme in terms of religious practices. I must mention that the Druze's religion is a mixture of Christianity, Judaism, and Islam. The point I am trying to make is that they accept various doctrines into their beliefs. There is no disrespect of religion or race and yet they pay homage to the three great religions of the world by incorporating them into their society. Moorish Science operates the same way with the exception of one thing; they honor the prophets by acknowledging their accomplishments. Ninety years after it emerged in New Jersey, the Moorish Science Temple of America has continued to receive criticism in terms of establishing itself as a legitimate branch of Islam. However, this issue is not limited to Moorish Science. Over the years the world view of Islam does not recognize the American born institutions of Islam. Perhaps now that the we are living in the 21st century, there have been some changes for the better by establishing relationships and friendships with the Islamic world community. Such relationships cause a mixture of emotions for the non-islamic community. Moorish Science does not resemble mainstream scriptural Islam or the beliefs and practices of Muslims. Unlike mainstream Islam, Moorish Science offers a mixture of a variety of doctrines ranging from Rosicrusianism, Judaism, Freemasonry, Christianity, as well as Islam, which gives it its final ingredient. Perhaps Moorish Science can be defined as more oriental than Islamic. Nevertheless, if you believe in a God and define him as Allah, and if you honor Muhammad as a divine prophet then those are two major essentials that qualifies you as a Muslim.

Islam in America is not to be confused with the world view. In America it is rapidly growing especially among African Americans. The next question is why are African Americans leaving the church in order to embrace the religion of Islam? Perhaps this is an issue that can traced back to slavery, because slavery deteriorated the mind and the spirit. Dr. Yvonne Y. Haddad writes in her article, A Century of Islam in America, "The muslim discovery of America is a little explored topic. Some believe that it predated the Columbus expedition.

Records note the arrival as early as 1717 of Arabic speaking slaves who did not eat pork and believed in Allah and Muhammad the Prophet. According to some estimates, as many as a fifth of all the slaves introduced into the Americas from Africa in the 18th and 19th centuries may have been muslims. Many of them went to South America, and those who went to the American colonies were by and large quickly converted to Christianity. Only a few vestiges of Islam, such as Qur'an, which was apparently written down from memory, remain from this period. So what has been observed from this historical statement is the converting of Islam to Christianity and now back to Islam. Perhaps this is what the prophet Noble Drew Ali had come to understand. The possibility that Africans who were muslims at the time they were taken from the western hemlsphere of Africa, captured as slaves and brought to America, were settled under the strong oppression of the slave masters. We cannot forget their trials and tribulations and this is what the prophet understood when he began calling all blacks in America, "Asiatics." However, they did not become Asiatics because of their country of origin, because Asia is not in Africa. However, Africa is in Asia and I will explain this in a later chapter. Blacks in America are not Asiatic by birth but are Asiatic by way of religion. Islam is an Asiatic religion with African Hebrew origins. Religion has a way of changing the destiny of people. Perhaps the prophets way of changing religion in America was to forsake our African origins and embrace that of an Asiatic origin. Or perhaps the prophet believed all life and all existence began in Asia instead of Africa. We may never have understood the prophets emphasis on the Asian continent except for the numerous references that he displays in the Holy Koran Circle 7.

Let us focus even deeper into the concept that we call religion. First of all, what is religion? Webster's Dictionary defines it as "man's relation to divinity, to reverence, worship obedience and submission to mandates and precepts of supernatural or superior beings. In its broadest sense, religion includes all forms of belief in the existence of superior beings exercising power over humans by volition, imposing rules of conduct with future rewards and punishments. A bond and virtue whose purpose is to worship God as the source of all being and principle of all things." Everything stressed in the preceding passage is emphasized in the Moorish Science Temple of America.

When prophet Noble Drew Ali came to us he laid an everlasting foundation that does not limit it to only Moorish Americans but to all people that he would describe as of Asiatic origin. With influences ranging from various religious doctrines you now have a foundation that creates a sense of motivation and enthusiasm among those who are exposed to his wisdom. Before the arrival of Islam, Christianity was the only means of salvation that black people had. Day in and day out people often prayed for salvation and yet for the black man in America it did not arrive until one individual decided to go against the norm. This man was the prophet Noble Drew Ali.

While he was not the only man to embrace the religion of Islam, it was from his seed of learning that sprung forth other leaders with an entirely new concept of beliefs. These beliefs turned into a movement for those individuals who decided to approach civil rights with a militant point of view. Elijah Muhammad, Malcolm X, Clarence 13 X and Duse Muhammad Ali were all either militant or Pan Africanist, whose main ideals were to attain the ultimate black awareness. It is amazing to see such acts enhanced with religion being the tool of origin or that spark which binds men together for a major cause. A cause which is enhanced by way of divine intervention. Holistically, we observed the numerous religions sects which are formed from just one idea and that idea has captured the hearts and souls of a people who yearn for a change.

I mentioned the converting of Christianity to Islam and the above mentioned individuals, with the exception of Duse Muhammad Ali, all were at one time affiliated with Christianity. Elijah Muhammad was a Baptist Minister and his father was a preacher. Malcolm X's father was a preacher, so Malcolm was born into a Christian background. Clarence 13 X was also born into a Christian family. However, these men rejected the total ideology of Christianity and embraced a religion that is similar in foundation but far different in philosophy. This passage is not meant to degrade or disrespect any of the teachings of Christianity, but we must study the history of the church and its doctrines.

The doctrines of Christianity linger on the word, salvation. Christian doctrines speak to the mind of a soul about accepting Jesus Christ as your Lord and personal savior. Now focus more in depth on how this message is given to someone with no knowledge of Christianity and its teachings. Imagine the culture shock for an African slave who is being forced to accept this and deny all that was his idea of salvation. Christian doctrines teach the concept that anyone who refuses to accept Jesus Christ as their personal savior will continue to live in sin forever and suffer total damnation. This was the tool that Christian slave owners used against the Africans in their attempt to divide and conquer. This is a prime example of how one may use religion as a tool to keep the mind from wanting to learn new ideas. I believe Jesus Christ did not intend his teachings in such a way. I believe Jesus wanted salvation for all men whether they be Christian or not. However, we must remember that Jesus did not write the bible, but it was written by other men who involved their own ideas and doctrines.

What I say next may cause some alarm. Islam has had the same effect as Christianity. It was also a religion forced upon African people. Dr. John Henrik Clarke writes of this. Dr. Clarke speaks of Africa's ancient glory and eventually the conquering of Africa by several outside groups. He writes, "In the years of the slave trade, Africa lost, over one hundred million people. For every African captured, three were killed. The Arab slave trade in East Africa that started a thousand years before the European Atlantic slave trade and the Atlantic slave trade that lasted approximately 300 years was a holocaust against African people, which started 500 years ago and is not completely over to this day." More importantly, the holy Roman Empire was the first to convert Africans to Christianity. They made the Africans slaves and oppressed them in the name of Christianity. We had Christian missionaries traveling to Africa to set-up churches and monasteries and ordaining new priests, setting up the process of converting the Africans to Christians. From this time on there were small Christian kingdoms who were required to pay heavy taxes to the Roman Empire. All this occurred between the 1st century A.D. to the early 6th century.

The prophet Muhammad then began preaching this new religion of Islam and established it in Arabia. Arabs began invading several countries ranging from Persia, India, China and Africa. Dr. Clarke says that Africans were being so oppressed by the Romans with heavy taxes that they decided to make a deal with the Arabs in exchange for their freedom. So the Arabs freed the Africans from Christian control but at the same time they became enslaved by the Arabs and once again forced to convert to a new religion. This time it was Islam. The Arabs were just as vicious as the Christians. They too enslaved and converted Africans and took possession of their land and levied heavy taxes on those Africans who were not Muslim. They invaded the northern hemisphere of Africa and that is why the northern part of Africa to this day is predominantly controlled by Arabs. Once the Arabs invaded Africa, they acted just as other invading groups had before them; they claimed the identities of that territory. Imagine Arabs now referring to themselves as Egyptians and claiming to be descendants of the mighty pharaohs. This is far from the truth. Next, they conquered and settled into areas of Egypt, Libya, Tunisia, Sudan and Morocco and these countries are all under Arab control. The issue of racial identity in Egypt past and present has been subjected to distorted politics and scholarship. Today Egyptian society is regarded as white-Arab and its black-African roots and population marginalized and in many instances denied an existence or any association with the civilization that made the greatest contribution to mankind. Napoleon Bonaparte's destroying the black African portraiture in the faces of the sphinx in the 18th century (1798) is but among the plethora of direct actions to disassociate the glory of Kemit, known today as Egypt from the Africans who founded this civilization of civilizations. Currently, reclaiming Egypt's African past faces opposition from its overwhelming Arab present and Europeans internationally in all spheres of power who find it more profitable and believable to imagine that ancient Egypt was not African. Not to be discouraged by these efforts, African scholars continue to reaffirm Egypt's African-ness in order to foster "...human capacity, potentials, and possibilities" in Africans everywhere.

However, let us not forget the main purpose of this scholarship; to understand the basic concept of Moorish Science. I want to conclude, that anyone reading this book should understand religious doctrine, its history and its origin.

The study of Moorish Science is as complex as any other doctrine that preaches a different idea. Unlike mainstream religions, Moorish Science emerged during the Black Nationalist Movement, and perhaps acquired some of the black nationalist themes in its doctrines. Even the prophet Noble Drew Ali acknowledges one of Pan Africa's greatest black nationalists, Marcus Garvey.

From the Holy Koran Circle 7; "in these modern days their came a forerunner, that was divinely prepared by the great God Allah and his name is Marcus Garvey, who did taught and warn the nations of the earth to prepare to meet the coming prophet; who was to bring the true and divine creed of Islam, and his name is Noble Drew Ali; who was prepared and sent to this earth by Allah to teach the old time religion and the everlasting gospel to the sons of men. That every nation shall and must worship under their own vine and fig tree, and return to their own and be one with their father God, Allah.

In this verse, Noble Drew Ali compares his arrival to that of John the Baptist and Jesus Christ when he acknowledges Marcus Garvey as his forerunner. So perhaps the Moorish Divine Movement at the time was acknowledged as a nationalist movement and not a religious one. Author Susan Nance, in her article, Mystery of the the Moorish Science Temple states, "seventy five years after it emerged in Chicago, the origin of Moorish Science is still a long standing puzzle of American religious history. In much of the literature on the faith, there is an overwhelming focus on the Moors black nationalist teachings, an approach that reduces believers motivation to anti-racial sentiment and does not give them credit as sincerely spiritual people.

I think the Moorish movement can combine both worlds, taking into consideration that every religious doctrine has some form of nationalism, then why not allow the Moorish Divine movement to incorporate such acts into it own doctrine. We must understand the situation of America and the inner city black communities in order to grasp the thinking of the prophet and others like him. In other words, something new and different needed to be created and that was what is now called Moorish Science. We must also remember that the prophet continued his loyalty to America and never spoke against the government or country. The prophet placed an American flag next to the Moorish flag in every Moorish Science Temple. Originally the two flags symbolized the agreement made between America and the country of Morocco; a peace treaty was established between them in 1787, and that treaty allowed anyone of Moorish descent certain privileges and rights on American soil. The prophet, Noble Drew Ali, issued to his members identity or nationality cards to show proof of their Moorish identity. The prophet asserted that American blacks are Moorish Americans because they are descendants of Moroccans and born in America; a distinct subgroup of the Asiatic nation.

Perhaps the prophet felt we had earned the same rights as Moroccans. Susan Nance writes, "Ali's belief that Moroccan subjects could and did enjoy special rights in the United States not allowed African Americans was not farfetched. Black popular culture contained stories of black North africans escaping racial discrimination in the United States."

Booker T. Washington writes about an incident in his book, Up from Slavery, where a black man in 1879 was refused service in a white owned hotel in a southern town. Because the man spoke English, he was assumed to be African American. However, after he proved his Moroccan citizenship, the hotel staff apologized and granted him service. Washington writes, "I happened to find myself in a town in which so much excitement and indignation were being expressed that it seemed likely for a time that there would be a lynching. The occasion of the trouble was that a dark skinned man had stopped at the local hotel. Investigation, however, developed the fact that this individual was a citizen of Morocco, and that while traveling in this country, he spoke the English language. As soon as it was learned that he was not an American negro, all the signs of indignation disappeared. The man who was the innocent cause of the excitement, though, found it prudent after that not to speak English."

Susan Nance further states, "that many African Americans recognized that Americans had constructed blackness such that black identity had specifically to do with being American, particularly if one was from the south. Further, while many Moroccans were ethnically Arab, enough of Moorish or Moroccan citizens were black that the exact racial characteristics of a Moor were fluid, leaving the door open for a black American claims of Moroccan ancestry."

Moorish American identity had another advantage for African Americans; in black traditions of ethiopianism, the stories of American black origins in the ancient holy land (Egypt or Ethiopia) were particularly compelling since they provided a noble black heritage divorced from stereotype images of the African savages. Examples of this would be seen in the Hollywood movies where they depict Africans as savages and cannibals. This was placed in movies to make Africans believe untruths about our heritage and our ancestral roots. The movie Tarzan of the Jungle is an example of this. A caucasian who was raised by apes was called "Lord of the jungle." On the movie screen, Tarzan would often battle the so called black savages who ran around with spears, half-naked and chanting loud noises. This stereotype has lingered throughout the ages as a different form of racism. Groups like the Moorish Science Temple of America at least try to give its members a sense of the life of Africans before the Diaspora.

I am a believer in having a strong bond to ones country of origin. Black nationalist groups usually instructed its members on history, current events and world issues so that their primary directive was education and unity. Perhaps this took on a fraternal atmosphere and in some cases, that is what the Moorish Americans lean toward.

During the 1920's, Moorish Americans would often dress in elaborate clothes of Arabian nature, but more often they wore a fez as a symbol of their Moorish pride and faith. It's obvious that the outside appearance drew the attention of people who found their displays of oriental flamboyant themes extremely different. Author Susan Nance writes, "Noble Drew Ali seems to have understood that observers of his religious movement would view their presentation of themselves as representations of Morocco and their public behavior as a package, to draw the attention of inner city blacks to come and join, or at least to inquire about their messages to uplift black Asiatics."

During the 1920's, the prophet was one of the most publicized men in Chicago. This stemmed from constant media coverage from the Chicago Defender newspaper. In the library, I found several articles pertaining to the activities of Noble Drew Ali and the Moorish Science Temple. The newspaper recorded every event ranging from the prophets travels to mexico and Cuba, to his last years on earth. It appears that Noble Drew Ali became a very important figure in politics. There are stories of him attending government inaugurations and U.S. Postal offices encouraging blacks to vote for certain candidates. In other words, becoming active in their community.

Susan Nance writes, "The Moorish prophet Noble Drew Ali had been drawn to the rich popular intellectual scene that developed in the black store front churches and street universities of the urban north during and after the great migration. At least three thousand nationwide, and no doubt a considerably larger number of sympathizers. The Moors pragmatically put their beliefs into action by publishing a newspaper and running their own businesses and developing a prominent if ephemeral national public profile. Overall the Moorish American's success was due precisely to their ability to speak to African American's desire for a changed alternative spiritually grounded in local religious culture."

Nance further states, "highlighting contemporary black investigation of non-western religions, the Moors were partly a product of and partly further inspiration to the vibrant experimental religious scene of interwar Chicago. Acknowledging the problems inherent in labels, Moorish Science is most accurately described as a black spiritualist style religion steeped in the philosophies of Eastern mysticism."

So far, I have discussed my personal opinions of the Moorish Science temple, its purposes, its challenges and its primary directive to come into existence are all essential in the writing of this book. My goal is to not only explore the history of the Moorish Science Temple but to explore the origins of Asiatics from the very beginning to modern times. When prophet Noble Drew Ali came up with the term, "Asiatic" I wonder if he fully realized the power of that word. I mention this because the Asiatic race is so rich in history and culture, not to mention it is deeply rooted in African traditions. In many ways, this research is built from a foundation of other prominent writers. With their help, I have composed a research book filled with as much information as I can find on the subject of Moorish Science. So, let us begin our journey.

1. Sultan Abdul Aziz Ibu Suad

1. Sultan Abdul Aziz Ibu Suad a descendant of Hagar and ruler of the holy city of Mecca. Source holy Koran circle 7

Sultan Sayyid Khalifa Ibn Harub

2. The Sultan of Zanzibar this is the man that Booker T Washington spoke of in his book up from slavery this man because of his nationality was granted special treatment Source

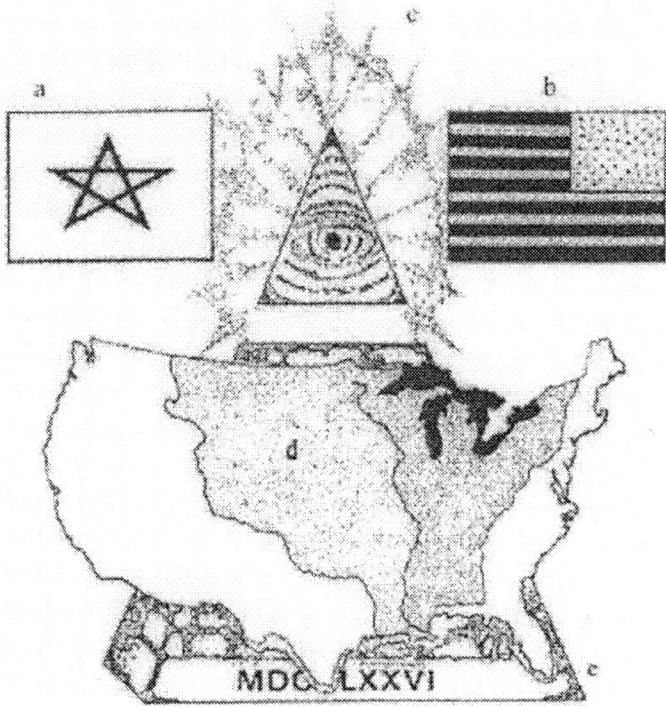

Moorish Map. On the map, *a* and *b* represent the Moroccan and U.S. flags; *c* is the Masonic Eye in the Pyramid; the map itself, *d*, is said to show Moorish population distribution in the U.S. (although I can't understand why it seems to indicate none in the East); and *e* is the date 1776, carved in the base of the Pyramid. From *Moor Sense*, 1971, reprinted in al-Mahdi, op. cit.

3. Moorish Map explains the connection between
the united states and morocco

UNITY

ISLAM

7

ALLAH

------------------------- 198--

This is your Nationality and Identification Card for the Moorish Science Temple of America and Birthrights for the Moorish Americans, etc., we honor all the Divine Prophets, Jesus, Mohammed, Buddha and Confucius. May the blessings of the God of our Father Allah, be upon you that carry this card. I do hereby declare that you are a Moslem under the divine Laws of the Holy Koran of Mecca, Love, Truth, Peace, Freedom and Justice. "I AM A CITIZEN OF THE U. S. A."

NOBLE DREW ALI, THE PROPHET, 6319 ST. LAWRENCE, CHICAGO, IL.60637 (312)684-4914

ASIA

ISLAM   OFFICIO: CUBAN-AMERICANO HEADQUARTERS   ALLAH

7

....192......

Estes No su nacionnales Y miembros Cacao Por El Moorish Holy Temple de Science Y nacimiento Obrarbier Por El Moorish-Americano. Ets nos honor todo el Toleogia Propheta Jesus, Mohammed, Buddha y Confucius. Puedo El blessing de El Dias de nuestro. Padre Allah ester sobre Que tengo Este Cacao Yo Hago aqui por Declare Que v Quire Un Moslem Debajo el Toelogia Ley De el Holy Koran de Mecca Ama Verdad pos Fredom y Justicia.

NOBLE DREW ALI, FOUNDER, 3603 INDIANA AVE., CHICAGO, ILL.—TEL. DOUGLAS 5909

4. *Moorish Nationality Card in English and Spanish*

Chapter 1
Asiatic Origin Among People of Color

I only make passing reference in the work to blacks scattered outside of Africa over the world not from a slave but dispersions that began in prehistory. The fact alone indicates the great tasks of future scholarship on the real history of the race. We are just on the threshold, gathering important missing fragments, and the biggest jobs are still ahead. Ancient China and the far east, for example, must be a special area of African research. How do we explain such a large population of blacks in southern China that are powerful enough to form a kingdom of their own? The black people of the Malay Peninsula, IndoChina or the heavy concentration of Africans in India both open still more interesting fields for investigation. Even the negroid finds in early Europe appear not to be as challenging as the black population centers in Asia. Our concern is with great populations; the blacks who have puzzled western scholars. Some theorize that Asia or Europe may be the homeland of Africans after all. The African populations of Palestine, Arabia and Mesopotamia are better known, although the centuries of black rule over these places should be studied in more detail. All of this calls for a new kind of scholarship, one without any mission other than the discovery of truth and one that will not tremble with fear when that truth is contrary to what one prefers to believe. Source: The Destruction of Black Civilization by: Chancellor Williams

We know from the works of some of the greatest African historical writers of the continents beauty and glorious past, yet we fail to acknowledge the accomplishments of blacks that are present on other continents. The presence of early Africans are known throughout other continents, such

1

as Europe, North America, South America, Australia and especially Asia. Since Asia is a close neighbor of Africa it is only fitting that people of African descent migrated into parts of Arabia, India, Mesopotamia and China. Scientists believe that this process may have taken place some 4000 years ago, before the dawn of civilization. In this passage, let us follow the migration of African people into other continents. Let us learn of their contributions toward world civilization and try to imagine the glory and beauty that it possessed. Let us learn the story's of individuals who stood out and what made them unique.

When prophet Noble Drew Ali states that we are descendants of Asiatic people, he only scratches the surface by only mentioning the Asiatics of North Africa, namely the Moors. However, it is far more complex and should not be limited to the Moors of Spain and North Africa. An Asiatic can come in the form of different shades of color; from the darkest skin to that of yellow complexion, and can exist in all types of climates. However, we must not forget that Africa gave birth not only to the Asiatic cultures but also to other cultures and races of people. Just as Africa is the birth place of all races, it is also a recognizable point of origin for each individual man. If we were to trace the origins of black Asiatics we must look to a place called, Nubia. The Nubians gave birth to the egyptian civilization and to black Asiatics.

If we focus on the continent of Africa, the Nubian civilization was located in the eastern part of Africa settling between the borders of Ancient Egypt and Ethiopia. Further east of Nubia is the area of what is now known as Arabia. Scientists believe that Africans migrated from around the area of Nubia into Arabia and further into the Asian continent, until they settled into India, China, Nepal, Persia and other parts of Asia. Next, they established cultures and eventually small kingdoms. There is a distinct difference between the Africans and the black Asiatics, and yet in most cases they both possess the same skin color. They differ in bodily features because of the climate they dwell in. Needless to say, we must develop more research to further explore the land of Asia and its roots in Africa. Perhaps the prophet Noble Drew Ali saw this in his early travels to Egypt and he acknowledged the link between blacks in America and Asiatics. This can be defined as a rebirth into new ideas about people of African descent. However, blacks are not limited to Africa. The prophet Noble Drew Ali called this the uniting of Asia, and so since this is the uniting of Asia part of this chapter it requires me to explore the earliest known black Asiatics.

This chapter will primarily focus on early Asiatic cultures. Over the years scientists have theorized that the very root of the Asiatic culture began with a group of nomadic people known as the Aryans, and it was the foundation of the Aryans that gave birth to the modern day religions of Asia. However, even though the Aryans contributed to modern day Asia, they were not the founders of the civilization. Perhaps I can go as far as to say that Asia owes its development to the earlier inhabitants of Africa. But what both the Africans and the Aryans brought to Asia was the foundation of religion. Examining the cultures of Africa we can find similarities of African religions in the cultures of Asia. We find the remnants of egyptian beliefs and cultures. We can observe similar coincidences between the pygmies of Africa and the Bramins of India. In both Asia and Africa, we find the concepts of polytheism and the manifestations of many gods and goddesses into one supreme deity represented by three individuals. We further acknowledge the concept of the son of man, and man will continue to live on. We find the supreme lord Krishna of Hinduism sharing the same spotlight as Lord Jesus Christ who is a product of egyptian Judaism. In all this we find the influential concept of the son of the almighty. Man's invisible spirit force is subject to incarnations, as is man. Our ancestors do not die because their spirits live on forever. Both the Africans and the Asians believed in this concept of immortal life. it is obvious that the Asiatic customs has a strong African background. So let's find out more of this in the following pages. Let us trace the origins of man in Asia and Africa.

Section 1

This is the first of many examinations I have written on early Asiatics. The first of these are the earliest group called the Dravidians. The Dravidians are a special group because from them came forth the other races and cultures of Asia. I must also include the origins of the Dravidians and their connection with the civilizations of Africa. It is a fact that Africa is the birth place of man and civilization, and the black Dravidians of India are a branch of that original group. To understand the origins of the dravidians we must first learn of their migration and where they settled. Archeologists estimate about 4000 b.c. a group of Africans traveled thru Arabia, Persia and Mesopotamia and settled throughout parts of India. There the Dravidians dwelled in peace for hundreds of years. Long before there was an infiltration of Aryans, who invaded around 2500 b.c., and before there was a caste system which separated the different shades of color, which gives us one of the earliest presences of racism, there was a foundation of a thriving culture beginning to take fold. Imagine a culture so vast and well established, and yet it was invaded by outsiders whose

3

primary goal was to plunder, pillage and take control of the people and the resources of the land. Before the infiltration of the Aryans, Dravidians wealth, culture, architecture and civilization was legendary throughout the ancient world. The Aryan invasion did not just happen overnight but was a process which occurred over a period of time. Author George Wells Parker has some interesting words to say about the history of Asia in his lecture, The Children of the Sun. Parker writes, "it is still current opinion among those not in touch with the latest scientific exploration that Asia is pre-eminently the home of the yellow races. These races are grouped under the term Semite because it was accepted that they were descendants of Shem, one of the sons of Noah. But today the term means absolutely nothing. So many strange and perplexing problems have arisen that there is only a distant hope of ever settling matters to rights. One thing which has been discovered, and which is creating so much surprise, is that it appears that the entire continent of Asia was originally the home of many black races and that these races were the pioneers in establishing their wonderful civilizations that have flourished throughout this vast continent. At different time invaders have come from the North and tried to conquer many of these peoples, but in most cases they found them too strong and compromised by settling among them. This amalgamation has had a tendency to lighten the color of these Asiatic races, but in no instances has the complete obliteration of the African characteristics been effected."

Parker acknowledges the impact that the invaders had on the Dravidian Indians society though their skin color had changed, the African characteristics still remain. Further explaining the Dravidians, I can trace their origin to the Kushsite African race, still numerous in various parts of the world. They spread from india in the east to Nubia in the west. For example, this group of ancient blacks, the Naga people were and still are the largest sub-group of the Kushic speaking branch of the black African race. In fact, the Naga title is still retained in various forms throughout Africa and Asia including describing the Kushitic branch of the African race. The Naga are just one of many tribes that are located in India and we find numerous links between Africa and Asia in terms of geological relations because all of them are classified as Dravidians. These Dravidians are approximately a third of India's population with negroid like complexion. They tend to be placed in the lower caste of India's system of racism. To my knowledge, the black Dravidians situation in India resembles that of many Africans worldwide. They need to lobby for equal rights just as blacks still do in America.

Let us examine the Hindu caste system. The black Dravidians represent the lower class despite the fact that they were the first inhabitants of Asia only to be invaded and oppressed. When the Aryans invaded, the result was the weakening of the great Dravidian empire. Their kingdoms eventually fell to the Aryans. The caste system was introduced to further divide and control the black Dravidians while the Aryans established themselves at the top of the system with full control over the rest of the population. This perhaps can be considered the foundation of absolute world power claimed by Europeans. Notice that when the Aryans took power they transformed what was a peaceful civilization into a place where drinking, free sex, gambling and other evils were practiced. Many rites of worship to invoke their gods were practiced and in due time these practices began to influence others. The black Dravidians were pushed to poverty, ignorance, hunger and unemployment. Due to their situation, robbery, looting, murder and prostitution, which were previously unknown in their culture, began occurring in Dravidian society. However, there is a positive aspect of this Dravidian/Aryan culture.

"If we should look at the records we would see that the early Aryan language-groups stemmed from the black Dravidians who occupied southern India in remote times, two peoples mingled freely. Thus, the so-called Indo-European movements around 2,500 B.C. were basically migrations of a Negroid folk which pooled itself in southern southeastern and southwestern Europe, around 2,000 B.C. Indeed black African races, had already covered most of Europe as early as 20,000 B.C. They left a secondary African base for art in ancient Hellas (Greece) and a primary African base for color in Austria, Italy, France, Spain and Portugal. This explains why you have some Europeans with dark tan complexions." -- John Henrik Clarke

The Dravidians continued to exist, and glory must be given to those African ancestors who gave birth to the religions and cultures of the civilization. Like all religions and cultures, occasionally outside influence will bring about change. West and Eastern Africa alien religions introduced by the enemies of Africans, worked well implementing the invaders divide and conquer schemes. In many cases, Africans allowed such religious concepts to be blindly followed by their people without examining the consequences on the original African Asian culture and system of beliefs, which are more adaptable to the African Asian way of thinking. Take the ancient writings of the Rig Vedas. The Rig Vedas are a collection of writings that were composed over a period dating back as far as 5000 b.c. Contained within it writings are moral stories of life the attainment of pure transient knowledge. Such writings are an inspiration to anyone who reads it rich abundance of knowledge. All vedic scriptures were written by Dravidian Indians. Modern day scientists have written theories that the vedic scriptures were written by invading Aryans. However, the real truth about the writings was the thriving culture of the Dravidians that gave birth to this sacred literature.

According to Drucilla Dunjee Houston, the Vedas were originally written by black Kushites whose literary works were stolen by the invaders and corrupted with racist ideas. She explains in Wonderful Ethiopians of the Ancient Kushite Empire, "5000 years ago we have shown there was no branch of the Aryan race that could have produced the Rig Veda. Years ago no Japhethic nation possessed blacksmiths, chariots, in the civilization the Rig Vedas reveals." I was once instructed that religious scriptures are the key to ones history and point of origin. The Vedas, for example, have an epic within their history that I recommend called the Bhagavad Gita. Its scriptures are based on a conversation between two Dravidians, Lord Krishna and his devotee, Arjuna. The writings are filled with an age old knowledge of understanding and realization. Though the Gita is just one small portion of the extremely large Rig Veda, it contains several different stories and epics of well known Hindu Deities. Most notable is Lord Krishna, who is considered as one of the more favorable deities. Krishna was the savior and redeemer of the Hindu people. I compare him to the Lord Jesus Christ. Like Jesus, Krishna healed the sick, preached to the poor and provided comfort and salvation for those who looked for it. I am surprised that prophet Noble Drew Ali did not acknowledge Lord Krishna as of the mentioned divine prophets. Buddha, Jesus, Muhammad and Confucius all learned from the teachings of Lord Krishna and the Hindu religion. We must acknowledge this scholarship in order for the truth about Africans in Asia. "In the latter Sanskrit literature the invaders made alliances with the aboriginal princes, after they found they could not conquer them, and when history at last dawns upon the scene, we find some of the most powerful kingdoms of India ruled by dynasties of African descent. In the epic which narrates the advance of the invaders into southern india, one of the chieftains describes his race as of fearful swiftness, unyielding in battle and in color like the dark blue clouds. This blue- blackness appears in ancient pictures which illustrate the epic. The fact that Krishna, their for the Sun god, means "the blackener" may have some significance." --Author George Wells Parker

Dr. Muata Ashby wrote a three volume book on African origins. He writes, "From its beginnings, European indological scholarship has tended to focus on languages, text and traditions of Indo-European origin while overlooking indigenous and Dravidian sources or down playing their role in the evolution of Indian thought. The present study also aims to re-approximate the archaic world view, alone from which archaic cults draw their soul inspiring vision and vitality and outside of which they appear to the modern mind as mere belief systems with no ontological basis in what we modern people fondly cherish as reality."

In these modern times we discover the roots of Africans in other parts of the world, and that brings on a new wave of ideas and thoughts. Even in the 1920's, when the Moorish Americans were making an impact in society by displaying orientalism, the average black experienced something different from the normal exposure in society. It was the goal of prophet Noble Drew Ali to influence that which was not known, and such knowledge in the hands of black people could stir up a variety of conflicts between them and the controlling group. Such knowledge needed to be pure and untampered in order for blacks to understand its message. For example, the Holy Koran Circle 7 is one of those books that needs to be fully analyzed and studied. The prophet began to explain the history of the Asiatics by acknowledging several groups that can trace their origins to Asia. The Holy Koran Circle 7, chapter 45 states,

1. The fallen sons and daughters of the Asiatic Nations of North America need to learn to love instead of hate, and to know of his higher self and lower self. This is the uniting of the Holy Koran of Mecca, for teaching and instructing all Moorish Americans etc...
2. The key of civilization was and is in the hands of the Asiatic nations. The Moors, who were the ancient Moabites and the founders of the city of Mecca.
3. The Egyptians, who were the Hamitites, and of direct descendants of Mizraim, the Arabians, the seed of Hagar, Japanese and Chinese.
4. The Hindus of India, the descendants of the ancient Canaanites, Hittites, and Moabites from the land of Canaan.
5. The Asiatic nations and countries in North, South and Central America; the Moorish Americans and Mexicans in North America and Brazilians, Argentineans and Chileans in South America.
6. Columbians, Nicaraguans, and the natives of San Salvador in Central America. All these are Muslims.
7. Turks are the true descendants of Hagar, who are the chief protectors of the Islamic creed of Mecca, beginning from Muhammad the first, the founder of the uniting of Islam, by the command of the great universal God-Allah.

This small scripture speaks of a variety of races, all whom Drew Ali calls and defines as Muslims. In order for me to trace their Islamic origins I would have to trace each group individually. However, I must say that some of these groups were in existence long before the religion of Islam was established. First I must acknowledge the Asiatics origins of these groups. We can trace the native Americans from Asia by tracing their migration some 4000 to 5000 years ago from the Asian continent. From the native American, or native Indian, we now have, with the help of other invading groups, separate groups such as Mexicans, Brazilians, Puerto Ricans and other Latin Americans. As for them being Moslem, we must begin to understand the numerous interactive mating between Europeans, African slaves and native Indians. Since the majority of the slaves were taken from the northern area of Africa, some of those slaves were probably Muslim. This is why the prophet Noble Drew Ali theorized that all Latin Americans were Muslims. The prophet further proved this by travelling through the various countries of Latin America setting up temples and issuing charters to Spanish speaking Moors, as he defined them. He further acknowledged the Arabs and Turks as the true descendants of Hagar, the consort of Abraham, who bore him a son called Ishmael and Ishmael became the father of all the people of Arabic descent, even Moors. The prophet writes that the Moors are the descendants of the Moabites. In the Holy Koran Circle 7 it states that the Moabites from the land of Moab, received permission from the pharaohs of Egypt to settle and inhabit North-west Africa. They were the founders and are the true possessors of the present Moroccan empire.

Moorish American doctrines are very complex, to the point that every theory and every source of information must be researched. It is a jigsaw puzzle that needs to be put together. But like all puzzles, time is needed in order to solve the mystery and to uncover its abundance of wisdom. I have explored the theory of the role the black Dravidians played in the understanding and development of Moorish Science because it was the development and knowledge of the Dravidian civilization that sprung forth the various groups that the prophet Noble Drew Ali acknowledges in his Holy Koran Circle 7. So Moorish Science owes a great deal to the Dravidians and their existence should be acknowledged by all Moors in the future.

Section 2
The Cultural Relationship between Egypt and India
The Theory of a Moorish Science Adept Chamber

Self Knowledge is the basis of true knowledge Soul to heaven, body to Earth. Man is to become God- like through a life of virtue and the cultivation of the spirit through scientific knowledge. Salvation is accomplished through the efforts of the individual. There is no mediator between man and his/her salvation. Salvation is the freeing of the soul from its bodily fetters, becoming a God through knowledge and wisdom, controlling the forces of the cosmos instead of being a slave to them. Subduing the lower self and through awakening the higher self, ending the cycle of rebirth and dwelling with the neters who direct and control the Great Plain. Egyptian Philosophy

A short time ago I was looking through some of the writings of the prophet when I came across one particular passage. The prophet referred to himself as professor drew of the egyptian adept. The word, adept, can have several meanings and several different understandings. For example, an adept can be someone who has been instilled certain rites and knowledge. Reflecting on the prophets history, he was said to have received certain mystical knowledge from an egyptian sage. Whether this is true is yet to be discovered, nevertheless the prophet did travel to egypt and perhaps what he discovered was that link between Africa and Asia. So perhaps the egyptian adept was the prophets way of explaining the connection between egypt and Asia. According to the Sidjul Papers the prophet had founded a temple prior to the Moorish Science temple. It was referred to as the canaanite temple and was in Newark, New Jersey. The Sidjul Papers stated that in 1913 Noble Drew Ali founded the canaanite temple and at the time he was known as Professor Drew, the egyptian adept. Ali officially began his mission to uplift fallen humanity. Reportedly, Noble Drew Ali also established the adept chamber of the Moorish Movement. It is logical to assume that the original adept chamber had an egyptian connection because Drew Ali referred to himself as an egyptian adept. We can assume he used the term canaanite as a generic racial term because canaanite was synonymous with Kushite, because Canaan, like Egypt and Arabia, were originally colonies of Kush. Like Kush, Canaan can refer to a land nationality or Phenotype. Moorish Science rejects the biblical lie that Canaan was cursed. It is Moorish Science's contention that ethnic slander was inserted into the torah to justify the genocidal war the Israelites waged against Canaan. Jesus and King david were both descendants of Ruth, The Moabite, and were therefore both of Canaanite descent.

We know from the writings of some of the greatest African historians of the greatness and beauty of the egyptians. Their history, knowledge and origins are all the product of black Africans. Taking a different approach, my next challenge is to from a link between the glory of Egypt to the land of India. However, first I must explore the origins of the Egyptians.

Before there were the egyptians there were nubians, and these ancient nubians gave birth to several different colonies of people of dark color. The nubians gave birth to the egyptians and also the black dravidians of

9

India. This section will answer the question of the contact between ancient Egypt and India. There is proof that the egyptians traded with the Indians, however, they have cultural differences. In both religious doctrines we find stories similar in nature in terms of the handed down stories of religions and tales of great battles, and stories of great heros both past and present.

The greek philosopher, Diodorus, writes that the egyptian deity, Osiris, traveled through Egypt, Arabia and India. He states that Osiris passed through Arabia bordering on the Red Sea to as far as India and the remote inhabited coasts. He built many cities in India one of which he called Nysa. In Nysa, he planted ivy, which continues to grow there, but nowhere else in India or around it. He left many other marks of his presence in those parts by which the latter inhabitants are induced, and do affirm, that this god was born in India. He addicted himself to hunting elephants and took care to have statues of himself in every place as lasting monuments of his expedition. Next, we find stories of egyptian pharaohs forming trade agreements with the Dravidian kings. All this we can find in the Hieroglyphs on the pyramids of Egypt. Perhaps a trade agreement was formed between them because they both shared a common heritage and even a relationship in terms of blood lines.

The greek historian Herodotus writes that all Indian tribes mentioned their skins are all of the same color, much like the Ethiopians. Next he states, "and upon his return to Greece, they gathered around," (meaning his students) and asked, "tell us about this great land of the blacks called Ethiopia?" Herodotus said, "there are two great Ethiopian nations, one in Sind India and the other in Egypt." All this is proof of India's connection with Egypt. However, the expansion of Africans throughout the ancient world did not stop in India. There are two stories of Africans in other parts of Asia. We find remnants of African presence in ancient Persia or Mesopotamia as it was defined. Author Godfrey Higgins writes in his two volume research book, Anacalypsis of the Findings of Ancient African origins, "Take the ancient Persians and Babylonians for example, it has been said through the study of biblical scripture that the hebrew all father, Abraham, came from the persian city of Ur and we must reflect on the story of Abraham. Scripture tells us that Abraham and his family traveled from Ur to parts of Arabia and finally settled in Egypt."

Perhaps I can conclude the following theory on Abraham, but first Higgins points out that the gods that Abraham worshipped and coincidentally we find the same remnants of Dravidian influence. Higgins states, "the fact that Abraham worshipped several gods, who were, in reality the same as those of the Persians, namely the creator, preserver and the destroyer (the Hindu trinity) has long been asserted throughout other religious doctrines. Next we find that Abraham traveled to Egypt where he learned the ways of the Egyptians. It is possible that he studied along side other Egyptians and learned the secrets of the adept.

"Christianity itself can trace its roots to the various ancient religions of the Hindus and Persians; for example; the holy trinity is a reflection of two distinct trinity's of old. In Egypt it is the trilateral representation of Osiris, Isis, and Horus, and in India, it is the trinity of Brahman, Vishnu and Shiva. Both are represented by the solar energies of the sun, the creator, the sustainer and the destroyer. The mysterious doctrine of the trinity loses the character of mystery when we consider its origin. In ancient Egypt the sun was worshipped as a god. Since there can be no life without sunlight, the sun was recognized as the creator of life, and since without adequate sunlight living things wither and die, the sun was regarded as the protector, or preserver of life. An excess of sunlight destroys life, so that the sun was also known as the destroyer of life. The sun, considered in its three aspects of creator, protector, and destroyer was indeed a trinity in unity. Solar and stellar symbolism have profoundly affected the Christian religion." John G. Jackson

Abraham was a monotheist and Egypt was the land of monotheism. This can be traced back to the pharaoh Akenaton who decided to eliminate all the gods and goddesses of the Egyptian pantheon. The Egyptians were one of the earliest cultures to practice monotheism, if not the earliest. The practice began around 1500 b.c. when the Egyptian ruler decided to remove all the existing deities and replace them with the sun god, RA. From the worshipping of RA came the foundations of monotheism, which is where the Christians, Jews and Muslims received their gods from. Abraham was indeed a father of many nations. However, he owes a great deal to the egyptians because it was the blood line of the egyptians that allowed his seed to grow as a nation. From Abraham's consort, who was an egyptian slave, to the mixing of Jacob's family with Egypt. In the bible, the term for egypt is Mizraim or Kemet. They are the descendants of Ham, son of Noah. The name Mizraim, means two territories; this dual territory idea has been a dominant feature of egypt's life from the earliest times to the end of it civilization. Egypt's influence during Israel's creation period is very significant to full understanding from its beginning to the foundations of its covenant with God. Egypt was in effect the father of the Jewish nation. To understand the egyptian factor in early Israel's experience, three things need to be first understood.

1. God speaks inerrantly but always within the conceptual framework of his audience for he speaks to be understood.

2. A culture like Israel for instance will always tend of absorb from its environment such as Egypt into its own conceptual frame work.

3. Common elements between cultures may indicate a common source as much as they may indicate borrowing, unless evidence indicates otherwise. Egypt was a dominant regional power during the nomadic life of Israel's three great patriarchs. It also served as the refuge for the family of Jacob in the seven years famine. It also was the home of Israel for more than three hundred years before they became oppressed and eventually were liberated in the exodus. Dr. Muata Ashby of the Sema Institute of Yoga says of the ancient egyptians in his book The African Origins, "through their association with Egypt from the time of Abraham, Moses, Joseph and the early years of Jesus, the early Jewish and Christian faiths shared a common bond and point of origin."

So, in knowing this perhaps I can shed further light on the subject. This is where the prophet Noble Drew Ali received his ideas on the egyptian adept. I can briefly explain the origins of the adept chamber of the Moorish science temple. To take this subject a step further, we can explore other major contributions to the three great world religions; for example, the patriarch Moses. Of all the great biblical patriarchs, Moses stands out as being a product of egyptian knowledge born in the land and raised by an egyptian princess. Moses was accepted by the egyptians as one of their own. While in Egypt Moses learned the ways of the egyptians and absorbed as much knowledge possible and the results were phenomenal. What developed from this was the origins of things to come and these things are considered the foundation of the Jewish faith, which gave birth to Christianity, Islam, and finally Moorish Science.

And Moses became learned in all the wisdom of the egyptians and was mighty in words and in deeds. -- Act 7:22

Moses Kabbalism or esoteric knowledge which he first learned as a pharaoh in training was reinforced by the teachings of his father in law, Jethro, the renowned Ethiopian magician. Moses adopted his Ten Commandments from the ancient 147 egyptian laws called the Negative Confessions, and gave the hebrews credit for African customs. Some of them were already quite ancient during his time. One classic example was the adoption of the rite of circumcision-an egyptian custom thousands of years old by Moses' day. -- Author Naiwu Osahon

Moses simply means "born of." The name required another name prefixed to it such as thothmoses (born of Thoth), Rameses (born of Ra) or Amenmosis (born of Amen). Whilst the Moses Element is spelt slightly differently when rendered in English, they all mean the same thing and it seems very likely to us that either Moses himself or some later scribe dropped the name of an egyptian from the front of his name. --Christopher Knight and Robert Lomas - The Hiram Key

Referencing Moses's knowledge of the egyptians, Sir E.A. Wallis Budge writes in his book From Fetish to Gods in Ancient Egypt, "Moses was a skilled performer of magical rituals and was deeply learned in the knowledge of the accompany spells, incantations, and magical formulas of every description. More over the miracles which he wrought suggest that he was not only a priest but a magician of the highest order and perhaps even a Ker heb or egyptian high priest."

An example of this would be the turning of his rod into a serpent which then ate the serpents of the egyptian priests, mentioned in the holy scriptures. In egyptian mythology the serpent is revered as a sacred animal and this animal can be seen in all of the Hieroglyphs. The serpent was not only worshipped by the egyptians but was also used in various ritualistic services. Even Queen Cleopatra has experienced the venomous bite of the serpent, which caused her death. Even Moses once again utilized the serpent by placing it upon his staff so the children of Israel could gaze upon its healing factors so that they may be healed of their wounds, which were caused by a snake bite. We can recognize this part of biblical history in the more elevated degrees of freemasonry. Author Rex Huchens writes in his book A Bridge to Light, "The symbolism of the serpent derives from a story in the bible in the twenty first chapter of the Book of Numbers, which tells of a plague of serpents sent by the Lord to chastise the hebrews for their lack of faith. The people appealed to Moses, who is commanded by the Lord to erect a brazen serpent upon a pole. Moses is promised that anyone who was bitten and gazed upon it would live. The brazen serpent would survive for eight hundred years until its destruction by order of Hezekiah because the people had begun to burn incense to it." 2 Kings 18:4

The use of the serpent is mentioned three times throughout the five books of Moses. The first being the temptation of Eve in the Garden of Eden. The second is the transformation of Moses's rod into a serpent and finally the plague of the brazen serpent. Perhaps these are all results of egyptian magic. The Jewish faith is rooted deeply in both egyptian symbolism and the egyptian mysteries. The torah is both an example and a reference of Jews dealings with the egyptians. If you notice the shape of a typical torah compare and contrast it with that of an egyptian papyrus scroll and notice the similarities, they look the same. When reading the torah it is never touched by hand but by a tool called a yod similar to what the egyptians used when viewing their documents. Let's focus on another story of the torah, The Exodus, the second book of Moses. The torah tells us of how the children of Israel were delivered out of bondage is Egypt and the jews commemorate this day and celebrate it. If we were to examine all the historical events of the Egyptians there is no known written evidence of the Exodus except the torah. Not even in the hieroglyphs of the pyramids will you find a story or perhaps they did not record this section of history. "The earliest opportunity for a coalition between Blacks and jews came in 1675 B.C. when an African people, called the Egyptians, took in the sons and daughters of Abraham, who were fleeing from hunger and starvation in Western Asia. After receiving food, clothing and shelter as well as the foundation for Judaic culture, language and religion, the majority of these guests joined the invaders, the Hyksos (or Shepherd Kings) rather than form an alliance to defend the country of their African benefactors. They had found a greater acceptance in Africans than Africans have ever found in a European-dominated country. With this visit to Africa, the people who would later be known as Jews conspicuously entered world history." -- John Henrik Clarke

Over the years the Jews have distinctly profiled themselves as God's chosen race of people. Pure and untouched and in some cases above races of other men because of their identity. This is far from the truth. A race so pure but yet purified by the blood of the Egyptians. The Jews and the Egyptians shared the same concepts of belief and customs, for example, a single creator.

According to one unknown author he writes, "In contrast to other near eastern cultures, the ancient Egyptians in spite of regional differences in names, believed in a single creator and a source of divine power."

The second is the method of creation. Again, ancient Egyptians believed the act of creation was not a result of contest between Gods, but in their Memphite theology it was believed that the creator spoke creation into existence out of nothing. When I explore the theories of an Egyptian adept I can only find stories pertaining to the mysteries and sciences of Egypt. An adept is an individual who through serious study and accomplishments is considered highly proficient in a particular magical system. Author Susan nance speaks of various magical acts performed by the prophet during Moorish open house meetings. After all there are theories of the prophet being a practicing magician.

Earlier I stated that Moorish science is composed of a variety of religions and esoteric doctrines, but more notably rosicrusianism, which is where the prophets received the majority of his egyptian learning. Rosicrusianism is deeply rooted in egyptian knowledge. When asking members of the order, most of them will tell you that its origin dates back to mysteries of Egypt and the pharaohs. In truth, it dates back to the

16th century to an allegorical character by the name of Father Christian Rosencruz. Through the study of alchemy and egyptology and other occult sciences thus was born this science. The Egyptian adept is a science within Moorish Science that I cannot understand nor can I decipher its purpose. However, I can relate this to the study of science in general. In ancient times science was mostly transmitted orally from one individual to another; from teacher to student and from philosopher to student. If we reflect on the ancient mysteries schools of Greece, Rome and Egypt we will find that great philosophers like Socrates, Plato, and Aristotle often lectured to a group of students trying to absorb as much information from them as possible, and then these students will become masters and lecture to the next generation of students. Moorish Science operates in that same manner. When a new member enters into a temple he is instructed by the prophet and is therefore taught all the mysteries of the Moorish Science Temple. The temple itself is a universal learning tool. To the outside world, it is just a building but to the spiritual moor it is the beginning of life and birth and the end of death and departure. Moorish Science is a science of the mind and a science of spiritual life. In the spiritual world the Moors are taught that from one life, formless and uncreated, proceeds the universe of life. Man alone is one with the universal world and his universal God all exists on the spiritual plain of one reality. Is it enough for man to know that he exists? Is it enough to be formed into human flesh to enable him to observe the gift of life or to become part of the universal spirit? I was once told that neither heaven or hell existed. The individual that relayed this intelligence to me did not understand that these terms we used to enslave the mind to believe the paranoia and live in fear of it. I can neither believe in this doctrine nor can I foster it. What I can cypher from this is knowing that we must understand that truth is always present in the hearts of all man.

In this age, man is constantly challenged with the existence of a universal god and how to acknowledge his presence. Remember the mind of the man has no limitation on what he should believe in, but we must also understand that a man can have no god that is not bounded by his own human conceptions. The wider the sweep of his spiritual vision, the mightier will be his deity. But where can we find a better demonstration of him than in man himself. The holy books constantly remind us of the noble deeds that god has performed before man and his brethren.

Albert Pike, in his book Morals and Dogma, writes "these were the ancient ideas as to this great god, father of all the gods, or of the world; of this being, principle of all things and of which nothing other than itself is principle, the universal cause that was termed god. Soul of the universe, eternal like it, immense like it, supremely active and potent in its varied operations. Penetrating all parts of this vast body, impressing a regular and symmetrical movement on the spheres, making the elements instinct with activity and order, mingling with everything, organizing everything, verifying and preserving everything, this was the universal-god which the ancients adorned as supreme cause and god of gods."

What Pike is saying is man has been shaping an image of god from his own thought patterns and from this one thought pattern came many thought patterns. In the beginning there was a single god existing of himself and there was no other, but after existing for along period by himself, desiring to manifest himself, he created other souls to dwell with him in this universe so he would not be lonely and thus began the creation of life. This is basic knowledge of an adept. The individual was trained to be god-like while on earth and at the same time to qualify for everlasting happiness. Around 5000 b.c. Africans of the Nile valley decided to bring their cultural, traditional, spiritual and other learning acquired over thousands of years together under one formal educational arrangement for the spiritual development of mankind. They called what they put together, The Mystery System, a secret order with membership gained only by initiation and pledge to secrecy. An adept must contain the knowledge of the ages. The Egyptian adept can only be created in two places; the first place is in the heart and the second is within Africa. Naiwu Osahon writes in his article, African origin of Religions, "the origination of an adept came from the civilizations of Africa and the mysteries of Egypt. Traditional African religion is the oldest in the world." This is obvious since Africans are the oldest human beings on earth. African traditional religions led to the system of alchemy founded some fifteen thousand years ago by the first human genius whom Africans described as the "Thrice Greatest." The greatest of all philosophers, the greatest of all priests and the greatest of all kings. His African names included, Thoth, Tehuti and Theuth. The West knows him as Hermes Trismegistus. He was the worlds first adept, or master, and he created the science of alchemy for the spiritual development of humankind. He built the great pyramid of Giza. It was the first pyramid built in Egypt and it serves as his shrine and academy. Wise men journeyed from all over the world to study at his feet. From this passage we can conclude that this is where an adept was created, and Egypt was the school for which all other races learned.

According to Moorish literature while the prophet was at the Pyramid of Cheops, his followers believed he received initiation and took the title, American Muslim name. In America he would be known as Noble Drew Ali. On his return to the United States in 1913, he had a dream in which he was ordered to found a movement "to uplift fallen humanity by returning the nationality, divine creed and culture to persons of Moorish descent in the Western Hemisphere." He organized the Moorish Science Temple along the lines similar to Masonic lodges, with local temple branches and "Adept Chambers," teaching the esoteric wisdom derived from the secret circle of Eastern Sages, the Master Adepts of Moorish Science.

My guess is that the adept chamber served as a mystery school for the Moors in order for them to learn and study those mysteries that are only open to a select few. I believe the Moors still use this system of learning in order to teach its members that knowledge that is sacred only to them. So when one speaks of an adept, he is speaking of one who is full of the wisdom of the ages and of the future to come.

Section 3
The Buddha, The Enlightened One A Man of Dark Color.

It would seem that Buddha was an Egyptian (adept) priest, chased from Memphis by persecution of Cambyses. This tradition would justify the portrayal of Buddha with woolly hair. Historical documents do not invalidate this tradition...there is general agreement today on placing in the Sixth century not only Buddha but the whole religious and philosophical movement in Asia with Confucius in China, Zoroaster in Iran. This could confirm the hypothesis of dispersion of Egyptian Priests at the time spreading their doctrine in Asia. -- Dr. Cheik Anta Diop

Manifestations of the Buddha in Asia are black with woolly hair. They all appear to be Egyptian- Nubian Priests who fled Egypt.The priest carried their spiritual knowledge but lost much of the scientific knowledge for obvious reasons. The well-known aspects of Buddhism and its companion, Yoga, are all simply Egypto-Nubian Priesthood practices, meditation and the belief that one could attain a god-like state if the soul was liberated from the body through knowledge and denial. -- Dr. Vulindlela Wobogo

This section is based on the life and origin of Siddartha Gautauma, whose name was later changed to the Buddha. Never before has there been such an individual who has made a larger impact on the continent of Asia than the Buddha. His teachings and his ideas of obtaining enlightenment all have affected the lives of the Asiatic people who embrace his degrees of knowledge. The buddha, of course, is a Dravidian Asiatic, who began teaching in parts of India around 6 century b.c. According to buddhist scholars the life of Buddha began in a small kingdom in southern Nepal. His father, Suddhodana, was a rajah of the sahya clan. His mother, Maya, died a few days after his birth. He grew up in a life of luxury and happiness,

17

and eventually married and had a son. Legend has it that because of his nobility he was protected from viewing poverty, famine and other forms of discord until one day, while venturing outside his kingdom, he observed an old man, a sick man, a dead man and an ascetic. He was so struck by these sights that he abandoned his family to become a wondering monk. During this time, he began studying under Hindu bramins and other priests throughout Asia. Placing upon himself the cruelest of cruelties to his body and mind. He virtually starved himself and lived on only water and bird droppings. A complete and total denial of all of lifes pleasures, or total asceticism. After six years of searching for peace through asceticism, Gautauma came to a town in northern India. He sat under a bodhi tree (a gigantic fig tree) and was determined to stay there until he received enlightenment. Forty nine days later, he was illuminated, became the Buddha, which means enlightenment. After receiving enlightenment the Buddha began converting people to this new religious doctrine. But where did he learn these teachings? Perhaps through self-discovery he created the foundations of what was to become modern day Buddhism. As for religious philosophy, the Buddha based his teachings on four noble truths and eight noble paths, which are composed at a mixture of philosophical truths. I will quote briefly some of the teachings of Buddha.

In Buddhist teachings there is a wheel of life and within this wheel there are eight noble paths which are described as the following wisdom.

1. Right understanding is learning how to see the world as it truly is.
2. Right thought is understanding that thought has great power on one self and others, and that whatever one focuses on gains more life; one becomes it.
3. Right speech is knowing what to say, how to say it, when to say it, and when to remain silent.
4. Right action guidelines for controlling one's behavior and allowing calmness of mind to pursue enlightenment.
5. Right livelihood is making a living in such a way as to benefit oneself and all other beings.
6. Right effort is determination and perseverance in one's spiritual discipline to transcend one's lower nature.
7. Right mindfulness is learning how to be aware of everything that one does at all times, not acting automatically, reacting to events as an animal.
8. Right meditation is a way to transcend into higher forms of consciousness including the four stages with form and four stages without form.

Notice the similarities between the teachings of Noble Drew Ali and the Buddha. It is obvious that Moorish Science borrowed from the Buddha's teachings, primarily with subjects dealing with rightful and moral character. All the topics that are discussed in the wheel of life are also discussed in the Holy Koran Circle 7. Buddhism and Moorish Science are both oriental religions that incorporate a variety of teachings from other oriental religions. Buddhism derived its beginnings from the established Hindu doctrines. We must remember that the Buddha was a black Dravidian who was born into a hindu caste influenced culture. Moorish science on the other hand is both Islam as well as oriental doctrines. So my conclusion would be that Moorish science is a religious philosophy in its own right. It is composed of a variety of sources and buddhism is one of those sources. With the studies and theories of buddhism and Moorish science, their doctrines can be traced to an older and greater civilization; Egypt. I have referenced Egypt's presence in the Asiatic religions previously. Great writers like Gerald Massey have referenced the buddha as being black with negroid features, and in some cases may have learned from an Egyptian sage. One theory is Dr. Diop's theory discussed earlier in this chapter of buddha religious teachings. There is also a theory of Egyptian priests fleeing Egypt during the invasions of the Persians. Hysokos and other middle eastern groups travelled to parts of Asia and Europe and spread their teachings to the neighboring inhabitants. That is why we see remnants of Egypt in other cultures. Thar is why the concept of the trinity in the hindu culture and the presence of the lotus flower in the study of Krishna consciousness can be traced to the pyramids of Egypt and the hieroglyphs. We find that philosophers like Plato, Aristotle and Socrates preaching a philosophical doctrine older then their civilization had learned from the Egyptian sages of the time. We have Greek Hippocrates taking all the credit for being the founder of medicine, when in fact, the Egyptian viser Imhotep was the founder of the craft. More and more we learn of the glory of the African presence in other parts of the world, especially the origins of buddha.

Gerald Massey writes, "It is not necessary to show that the first colonizers of India were black, but it is certain that the black buddha of India was imaged in the Africoid type. In the black African God, whether called buddha or Sut-Nashi, we have a datum. They carry in their color the proof of their origin. The people who first fashioned and worshipped the divine image in the Africoid mold of humanity must, according to all knowledge of human nature, have been African themselves. For the blackness is not merely mystical, the features and the hair of the Buddha belong to the black race."

The Buddha was a man of many mysteries. In religious doctrines people tend to design their God like figures into the images of themselves and this is found in all cultures and civilizations. However, in some cases, the founder of the religion is not of the origin of that ethnic group and there are several people that can be mentioned that fit that description. In Christianity, we find Jesus who is of Jewish descent or should I say African jewish descent. His teachings are being practiced by more than 2 billion Europeans worldwide and yet they portray him as a blond haired, blue eyed caucasian male. Also Muhammad is a mixture of two races, African and Arabic. Muhammad had an ethiopian mother.

In the Islamic culture, there are no known pictures of the Islamic prophet, Muhammad. There are only images of his body, but never his face, perhaps this was the muslim worlds way of hiding his true image in an Arabic one. Now we have the buddha who is a negroid and his doctrines are practiced by different shades of colored people.

The religion of Buddha, of India, is ancient. In the most ancient temples scattered through Asia, where his worship is continued, he is found black as jet, with the flat face, thick lips and curly hair of the African. -- Godfrey Higgins

The buddha is one of many Asiatics who we can identify with and trace his origins far back, so far that we arrive in the times of Egypt. We find numerous similarities between the cultures of Indian and Egypt and perhaps we can locate the use of enlightenment in terms of both the egyptian and the buddhist. Dr. Muata Ashby, in his book The African Origins, writes, "in light of the mounting evidence linking buddhism with ancient egyptian religion, it should be noted that the term, buddha meaning enlightened one, relates to the concept that spiritual knowledge is like a light which illumines the mind and shines on one's innermost soul. The buddhist term, bodhi or enlightenment, is synonymous with the terms awakening self-realization and liberation. Though the use of the term enlightenment was popularized by the discipline of buddhism as a means to highlight this concept, it was also used in ancient egypt in the remote periods of antiquity. In buddhism, the transcendal consciousness is likened to a light and buddha consciousness is understood as wakefulness or awareness of that light. Thus, anyone who achieves that form of illumination is called a buddha.

This concept is similar to that of an adept. Perhaps the buddha was a master adept who somehow obtained enlightenment during his trials of life, and perhaps with the knowledge of an adept the buddha was able to transform the minds of millions of people so they may obtain the enlightenment as well.

Section 4
The Rise of Islam and the Presence of African Influence

Never has there been such a mystery as the mystery of one's most intimate thoughts. Throughout the ages, men have lived within their own most intimate dwelling only for it to be released by some unknown phenomenon. Now this thought that man has created is somehow passed down, it then takes on many manifestations and new ideas. This is how religions are created. One idea from one individual is taken over time by someone else and they take it upon themselves to incorporate their own ideas, thus creating a new idea and a new religion. We can find examples of this in the three great world religions, which form a presence of a trinity. Within this trinity we find a foundation. In Judaism, and from Judaism came Christianity and Islam. Never have I encountered such theories in religion that I find in Islam. In most cases, a person who practices the Islamic faith will subject themselves to a strict moral loyalty to its doctrines; from the sayings of the prophet Muhammad to the five daily prayers that are required for each devout Muslim worldwide. Every religious doctrine has a point of origin and Islam is no different than any other religion in terms of spreading its teachings to anyone alien to its spoken words. Before the prophet Muhammad began preaching the religion of Islam, he would often learn and debate with the Christians and Jews, and from the intensity of these debates perhaps Muhammad reached a goal of salvation. Proclaiming himself a prophet of the most high God Allah. If we were to explore the history of Islam we would find, just like other religions, that it is composed of many religious doctrines. Islam has within its body of learning remnants of Christianity, Judaism, and especially the presence of various pagan religions.

I will explore all this in the coming passages, but first I will discuss the origins and revelations of Muhammad. According to the writings of the Al Quran, Muhammad was born around 570 A.D. in the city of Mecca to impoverished parents. His father died before he was born and his mother, Amina, died shortly after his sixth birthday. Muhammad was raised by his grandfather until he reached manhood. One day while working along the caravans of Arabia, he met a wealthy widow named, Khadija. He worked for her as a trading agent and eventually he earned her favor, and at the age of twenty-five Muhammad married her. He enjoyed a life of good wealth, which was money earned from various trading routes. Then, the course of his life changed; legend has it that it was a custom of Muhammad to venture off alone to a nearby cave to meditate. One day while meditating an angel appeared to him. The angel was gabriel and sent by God to deliver a message. Frightened by the Immaculate presence of this angel,

Muhammad paused in fear. Gabriel asked Muhammad to recite the words in the name of Allah. Muhammad did not respond. Gabriel asked Muhammad the same question again and for the second time, Muhammad did not respond. Gabriel grabbed Muhammad and choked him until he finally recited the verse in the name of Allah. Then Gabriel explained to Muhammad that he was called by Allah to be a prophet. His mission was to spread the new age teachings to all of Arabia. Muhammad's wife was the first to submit to Islam and over a period of time Muhammad received several revelations and each was passed down orally because Muhammad could not read nor write. Because Islam was a new doctrine it received opposition from numerous tribes, especially his own, the Quasirah. In 615 A.D. Muhammad was forced to leave the city of Mecca and this was the first pilgrimage in the religion of Islam. Muhammad and his followers settled in the city of Medina and in parts of Africa. Muhammad eventually won over the tribes of Arabia, conquered Mecca, and became its leader. Thus Islam was established and it still continues to exist.

When I examine various religious doctrines the writers of these doctrines fail to acknowledge the presence of Africans in their religions. We must acknowledge the contributions of Africans. Since the beginning of the revelation of the Quran that inspired and motivated prophet Muhammad, Africans have been pivotal figures in the development of Islam. Even one of Muhammad's most trusted companions was African. However, it does not stop at just a friendship. There are theories of African blood flowing through the veins of the prophet, and these theories can be proven with the acknowledgement of his Ethiopian mother. The prophet had several wives and some of them were of African descent. According to Dr. Akbar Muhammad, "the prophet acknowledges his uncle to be of very dark skin which further proves his African lineage." Dr. Akbar informs us that not only were the prophet's ancestors of African descent so were members of the Quarish tribe and many Africans were among the earliest followers. Needless to say, when we observe Moorish Science doctrines it must be acknowledged that Islam is rich in history and this history is not limited to the Arabs. Noble Drew Ali's Holy Koran gives us a brief presence of Islam within its writings by acknowledging the name of Allah. In his book, Ali replaces the name of God with the name of Allah. However, his book speaks of different stories of ancient times. The history of Islam is also the history of Africans and we must acknowledge one of Muhammad's most trusted and loyal friends, Bilal.

The story of Bilal is very complex. According to Islamic history, Bilal is the most celebrated African in Islamic history. He was the first caller to prayer and treasurer of the earlier Islamic state. He was an Abyssinian slave in bondage to a cruel master who mistreated him for accepting Islam. He also became an early follower of Muhammad in Mecca. In the story of Islam, Bilal was freed by Abu Bakr because of Bilal's beautiful voice; so beautiful it is only only fitting that he would be called the first muezzin. Bilal also was a statesman of political affairs and in later years he became governor of Syria, and was buried there. As Bilal, the black Abyssinian, whose voice was the mightiest and sweetest in Islam. In those first days, Bilal was prosecuted as the slave of the persecuted prophet of God.

"It is told how he suffered but after, our lord had departed into the chamber of Allah and the tawny horseman of the desert had ridden from Mecca even to the gates of India, conquering and to conquer, and the young crescent of Islam, slender as a sword had waxed into a vast moon of glory that filled the world, Bilal still lived with a wonderful health of years given unto the people of his race. But he sang only for the Caliph, and the Caliph was Omar. So one day it came to pass; the people of Damascus whither Omar had traveled on a visit begged the Caliph saying; O Commander of the faithful, we pray thee that thou ask Bilal to sing the call to prayer for us even as it was taught him by our lord Muhammad. Now Bilal was nearly a century old, but his voice was deep and sweet as ever, and they aided him to ascend the Minart." --Cafcadio Hearn

Bilal was influential in the establishment of Islam and even today he is acknowledged throughout the Islamic world as one of Muhammad's most trusted friends. Perhaps I can go further by saying that Bilal is one of the creators or developers of Islam. Dr. Yosef ben Jochannan writes in his book African Origins of the Major Religions, "Bilal was Islam itself; he gave it its paradise. He made its rewards interesting enough to make Christians and Jews alike, leave their own religion and convert to Islam. he made Muhammad the prophet. He managed Islam's treasury and built its capital resources. For Bilal was the founder of this religion for all Asiatic men and women."

Bilal's story has been told in the pre-written passages. He was a major contributor to Islam, however, it does not stop with his story. Early Africans were known to have been narrators and teachers of Islamic doctrines. Even non muslim Africans contributed to the culture of Islam. For example, there was the poet Antar who was an Ethiopian Arabian. He was so dark that his nickname was, "The crow." J.A. Rodgers writes in his book, World's Great Men of Color, 'that Antar accomplished great feats as a warrior and poet in pre-islamic Arabia. One of Antar's poems was accorded the highest honor possible for an African-Arabian writer. Antar's works hangs among the seven poems at the entrance of the mosque at mecca. The collection of poems, known as Millallakat, is cherished by Muslims around the world."

"Let me speak a moment of the Romance of Antar. I have searched in vain to find it quoted in any American book, although it is the greatest lyric poem of Arabia. Can it be because the hero describes himself as being "black and swarthy as an elephant?" Stranger still Antar was not Arabian born, but a negro slave, yet chosen among the Arabs as the fullest expression of their own ideas of a hero. Even in the cities of the orient today lounger in their cups never weary of following the exploits of this black son of the desert, who in his person unites the great virtues of his people, magnanimity and bravery. With the gift of poetic speech. It is the Arabic romance of chivalry and to it is due the spread of romance and chivalry throughout Medieval Europe." --George Wells Parker

Next we have the presence of Islam among Berbers who later became Moors. The Berbers/Moors became great propagators of Islam; they successfully crossed into Europe in 713 A.D. under the Moorish General, Tariq Ibn Zaid.They settled in areas of Spain and some parts of Portugal, and this is where the prophet Noble Drew Ali learned the history of the Moors.

To fully understand the term, Moor, we must first learn of their history. Most of us are not aware that the peoples whom the classical Greek and Roman historians called berber were black and affiliated with the contemporary peoples of East African areas. The word, berber, was used to refer to peoples of the Red Sea area in Africa as well as North Africa. It was such populations that in large measure comprised the Moorish people, but because of the attribute of blackness, which sharply distinguished them from the bulk of the European people, the word came to generally be used by Europeans to describe persons of black complexion in general. The word, moor, was used for people basically of berber in origin, but then came to include, during the Islamic period, the early Arabians. Both of these populations belonged to a physical type or types of men commonly referred to by early scholars as hamitic or brown Mediterranean. It is worth noting that the Moors of North Africa at first resisted the conversion of Islam and fought the Muslim armies before they accepted the religion and became its most ardent Caliphs, generals and scholars. By contrast, the flow of Islam into sub-sahara Africa took a completely different form. Inner Africa experienced no Arab conquest and Islam was spread through the peaceful work of African itinerant traders and peripatetic local teachers and scholars. The spread of Islam into Africa has impacted this great continent. Its teachings were passed onto Africans in two ways; the first was by force and the second, which was common with Africans, was to integrate Islam with traditional african cultures. Needless to say, we can further acknowledge Africa-established Islamic kingdoms.

Mansa Musa was the king of the Mali empire, a Muslim king who performed the pilgrimage to Mecca in such fashion that his fame was proclaimed because of the elaborate amounts of gold that he spend during his travel to the holy city. On 14th Century maps his picture is displayed on the legend as spending so much gold on his pilgrimage that he devalued the precious metal. Islamic influence is represented in all sections of early Islamic history. All this should undoubtedly explain and acknowledge their history and accomplishments. This scholarship is designed to understand the impact played in world african cultures. Earlier in the previous passage, I stated that Islam is a mixture of pagan religions with additions of Judaic- Christian doctrines. This combination of religions all contained remnants of egyptian religious beliefs as well as other beliefs from neighboring cultures. First I would like to explore the biblical origins of Islam's Quranic doctrines. They state that the Arabs are descendants of Abraham's eldest son, Ishmael. Biblical scripture states that Ishmael and his mother, Hagar, were banished from the house of Abraham. To further prove the African presence in Islam, Ishmael's mother was of egyptian origin and Abraham was from a land of dark people. This we can see in the tribes of black found in Palestine, Persia and other middle eastern civilizations. The Arabian peninsula first inhabited more than 8,000 years ago was populated by blacks and Abraham was from that region. There have been numerous debates on the legitimacy of the modern day Arabs. The debate has been the following;

1. Are these Arabs, who are very light in skin, the true original Arabs of old?
2. Are these Arabs the true descendants of Ishmael?

Author George Wells Parker writes a thorough opinion on this subject in his book, Children of the Sun. He writes, "And Ishmael, the son of Abraham by his hand Maiden Hagar, went into the far country of Yemen and there took unto himself a wife, and from them descended the pure Arabian race. This is the ancestry claimed by the southern Arabians for their race and whether it be true or only legend, they have contended for this ancestry throughout the centuries and to this day, from the north there came another people calling themselves Arabians. They were lighter in complexion than those of the south and they claimed themselves the real Arabians. The Yemenites, from whom Ishmael chose his bride, were a black race alien to the ethiopians, and the Arabs of the south were likewise black, and between the northern and southern Arabians there broke out a hatred which they carried to the farthest ends of the world."

Even today these groups of people are still fighting amongst themselves just to prove legitimacy of their origins. Now, I will again reference Islam's founder Muhammad. He acknowledges his own racial color by his relationships with the country of ethiopia.

Author George Wells Parker writes, "Note, too, the fact that Muhammad was one of these black Arabs. When he appealed to the Arabians he called himself, 'Arab of the Arabs, of the purest blood of your land, of the family of Hashim and of the tribe of Qurysha.' It was the family of Hashim that founded the house of the Abbasids, and thus are we brought face to face with the fact that the third of the world's greatest religions was founded by a man in whose veins flowed black blood. This is one reason why Mohammedism is so strong and will ever remain strong among races of Africa. The religion preaches absolute equality and one of the precepts of the Quran reads is a negro is called to rule over you, hear him and obey him, though his head be like dried grapes. From what has been written of the Jews and Hindus it will readily be seen that the African is now as he was I the dawn of history, the founder of religion."

Focusing on a different subject we must observe the presence of pagan religions by examining Islam's most sacred object, the Kaaba. In pre-Islamic Arabia 360 gods and goddesses were worshiped and a representation of these deities were placed around the kaaba, which is a cubed shaped box in a circle of 360 degrees. This is why the average Muslim pilgrim performs a circumambulation around the cubed box- that way each pilgrim could pay homage to his/her particular deity. In addition, these deities included ancient egyptian as well as greek and Hindu divinities. One of these was allah. Before the establishing of Islam, before the birth of the prophet Muhammad, Allah was actually a moon deity that the Quasirah tribe originally worshipped. When Muhammad conquered Mecca and became its ruler he removed all the deities from the Kaaba and proclaimed it an Islamic shrine.

"Before the advent of Islam, southern Arabia already possessed the sacred kaaba sanctuary, with its black stone, at Mecca. The kaaba was reputed to have been constructed by Ishmael, son of Abraham and Hagar the egyptian (a negro woman.)" -- Author unknown

Muhammad proclaimed the name of Allah as the supreme deity and this is the same Allah that was the chief deity of the Quasirah tribe. Therefore, it is only fitting that Muhammad adopted ideas from his tribe of origin and incorporated them into the newly established Islam. In modern times, we can observe the same events playing out over and over again. In the western world we observe various new age religious movements coming into existence by creating their own doctrines and views of that ancient

26

faith. In America, we observe the uprising of several religious orders that were created for the American way of life; that is religious sects ranging from the Mormon church to the present day Moorish Science Temple of America, which can trace its ideas to an ancient religion. Needless to say, Islam like any other religion has many contributors and I would claim that 80% of its foundations were created by people of African descent. The only conflict that Africans have is realizing what our ancestors have contributed to civilization.This is why Noble Drew Ali established the Moorish Science Temple. His ideas was to create a link to the origins of Islam. The Moorish Science Temple was and is the first major establishment of Islam among blacks in America. However, I must mention that Islam dates further into early American history. The next chapter, The Story of the Native American Moors, goes more in depth on this subject.

I am now faced with the question of establishing the Moorish Divine Movement as a legitimate branch of the Islamic faith. In this world, everyone has a different way of acknowledging his or her own deity. Some individuals may go to extremes in order to please their gods while others prefer a more conservative approach. In some cases Islam can be very extreme in its beliefs, but over time there are those who have approached its doctrine somewhat different. The Moorish Divine Movement is an example of this. There are two major branches of Islam; the Shite and the Sunni. The difference between the two groups is that the Shite Muslims follow the blood line of Muhammad from his only living daughter, Fatima. The Sunni follow the leadership of Muhammad's closest friend, Abu Bakr. Some how after the death of Muhammad the elite Muslim powers separated into these two major groups. Since the death of the prophet Islam has experienced the establishment of several different off-shoots, and in most cases each one of these off-shoots carried with it the foundations of Islam with the additional ideas of its founder.

When the prophet Noble Drew Ali began preaching his version of Islam he did not incorporate any remnants of the already established orthodox Islam. In fact, he could not read, write or speak the Arabic language. The Chicago Defender writes in Ali's obituary that he could scarcely read or write. According to Muslim scholar, Imam Isa, "although Noble Drew Ali was unable to teach Islam in its pristine purity due to his lack of knowledge of the Al Quran and the Arabic language, he did serve as a stepping stone in introducing Al Islam to a people who had totally lost the knowledge of their rightful way of life."

Noble Drew Ali was able to bring the black man and woman together for the common causes of uplifting the spirit and economic development of a nation. If we were to reflect on Islam and Moorish Science we would find absolutely no similarities between the two. However, my goal for this passage is to determine whether Moorish science should be considered a legitimate branch of Islam? There are major issues that need to be addressed before I begin my analysis of this question.

There has been opposition when a new religion is founded. Noble Drew Ali and Muhammad both endured oppositions from other dominant religious sects, and yet through endless trials and political battles their religions continued to exist. Situations such as this are not limited to the religion of Islam. We find this in the establishment of any new religious doctrine. We find stories in the bible of how the Jews persecuted and rejected the teachings of Jesus. they condemned him and his followers and finally crucified him upon a cross. The ruling parties of the time tried everything in their power to eliminate the Christian faith but failed to do so. Today, Christianity is the largest religion world wide numbering more than 6 billion followers. In these modern times, we observe the Mormons of Utah being persecuted by the American government for their religious practices of polygamy. Now, the Mormon religion expands over all parts of the globe numbering 10 million followers. There are numerous other examples. Just like Christianity and the Mormons, Moorish Science has the right to exist, and not only exist, but should be acknowledged as a legitimate branch of Islam. Everyone has a different way of serving God and Moorish Science is no different than the rest of the worlds religions when it comes to expressing the ideas on serving God. In the beginning, Islam was not accepted by the major religions, but eventually it became the worlds second largest religion outnumbering the Jewish faith and approaching the numbers of Christianity. Therefore, Moorish Science has been in existence for more than 90 years and seems to be well established taking into consideration that it has several off-shoots from its original doctrines. So Moorish Science speaks of a different doctrine from the teachings of mainstream Islam and yet it displays and acknowledges the presence and love for the almighty god, Allah. So it is only fitting to conclude that Moorish Science is legitimate. Here are some of the Moorish Science doctrines on its view of Islam:

Islam is a very simple faith. It requires man to recognize his duties toward Allah, his creator, and his fellow creature. it teaches the supreme deity of living at peace with one's surroundings. it is pre-eminently the religion of peace. The goal of man's life according to Islam is peace with everything. Peace with Allah and peace with man. It is obvious these doctrines have impacted those who embraced its abundance of learning. Therefore, the acknowledgement of Moorish Science is essential to the many different branches of Islam. Small in numbers as it may be, it does exist.

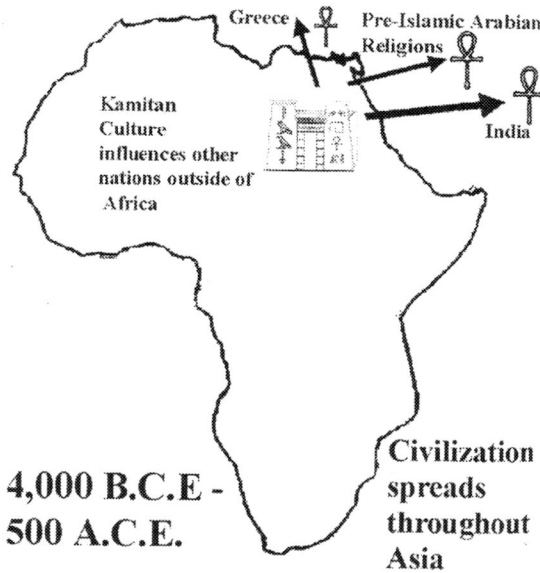

Greece

Pre-Islamic Arabian
Religions

Kamitan
Culture
influences other
nations outside of
Africa

India

**4,000 B.C.E -
500 A.C.E.**

**Civilization
spreads
throughout
Asia**

*5. Civilization spreads throughout Asia explains the birth place of
civilization was in Africa Source The African Origins by muata Ashby*

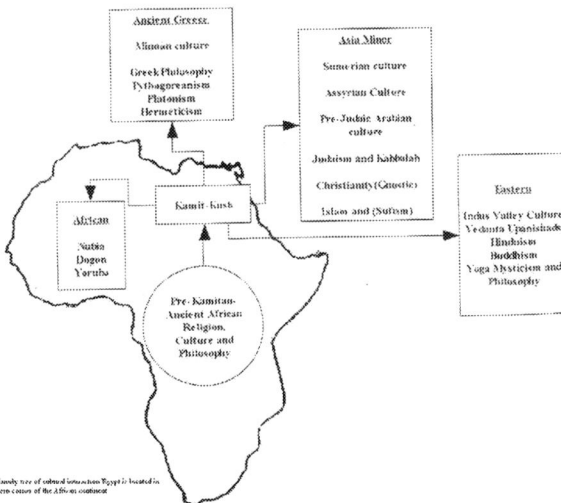

Ancient Greece

Minoan culture

Greek Philosophy
Pythagoreanism
Platonism
Hermeticism

Asia Minor

Sumerian culture

Assyrian Culture

Pre-Judaic Arabian
culture

Judaism and Kabbalah

Christianity (Gnostic)

Islam and (Sufism)

Eastern

Indus Valley Culture
Vedanta Upanishads
Hinduism
Buddhism
Yoga Mysticism and
Philosophy

African

Nubia
Dogon
Yoruba

Kamit-Kush

Pre-Kamitan-
Ancient African
Religion,
Culture and
Philosophy

The African family tree of cultural interaction Egypt is located in
the north eastern corner of the African continent

*6. The African family tree of cultural interaction Egypt is
located in the North Eastern corner of the African continent.
Source The African Origins by Muata Ashby*

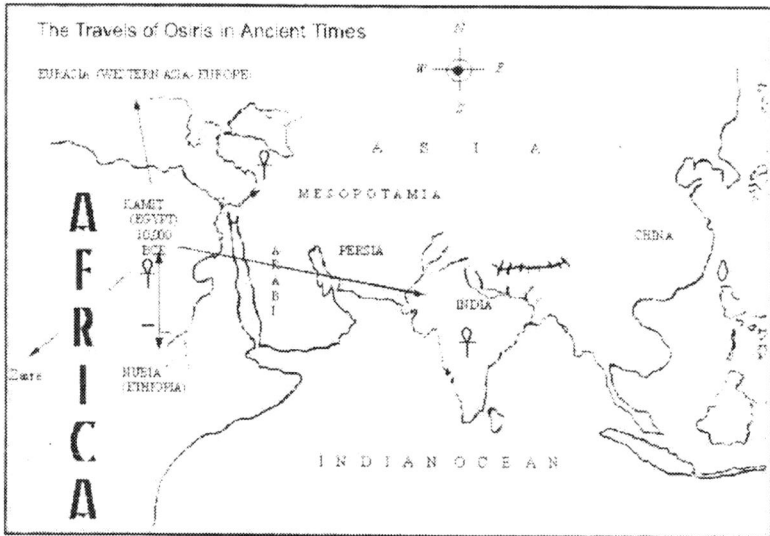

The Travels of Osiris in Ancient Times

7. *The Travels of Osiris in Ancient Times. Source*
The African Origins by Muata Ashby

The Black Lord Krishna

8. *Negroid Buddha and the Black Lord Krishna according to Hindu doctrines Krishna was known as the blackener.*

The Eyes of
Horus

The Eyes of
Krishna

The Eyes of
Buddha

9. The Eyes of Horus, Krishna and Buddha. Source
The African Origins by Muata Ashby

AFRICAN ORIGINS Of Eastern Civilization, Religion, And Ethics Philosophy

Below left- Amunhotep, son of Hapu, Ancient Egyptian philosopher, priest
and Sage at 80 years old in a meditative posture. Below right - Buddha "The
Enlightened One" of India.

Ancient Egyptian
Wisdom teaching:

"Passions and
irrational desires
are ills exceedingly
great; and over
these GOD hath set
up the Mind to play
the part of judge
and executioner."

Buddhist teaching:
Nirvana means

"Enlightened
Consciousness.
Bliss when the mind
is free of all desire"

10. Amunhotep and Buddha Source The African Origins by muata Ashby

Africus: net entire rakeless head is covered with woolly hair like that of Buddha's.

Venus of Willendorf

Buddha, 12th century (sitting), 9th century (top inset), and 11th century (bottom inset).

11. Negroid Buddha

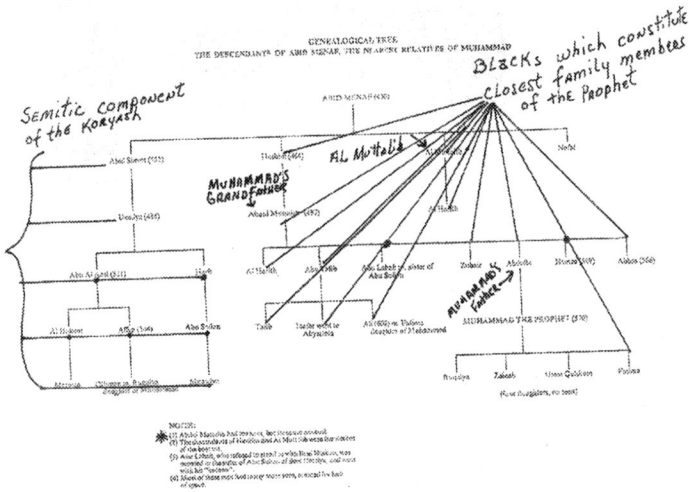

GENEALOGICAL TREE
THE DESCENDANTS OF ABID MANAF, THE NEAREST RELATIVES OF MUHAMMAD

Semitic component of the Koryash

BLacks which constitute closest family members of the Prophet

MUHAMMAD'S GRANDFATHER

AL Muttalib

MUHAMMAD Father

Figure 10. Genealogy tree showing the various branches of the Koreysh.

*12. Genealogy of Prophet Muhammad Tribe the Koreysh
this traces the African blood line of the prophet. Source
African presence in early Asia by Ivan van sertima*

13. *King Mansa Kan Kan Musa African king who converted to Islam and perform the pilgrimage to Mecca in such fashion that it became legendary*

14. *Bilal the first muezzin or caller of prayer in Islam and a close friend of Muhammad*

15. *Allegorical Picture of the prophet Muhammad
face is covered to hide his identity*

16. *Burial Shrine of Prophet Muhammad.*

Chapter 2

The Story of the Native American Moor

The descendant of the Ancient Moabites and the true national indigenous peoples of the continental United States, North, South and Central Americas (Al Morocs), including the adjoining islands in reconstructed history, the Moors have been labeled/branded the following wardship status names: negroes, colored, blacks, African Americans, latinos, puerto ricans, hispanic, Indians and west Indians. None of the brand names are true national names of any member of the human family.

It is very complex to speak of both the origin and the history of the native american people. The prophet Noble Drew Ali acknowledges this indigenous group of people as Moors and this he writes in the Holy Koran Circle 7.

"When we speak of native american Moors we must learn their stories, their trials and tribulations, and also their impact on Moorish history."

Earlier I stated that Noble Drew Ali had traveled throughout Central America establishing temples and issuing travelling cards to spanish speaking Moors. To understand the native american moor we must first understand that the native americans are composed of several different outside invading groups and of their migrations. According to scientists, about 4,000 years ago a group of Asiatics travelled along a short body of land called an isthmus. This land was somehow connected to the Asian continent. Next there are various migrations from Asia to North America. These migrations lasted for some 2,000 years. These Asiatics are now known as the original indigenous people of North America. For several centuries these people lived in peace, surviving on the resources of the land until the beginning of the european explorations. These explorations were the beginning of the the downfall of the Indians. These explorers were looking for wealth and new land in which to claim for their european monarchy. The Indians of North America resembled that of Africans and the great African civilizations. The Indians, like the Africans were the founders of science and were rich in gold. Both Africa and North America were plundered. History tells us there were several invading groups; they were the Italians, Portuguese, British and Spaniards. They comprised the melting pot of various ethnic groups we see today. However, these european groups moved in, battled the Indians with superior weaponry and were victorious in taking the land that was not rightly theirs. This is an old tale of divide and conquer. First, they drain the resources and then assimilate into the existing culture, thus creating new cultures and new people. We know for a fact that the latin communities are composed of the original people and the invading conquering groups. We find the mixture of european blood that gives such groups as the Mexicans, Nicaraguans, Venezuelans, and all other central american groups.

We must also discuss African slavery. This subject will tie to the connection of the nature of the native american moor. Perhaps the prophet understood this origin by figuring out the formula of their creation. Let's trace their origin. First, we have Asian descendants who crossed the isthmus which gives us a Asiatic point of origin. Next, there are captured African slaves who were taken from the western hemisphere from countries like Algeria, Mauritania, Senegal and Morocco, Even today we can see the remnants of the atrocities of slavery by visiting the existing slave castle along the west coast of Africa. It is worth noting that some of these slaves were practicing Muslims and were of Moorish descent. In his book, The Story of Prince Hall Masonry in Illinois, author William H. Hardy writes, "Long before European countries had achieved the status of nation and empire; and thousands of years before the birth of Christianity, Black Africans had been frequent visitors to the land now known as the Americas.

The ancient presence of the members of African Kingdoms in mexico and South America has been proved through the unearthing of Negroid skeletons, countless artifacts and huge sculptured Nubian heads. There is no denying their Negro-ness. The ancient Americans who sculpted them have been shown to be absolute masters of realistic portraiture, and did not arrive at these distinctive features through accidental stylization. The features are not only Negro-African in type but individual in their facial particulars, canceling out the possibility of ritual stereotypes of an unknown race produced by some quirk of the sculptor's imagination. At the time of the European Age of World Discovery, however, African

Kingdoms of advanced age were at various stages of cultural decline with the presence of disastrous wars over religion and territorial rights.

History has recorded 1501 as the year for the official introduction of Legal African Slavery in the Americas. Shortly after Christopher Columbus landed in the Bahamas in 1492 and claimed a piece of the new world for Spain, it was quickly understood that the native Indians were not agreeable to work in the fields and mines for the invading Europeans. Thus, the children of Mother Africa, weak from massive conditions of chaos, became easy prey for bondage. The seizure and transportation of human beings from Africa for the express purpose of selling them into slavery is a scar of shame that will never be eradicated by the human race. And, it is, and will continue to be an ever present reminder as to how, and by whom, the Americas were really built.

As the English Colonies of North America took shape, slaves were in demand to perform all types of work. The untiring European desire for rum, rice, cotton, and tobacco accented an even greater need for slaves on the plantation of central and southern colonies." Martin Delany, a great black nationalist writes in his opinion on Ancient African's in America, "The continent of America is an asylum for all the various nations of the earth. Among the earliest and most numerous class who found their way to the new world were those of the African race. And it is now ascertained to our mind, beyond a peradventure, that when the continent was discovered, there were found in central America tribes of black race, of fine looking people, having characteristics of color and hair, identifying them originally of the African race, no doubt being a remnant of the Africans who, with the Carthaginian expedition, were adventurously cast upon the continent, in their memorable excursion to the great island after sailing many miles distant to the west of the pillars of hercules (strait of Gilbrator.)"

Now the last and final ingredient of this mix is the conquest of the Spaniards. When you combine the indigenous people of Asia who migrated to North America with African slaves who were shipped over to America for labor (some of these slaves being arabic speaking muslims of Moorish descent), and the european explorers who assimilated into the indigenous indian population, combined with the conquest of the Spaniards, this process gave birth to Puerto Ricans, Cubans, Dominicans and Belizians and other latin groups that mixed with the blood of Africans.

The story of the Spaniards is interesting because they too learned from the Africans. We must understand the history of Spain and its contact with the African world and namely the Moors. History tells us that the Moors were the glory of Spain and it was the knowledge of the Moors that allowed Spain to become one of the most powerful european nations of the 14th thru 16th centuries. Over time the Moors were expelled from Spain and they took with them all the science and technology. However, the Moors had established their own civilization. I will discuss this in a later chapter but I must include that the African people which empowered Spain's empire all came from within Moorish imperial boundaries. Historical records reveal that in Africa, the Moorish empire once extended as far south as the Senegal River and as far east as the Egyptian border. Needless to say, the prophet Noble Drew Ali acknowledges these various groups of American Moors and in some aspects briefly traces their origins to the Moors of Africa and Spain. Since we acknowledged the latino's of Americas as Moors, I could never understand why there is racism among the various latin groups. There should be no strife between either of the spanish ethnic groups and yet racism is present in both outside and inside each others ethnic groups. We have Puerto Rican communities not getting along with the Mexican community and the lighter shades of Cubans discriminating against the darker Cuban population. This is also observed in countries like Belize, Brazil and Argentina. All these ethnic groups are descendants of Moors and at one time were Muslims.

"When Americas was discovered in 1452 by Columbus, it was already inhabited by a nation of people whom Columbus called or named 'Indians'. They too were descendants of a tribe of the ancient Asiatics and are therefore our brothers. The country was taken from them by europeans who had no right to take it lawfully and it rightfully belonged to our Asiatic brothers. So we have a perfect right to take it back." -- Moorish Voice, March 1943

The Holy Koran Circle 7 states, "The Asiatic nations and countries in North, South, and Central America; The Moorish Americans and Mexicans in North America; Brazilians, Argentineans, and Chileans in South America; Columbians, Nicaraguans and the natives of San Salvador in Central America, etc... All these are Muslims. --Chapter 45, verse 5 and 6

Racism among the latin communities is very common. However, the statement above gives us a reason why all native american Moors should come together. One unknown author writes, "It must be said that those persons known as latin and/or Spanish, more than likely possess the blood of Moorish (African) forebearers. There is most certainly a link between them and the former Muslim rulers of Al-Andalus- later known as the kingdoms of Spain and Portugal (The Moors). That fact certainly makes it quite difficult for such peoples to be racist against Africans or Muslims. Such Catholic communities should only argue theological differences and never racial ones. A Catholic Spaniard or latin is essentially attempting to skate on melted ice when they try to make an argument of racial supremacy or distinction. In addition, they would be denying the historic fact of the Islamic Moors primary role as scholarly tutors and beacons of civilized society for medieval Spain and Europe. There is much more which can be said about the legacy of Muslims in the early Americas. But this short passage was only intended to illuminate an area of the muslim experience which is all too often overlooked. In spite of what the proverbial mainstream Christian community may think, the presence of Muslims in the Americas is much older and more profound than many of them know.

To explore the history and origins of the native american moor further acknowledges the presence of Africans on the American continent. This scholarship is in no way limited to the native american moor and it goes far beyond the presence of the muslim speaking slaves. Have you ever wondered why the pyramids of America resemble the pyramids of Egypt? This is not coincidence and numerous stories have been passed down of early Africans visiting America prior to the great migrations of the european explorers. It is not a coincidence that there are dark skinned Indians as well as light skinned Indians. Perhaps it can be further observed noticing the various statues of indigenous tribes like the Olmecs, who seemed to have possessed certain negroid features. I must also conclude, just as other African writers have, the presence of African were here long before Columbus' so called discovery of America. Dr. Ivan van Sertima is renowned for his research on Africans in early America. Sertima has come to the conclusion that there were Africans that travelled from their homeland and created settlement colonies in the Americas. Perhaps the travelling Africans were establishing trade with the indigenous Americans. Contact between native Americans and Africans can be traced back to ancient antiquity. Gigantic black statues with negroid faces and other ancient monuments found in Mexico present undeniable evidence that African people sailed to America as early as 800 B.C. Dr. Sertima writes in his book, They Came Before Columbus, "what is needed far more than new facts is a fundamentally new version of history. In this new vision the atlantic is an open sea long before Columbus. But accidental drift voyages by African men, except in those cases where they brought fruit or grain with them, alien to America (and this happened in pre-history at least twice) would in themselves have a very minimal effect, if any. Planned expeditions, however, or expeditions intended for other destinations in Africa which were blown off course would be a different matter. They would bring not only a substantial but a select group of aliens to American slaves. This may account for the presence of negroid women in pre-Columbian America."

This statement from Dr. Sertima's work not only proves the presence of Africans in America, but it changes the American history books, which assert that most Africans arrived in Americas as slaves to the europeans. All this was essential in the exploring and conquering of the native American Indians. We should now understand how europeans arrived to an undiscovered country without any knowledge of its existence. In fact, I am sure that no european vessel could have made such a trip without proper navigation or coordinates. How did Christopher Columbus learn of the existence of this new continent? First of all every thing starts with a fable and half of the time that fable usually have some truths to it. There are theories that Columbus may have followed ancient maps created by Moorish seafarers. In 1492, when Columbus arrived in the new world, he was strongly influenced by the geography of the 13th century Arab scholar, Al-Idrissi, who served as an advisor to King Rodger of Sicily. Columbus had with him a copy of Al-Idrissi's works mentioning the discovery of a new continent by eight muslim explorers. He also had muslim crew members with him for translation and other services. It is obvious Columbus and most other european explorers lacked sufficient knowledge to travel the seas. Of all the european countries, The Spanish Armada were world renown for their large ships and sailing ability. All can be traced to the Moors of North Africa. The Moors were the teachers and trainers of the Spanish. They established schools of learning and universities to all european Spaniards, Jews and Moors.

The purpose of this chapter was to explore the rich history of the Asiatics in all parts of the world. Throughout this chapter, I have named several important individuals who gave the Asiatic religions their foundations. From the creation of the black Dravidians to the establishment of Islam, Asiatics have circled the globe to establish civilizations in distant lands. When one describes an Asiatic, you can surely acknowledge several different groups who either resemble or share a culture of origin. According to the Sid-Jul Moorish American papers, the name Asia is derived from the sanskrit usaa, meaning dawn or to rise, signifying, land of the dawn or rising sun. Asia's meaning is similar to the Arabic slang, meaning 'to rise' or sunrise, meaning eastward or toward the rising sun. The terms, 'saracen' and 'Asiatic' (Asian) imply that a person is eastern. perhaps this explains why most of the worlds major religions were established in the east. Overall, the various Asiatic religions and cultures have bestowed upon the world its immaculate wisdoms in which every race of men drew from in creating their own wisdoms and understandings, adding their own characteristics to an already established doctrine.

19. Olmec Head Statues compared to Egyptian head statues

Chapter 3

The Rise of Islam among Blacks in America: From its Origins to its Establishment in America

"Islam in African America has a history as long as memory, when Muslim slaves from Africa wrapped their faith tightly around them as invisible armor against daily degradation. But the practice does not seem to continue. Religious revivalists in the early part of the twentieth century, mostly in the North where large numbers of new migrants sought the strength of a community, found populations willing to listen and eager to believe. In 1913, Timothy Drew donned a fez and claimed Moroccan heritage for his people in the Moorish Science Temple. For all its imaginative reconstruction, the Moorish Science Temple has little under the surface to connect it to worldwide Islam. But its spirit of displacing the term "Negro" from blacks, of thinking of darker skinned peoples as Asiatics and Moroccans, of allying Drew Ali with "Jesus, Mohammed, Buddha, and Confucius" is part of the productive tension between separatism and universalism that will follow all African American Islam throughout the rest of the century. But it would be in the next decade, with the growth of future islamic communities that the Asian connection forges ahead." -- Moustafa Bayoumi, East of the Sun (West of the Moon): The Harmonic History of Islam among Asian and African Americans.

This section of the book introduces the reader to freemasonry and the religious background of the shriners order. In order to explain the topics in Chapter 3 I felt it was necessary to elaborate further on mysteries of the Masonic order. Since Moorish Science drew from this system of learning it should be known that Islam is rich in history especially when it comes to exploring the Wisdoms of the Masonic order.

If freemasonry truly is the builder of men then as members of this scared order we must come to the realization that there can only be one reality and that reality is wisdom. To man god has bestowed upon him Time and time is unlimited. This is the order of things, to be in tune and one with your creator the maker and sustainer of all things. The giver and provider of life's most precious Qualities. The mason is a builder of life and in order to build the mason must explore his mine because contained within it is the key to pure awareness. The mind is like a lake, when the mind is calm there is no agitation, no movement it is like a lake that can reflect an image clearly. However when the mind is agitated, the mental substances is put into Vibration and these vibrations are what constitute thoughts and perceptions of the senses. Thus consciousness in the state of rest reveals one image, one essence one being when the mind moves, seeking to fulfill desire after desire it is like a lake into which a rock has been thrown. Eventually the mind will manifest thoughts, and thought are what is needed to create, freemasonry posses the same qualities. It is both a system of building and a system of travel. We build from start to finish meaning a youth with absolutely no knowledge of self to a man who has obtained full enlightenment. We travel meaning not just from place to place but from the maternal World of energy and matter to a place of pure spirituality and with that bit of knowledge both will lead to creating a house not made with hands but eternal in heaven. A spiritual temple that we began erecting from our birth to our current status in life. Every man that is born is given the opportunity to explore and enjoy his time on earth. However I must note how we conduct ourselves determines our status when we come before judgment day. God created us from his thoughts and these thoughts manifested into life. Ancient philosophy tells us that the creation story is replayed every moment for every day. Every time our heart beats, a new moment of life is created. Everyday the sun rises another day is created and modern day science agrees with this assessment. It has been my desire to explore all the mysteries of Freemasonry and bring forth entirely new ideas and scholarship. So in my endless pursuit for this goal I decided to discuss a series of topics based not only on the craft but the outside sources that are composed within this vast body of literature and dogma. So now begins an endless journey into what I define as a quest for Masonic Enlightenment. When one speaks of Freemasonry, the first thing that comes to mind is a system of learning that is used to evolve the mind from a state of ignorance to intelligence. Once the mind has evolved a mason can now pursue an endless search for knowledge and this search for knowledge will require him to travel through all walks of life both mentally and spiritually. Freemasonry is a building science of the mind and of morals and this structure should be built from start to finish. The fist step of this universal structure is the beginning and it is here where the foundation is laid for future enhancements. Perhaps we can say that it is a building process for future things to come. When everything is complete and knowledge is obtained this process brings to mind the attaining of enlightenment. Enlightenment can be defined as total reaching for the ultimate wisdom or ultimate state of awareness. Author Albert Mackey defines enlightenment in his book encyclopedia of Freemasonry " illuminates and is frequently used to designate a mason who has been rescued from darkness and eventually received intellectual light". One new age writer states that enlightenment is men's emergence from self imposed immaturity. So, perhaps, that is what the mason experiences as he travels from degree to degree and each time he obtains a degree he becomes more enlighten until he reaches a state of mental perfection. At this stage, the mason now has developed what is called a universal conscience. Author Manley P Hall writes that the true disciple of Ancient masonry has given up forever the worship of personalities with his greater insight.

He realizes that all forms and their position in material affairs are of no importance to him compared to life, which is evolving within. To speak of freemasonry one has to understand the inner journey of the craft by way of the ritualistic work which I should say is only a men shadow of the big picture that is in stored for the spiritual man. The average well-learned mason should spend quality time reflecting on his life and the lives of his loved ones, because the master mason is a man of pure faith.

In the Ancient Symbols he is represented as an old man leaning upon a staff, his long white beard upon his chest as a symbol of his wisdom. This symbol of course represents old age. This can be deemed as more of a wisdom stage, because by now the mason has knowledge of all things that is stored within his environment of learning. A true master of the craft recognizes the value of seeking truth and obtaining knowledge which now brings us to the next subject. How do we go by obtaining knowledge or perhaps should I say where should we go to receive it.

Freemasonry is as universal as man himself. This sacred science serves as a formula for the building of himself and his brethren by way of the mystical symbols that we use to enhance our spiritual powers. Take the lodge, for example. The lodge is the main dwelling. Place for all levels of Masons and it is the lodge where all Masons should receive Instruction and knowledge of their level of working tools. The lodge is a place of brotherly love and unity so this should suggest that what ever is practiced in the lodge should be practiced on the outside world. In a profound sense, the lodge itself is a representation of the outside world. Just reflect on the universal symbols that are within the lodge room, for example The Ground Floor, the Earth the Celestial heavens, the north, the south west and east all are what I define as Earth based symbols. A Mason must and always will acknowledge the used of symbols because without them you have no masonry. Author Muata Ashby writes in his book the African origins it states. Symbols have a great Psychological significance because without them there would be no possibility for the mind to exist, function and interact with creation. A deeper examination of symbols reveals that they are more than just representations of images or ideas. The human mind understands things by first making a mental picture of it and then associating than mental concept with other ideas and thoughts. The true master mason is strengthened by the knowledge that is displayed within his inner lodge and it is that same knowledge that provides him with certain mystical rites and privileges. Let us now focus our attention on one of the Free Masonry's majors and important symbols, the east. In the Masonic ritual the east is a place of light. Therefore knowledge since light is the representation of knowledge it is only fitting that light should be the essential prize that all Mason's seek yet it has never been acknowledge in a worldly sense. To the outside world when I think of light the first thing that comes to mind is the Sun. The sun deemed a major symbol of Freemasonry serves as a symbol of light as well as a symbol of life and regeneration the Ancients believed that the sun would rise and set only to rise again symbolizes the birth and death and reincarnation of the cycle of life. In most cases the sun is usually related to religions. We can find stories of the sun in all the major world religions. Before I began this topic, I must point out that I am not a member of the Shriner's Order; However I must note that in order to compile this lecture I drew from various sources outside of the already established system of freemasonry. There is much more that meets the eye to what we know about the nobles of the mystic shrine. It has been the opinion of most outside viewers of craft that the shrine is considered the playhouse of the Masonic order in that it is a place where men can relive their adolescent tears of playing around, drinking, throwing wild parties and a host of network and charity events, but as most well learned masons worldwide will tell you that there is a much more serious side to Shrinedom. In this lecture I do not plan to rewrite the history of the shrine but only to elaborate on several theories and inconcealable facts. It is my intention to connect the modern day rituals of the order to his true African/Asiatic origins. It isn't unusual that I may receive criticism on the subject that I am about to write but in most cases truth is something that should never be concealed. I am not saying that

Freemasonry conceals truth but there is that truth behind the truth that I plan to explore. When we look at the make up of mystic shrine we will find a mixture of religious dogma taken from various faiths and philosophies, intertwining them into a combination of various teachings in which we as members of the Craft hold true because we know them to be as such. Before I continue let me speak a moment on the trials and errors of religion. I have come to the belief that men of all races have devoted their lives to the practice of religion especially those religions that are connected to the masses of peoples. We find them in every epoch and in all lands. In India, there lived those who transmitted to the world the Vedas. And there was also the great Gautama Buddha; China had its Confucius the Zend Avesta was produced by Zoroaster in Iran. The Ancient Civilization of Babylonia gave to the world one of the greatest reformers, the biblical patriarch Abraham. The three great world religions may rightly be proud of a long series of reformers: Moses, Samuel, David, Solomon, and Jesus among others. These individuals claimed in general to be the giver of a divine mission, and they left behind sacred books as a gift to the world for future generation to learn their stories. Overtime religion has brought a dark side to man-by way of wars. Massacres and genocides became the order of the times; causing more or less a complete loss of these Divine Scripture and as a result Scriptures were either destroyed or rewritten to fit the times or the controlling parties. In spite of this the human race has continued to embrace religious dogma and the result is the practicing of faiths in all parts of the world. This practice however manifested into various new age religions and well as the establishing of fraternal societies. It should be noted freemasonry itself is built on both the Jewish and Christian faith. Therefore I must conclude that everything that we practice as far as the Craft itself has been taught from a Christian stand point. So now comes to play the various origins of the Christian doctrines, where did all this come from! Over and over again modern day religions have been traced back to Egypt. And since Egypt is in Africa which at that time was inhabited by black Africans, it is only fair to come to the conclusion that they were the founders of what we know today as religion. Even the signs and tokens of freemasonry could be considered properly African Freemasons World wide already have laid claimed to trace its origins to the Egyptian mystery religion. Of all the ancient legends that of Isis, Osiris, and Horus of Egypt is very closely linked with certain ceremonies of the craft. In fact, those members of the craft who are students of the esoteric sciences would recognize its Egyptian foundations. Religious scholars will tell you that the ceremonies of freemasonry are of Egyptian origin but that following the enslavement of the Hebrew people in Egypt, Moses, because of his position of great power gradually transformed those ceremonies from Egyptian to Hebrew traditions. This explains why we find so much of Judaism in Masonic ceremonies. I would like to quote a passage from Dr. George Wells Parker in order to elaborate further on the subject at hand Parker writes "The Dawn of the Egyptian civilization is certainly a distinct proof of the important part played by Africans in the history of human culture. the religious ideas of a people often furnish us with more or less conclusive evidence as to their racial relations and many writers today who get no nearer to Egypt than the armchairs with their libraries, after trying to prove that because certain things in the Egyptian system of religion resembled the systems of other nations that, therefore, the Egyptians must have been something other than African. Yet even here they miss or deliberately overlook the greatest fact of all. The old idea of man having been created in the image of his maker is made manifest in all systems of religious worship and the gods are ever representative of their worshipers therefore when we observed the myths a beliefs of Egyptian religion that osiris the supreme god of Egypt was described as beautiful of face but with a dull black complexion it is by no means improbable to conclude that his color is an index to the color of his worshippers. Parker continues by saying." As flowers grow on a grave, so myths have sprung up around those solemn tombs. Osiris, the great, good god of Egypt, was slain by Typhon. Typhon attempted to possess himself of the throne and Isis, widow of the dead king; but Horus, the son of Osiris and Isis, opposed him and drove him from Egypt. And because the people were fearful that their enemy might return Horus transformed himself into a Sphinx and kept watch for the coming of Typhon." members of the shriners order should fully understand the mysteries surrounding the various symbols of their order this explains why the sphinx was incorporated into shriners ritual. Returning to the subject at hand it has been a long and endless search into what I define as the connection between Negro shrinedom and the various Asiatic Religions. There is a definite connection between the two and it is my intentions explore this link and perhaps discovering a new approach to embracing freemasonry most hidden truths. In order to discuss the origins of shrinedom we must discuss the origin of Islam. In order to accomplish this task I will first quote a section from Muslim scholar Muhammad Hamidullah. In his introduction to Islam, Hamidullah writes on Pre Islamic Arabia. It states "By the end of the 6th century, after the birth of Jesus Christ, men had already made great progress in diverse walks of life. At that time there were some religions which openly proclaimed that they were reserved for definite races and groups of men only. There were also a few which claimed universality, but declared that the salvation of man lay in the renunciation of the world. These were the religions for the elite, and catered for an extremely limited number of men. We need not speak of religions where there existed no religion at all, where atheism and materialism reigned supreme, where the thought was solely of occupying one self with one's own pleasures without any regard or consideration for the rights of others" from this point is where it becomes interesting because the outcome of the given statement was the beginning of Islam. At this point Arabia was a Pagan and idolatrous: Only a few inhabitants had embraced religions like Christianity Zoroaster and various others. However the Arabs did possess the notion of the one goal, but they believed also that idols had the power to intercede with him and these idols were placed around the sacred Kaaba. Preserved the Rite of the Pilgrimage to the House of the one God. This is the very house that was said to have been built by Abraham and his son Ishmael. What makes Islam so unique is its religious heritage. Ishmael's birth is what sparks this entire story his descendant being of the Babylonian Abraham and the Egyptian Hagar. Finally the birth of the prophet Muhammad the founder of the Islamic faith and ever since man has been building on his teachings both fraternal and religious.

"There is a history behind our so-called history that you cannot even conceive of. History has a deeper base. The periphery that we know as history is not the reality. Behind our so-called history continues another history, a deeper one about which we know nothing " - Author Mehmet Sabeheddin

By now I hope that you have a better understanding of the Moorish Science temple, its teachings and its doctrines, which are all essential to learning how Islam was introduced to blacks in America. I must note that instead of saying introduce, perhaps I should say reintroduce, because Islam arrived in America long before such groups like the Moorish Science temple, the nation of Islam, and several other orthodox Islamic groups were ever established. America is rich in Islamic history and it is not limited to the above named groups. In order to explore this topic further, I must reflect on a previous section of this book. In the section on native american Moors, I gave some details of how there were muslims present on the ships of Spanish explorers. Christopher Columbus himself relied on maps invented by Moors who were muslims, and these navigational maps are the reason Columbus discovered America. Additionally, he proved that the world was round, courtesy of the Moors of Spain. Great afro-centric writers like Ivan van Sertima would argue that muslim sailors were traveling to the Americas long before Europe began their explorations of foreign lands. There have been countless books and research articles on the arrival of Islam into the new world and van Sertima is one of many who have written on this subject. Let's not forget the dreaded slave triangle trades of Europe, Africa and North America. Remember, slaves that were taken from the northern hemisphere of Africa were in most cases practicing muslims and the areas of captivity were Islamic states. So my purpose for exploring this topic is to establish the presence of the islamic faith in the Americas long before Christianity arrived and was established and long before there was a colony of Pilgrims. Long before there was an established relationship with the American Indians, the muslims were sailing and trading with the Indians. So far, I have proven the presence of Islam in early America. Now I would like to explore how Islam was introduced to blacks in America. What we know about early Islamic influences in America is that various groups began calling themselves muslim. In the late 19th century and early twentieth century, there were several Islamic groups; one such group was the Amadiyat movement in Islam founded in the late 19th century. There was also The Muslim Brotherhood founded by Arabic immigrants in the 1900's. In order to explain the rise of Islam among blacks in America, I decided to explain their significance in chronological order within the assess timeline.

1100 A.D. - 1500 A.D. - Muslims explored North America at least 300 years before the discovery of the new world by Christopher Columbus, according to many researchers. Muslims were not only in the Americas, but very active there as well. Ivan van Sertima, in his renowned work, "They came before Columbus confirms that there was definitely contact between the ancient and early African people with the native Americans. Columbus arrived on October 21, 1492. When he was sailing past Gibara on the coast of Cuba, he saw a mosque. He also logged that remnants of other mosques were found in Cuba, Mexico, Texas and Nevada. Muslim seafarers were the first explorers of the seas. They traveled to foreign lands including America. These muslim travelers established trade and colonies and perhaps intermarried with the indigenous people. This explains why you have the various shades of color of people. Noble Drew Ali acknowledges these indigenous people as Muslims."

In addition to the known facts I must also note that Africans were traveling to the Americas long before the establishing of Islam as one of the world's great religions. Various African kingdoms were known to have sailed to the Americas.

Author Joseph J. Harding writes in his research article, "It has been accepted in today's society that europeans discovered the Americas following the native Americans. Yet there is evidence that suggests Africans were the first explorers to cross the Atlantic Ocean as early as

950 B.C. There have not been many scholars in the past that did research to confirm that Africans were among the first people to come to America, because African studies have only recently become a subject of social and scholarly interest. As a result, evidence concerning African social development is not common among historians. There is also the common idea among anthropologists that African cultures of that time were incapable of crossing the sea, on account of a lack of organization. There is much evidence to support that Africans came to the Americas before Europeans. This evidence includes documented voyages, archeological evidence, African elements in Olmec culture, and european explorer's records. The Olmecs were an ancient civilization in Central America around 1200 to 300 B.C."

An unknown author writes, "Documented journeys to the Americas are key evidence that Africans were in America before Europeans. Two different African civilizations have been documented making the journey to the Americas. The first documented voyage to the Americas was not planned. King Kushta, founder of the twenty-fifth egyptian dynasty sent out an expedition of ships in search of iron deposits off the coast of west Africa. They accidentally arrived in central America. This accident was attributed to the fact that Kushta's predecessor, the egyptian pharaoh Necho knew that the earth was round and that the sun was the center of our solar system 2,200 years before Copernicus rediscovered the idea. Pharaoh Necho used egyptian scientists and mathematics along with Phoenician sea power to organize great voyages into the Atlantic Ocean. A storm or an accidental ride in to one of the Atlantic's currents may have placed Kushta's in the heart of the Olmec civilization. My guess would be that the discovery of this new land to the egyptians was a way to expand their already vast empire into another continent. This explains the similarity in the pyramids. The existence of egyptian and west African elements in Olmec civilization presents evidence of a black presence in America. The technology needed to build pyramids and to move heavy sun blocks would have taken hundreds of years to evolve, yet there was no developmental stage to Olmec culture. Olmec civilization was like that of Egypt; it rose from nowhere and was completely modeled. This shows that the knowledge of building pyramids was brought over the ocean from Africa."

There are several other reasons that give indications of Africans being present in the Americas, including religion, tobacco, astronomy, and African animals that somehow surfaced in the Americas. All this can play a vital role in understanding the presence of the Africans arrival in America. 1500 A.D. - 1850 A.D. - After Columbus' exploration of

America there were several explorations to the new continent by various european countries. During the european explorations, colonies were established in the Americas at the same time the triangle slave trades were established. When the colonists first arrived there was a need for labor in order to till the land and grow crops. At first, they tried to enslave the indigenous people, but were unsuccessful in doing so. Thus, the triangle slave trade was born and it ran from Europe to Africa and finally America. Most of the slaves that were captured were taken from the north western hemisphere of Africa and these countries were predominantly muslim. The first African slaves were muslims that were taken and shipped to America. The slave trade would last for next 300 to 400 years, causing an assortment of problems for the people of African descent. Even today, there are major issues that still linger throughout our communities.

An unknown author wrote, "During the late 1400's and 1500's, Europeans began to establish trading posts in Africa. While the spread of Christianity motivated sincere Christians to establish numerous missions, gold and slaves eventually became the primary interest of the European interlopers. Ironically, the more that non-muslim Africans saw of Europeans, the more they gravitated to Islam."

1850 to 1929 A.D. - By this time blacks in America have no knowledge of their Islamic heritage. Blacks are practicing a new religion. Christianity which was forced upon them by their slave masters. In 1865, slavery ended and the reconstruction period began. During this time blacks were searching for an identity. Some continued to practice Christianity while others were searching for a different idea. This is how Islam re-emerged in the black community. Fraternal societies, like the Freemasons, exposed blacks to something different. Examining the mysteries of Freemasonry we find an auxiliary group known as the A aonms Ancient Arabic Order of Nobles of the Mystic Shrine. I must note that there are two distinct groups of masons; AFAM ancient free and accepted mason, which is predominantly caucasian and Prince hall masonry which is predominantly African American. The AAONMS or Shriners, are a branch of freemasonry that displays Islamic and Arabic themes, though the members of this order are not muslim. They dress like muslims and introduced an alternative arabic form of Islam, but most muslims call it a mockery of the faith. The history of the Shriners order began with William J. Florence and Walter J. Fleming in 1871. Florence was said to have traveled to Arabia where he received certain rites to a lost mystical order. This order was said to be of noble men who protect the innocent from thieves and robbers during their pilgrimage to the Islamic holy city of Mecca. Florence brought the degree back to the states and established it in the masonic order. The qualifications for membership to the Shriners are either being a thirty second degree Scottish rite mason or a knight's templar in good standing. To assure an association of men of the highest type and caliber, men who have been subjected to the vigorous test of all the degrees of masonry are allowed to join its ranks. members of the shrine participate in parades, charity work and various other philanthropic work. In Prince hall masonry, their version of the shrine functions in the same matter. The only difference between the two existing orders is the racial backgrounds. As for the Shriners of Prince hall this was the first exposure of Islam for blacks in America. An auxiliary order that is designed to be the playhouse of masonry served as a wake-up call to a lost religion.

The AEAONMS, Ancient Egyptian Arabic Order of Nobles of the Mystic Shrine, were founded by 33rd degree Prince Hall Masons in June 1893 at the Columbia Exposition in Chicago. For their rituals and texts, Black Shriners drew upon materials quietly expropriated from their white segregationist counterparts, whose own organizations were known as the Ancient Arabic order of the Nobles of the Mystic Shrine for North America. This original Shrine was established as a Masonic social organization in New York City in 1871, but in its irreverent legend lay claim to having been founded by "Caliph Ali" (Caliph ' Ali ibn Abi Tabib), cousin and son-in-law of the prophet Muhammad. This theory I will discuss later in the chapter.

The story of the Prince hall Shriners existence is far different than their european counter parts. The Prince hall Shriners were founded by John G. Jones, a 33rd degree mason of Chicago, Illinois who was the sovereign Grand Commander of the United Supreme Council of the Southern and Western Masonic Jurisdiction of the United States. After several years of correspondence made application to the grand council of Arabia to be initiated into the work and power and authority to institute temples in America. Permission was granted and negro shrinedom was born. His application was received and accepted in the city of Chicago. Several temples throughout the United States were established and its membership increased. Since the Moorish Science Temple is the first black Islamic group, its origins derive from the mystical Shriners. Noble Drew Ali was a freemason who received his knowledge of Islam from the masonic order. Author Imam Isa, in his book, Shaikh Daoud vs. W.D. Fard writes, "The honorable Timothy Drew (Noble Drew Ali, honorable is a title denoting fellowcraft or middle chamber in freemasonry) who became a Noble Drew Ali, raised to the degree of prophet in the negro Shriners. He was very learnt in egyptology, esoteric philosophy, and eastern theology. Before Noble Drew Ali began to build his nation, he went to Morocco and Egypt for initiation. When reading the teachings of Noble Drew Ali, you can see his ties to freemasonry. The movement initially started with the intention of bringing more negroes into freemasonry through their relationship to the Moors and escalated into the Moorish Science temple, The black muslims, and many others. The new doctrine was to be called Islamism so as not to be mistaken with Al Islam being taught in America. Their followers were to be called Moslem, in order not to be mistaken with muslims. And they were never to refer to themselves again as negroes, blacks, and colored."

It was this principle idea that allowed Noble Drew Ali's Moorish Divine movement to flourish in the 1920's. His asiatic philosophies gave birth to the ideas that sprung forth the rebirth of Islam, which at the time became a lost religion among blacks in America. This lost religion was restored because of Ali's exposure to the knowledge of the east and the mysteries of the freemasonry. However, Noble Drew Ali was not the only man exposed to freemasonry. There have been countless others that have benefitted from its teachings. Even the nation of Islam leader, Elijah Muhammad, was also a mason. In his writings, the Nation of Islam leader speaks of freemasonry and his experiences. Over time, especially given the ignorance of traditional Islamic practices in the U.S., Islam and freemasonry occasionally came to be identified as one. A practicing freemason for seven years prior to his joining the NOI, Elijah Muhammad once described the relationship between freemasonry and Islam in the following way. "Before the coming of Allah, i.e. W.D. Fard, Islam as sold to the so-called masons. This order made up of thirty-three degrees, and it is sold by degrees. If a member is eligible and able to pay for all the degrees he may do so, but only those who take the 33rd degree are called moslem Shriners." Freemasonry is an order that is deep rooted in every continent and every country. But it seems that when it arrived in America, it took on various levels from establishing lodges in every state to its teachings being the foundations of various new age religions.

Now approaching the very climax of masonic wisdom the degree commonly known as the shriner's degree is neither original nor derived from the teaching of the more elevated degrees namely the york and scottish rites of freemasonry, but rather it is a europeanized and mangled version of Islamic ideologies. In fact it is a merger of the esoteric biblical foundations of the Christian knights of the templar with mystical Quranic teachings of Islam. Throughout the previous section I elaborated on the origins of the Shriners degree. As in most situations I have quoted what was presented to me in terms of information given from a European perspective. Now I must approach the subject from a different point of view. Utilizing other masonic theories, I have come to believe that the true origins of the Shriners may have come from the very source in which its teachings are derived from, which is Islam. For you brothers of the craft (meaning of the masonic order) and those individuals who read this book, I want you to pay close attention to the following theories.Is it possible that the Shriners order was established long before its creation in North America? This allegorical story of the Shriners began after the death of the prophet Muhammad and after his ascension into heaven. Many political and religious turmoils arose amongst the various Arab and Persian factions. In a previous chapter I briefly discussed two primary religious groups that emerged. They were the Shite's and the Sunni's.

The Sunni's, who take their name from heir high reverence for the traditions of the prophet which in Arabic is referred to as the Sunnah, were the majority ruling class in both aristocracy and economic power. The Shite's, on the other hand were a smaller group that pledged undevoted allegiance to the Caliph Ali and his family. Ali was the adopted son of Muhammad and the only person to ever be born inside the Kaaba in Mecca, as well as the only male to grow up in the house of the prophet. Islamic tradition and history states that while growing up in the prophets household, he secretly collected in writing the revelation that would come from time to time to Muhammad. Shite historical records tell that this collected information was not just any writing, but rather it was the entire Quran. This Quran is far different than the Quran that the masses were allowed to compile. The Shite Quran is said to have carefully guarded secrets of literal, allegorical and future implications. I must note that with the prophet's death the Sunni's and Shite's fought against each other constantly over which branch is legitimate. Over time the Shite's retreated from war and settled into persia or modern day iran. it is in these hills that the specific ideology of the Shite school of thought was beginning to brew. The first noticeable group of secretive knowledge seekers were called the Ishmaelites (meaning a direct descendant to Ishmael, Abraham's oldest son). The Ishmaelites were a group who claimed direct lineage to the Caliph Ali, whom allegedly held the source of all the keys to ancient wisdom. The Ishmaelites doctrine consisted of stages specifically referred to as degrees, just as the stages in masonry will later be called. Their order was based primarily on deciphering of the laws of the universe and man, the teachings were designed to explore esoteric teachings which were passed down from generation to generation. While the old Ishmaelite teachings were being further defined into degrees the Ishmaelites began calling themselves Assassins (which in old Arabic implies guardians of some type of knowledge) and incorporating clandestine signs as well as symbology.

They refined their secretive teaching into 9 clear cut degrees with signs and passwords for each level. All this can be observed in modern freemasonry. Reflecting on medieval history, I will quote a passage from a brother Faison 19X Moamin. In his lecture called Nobles of the Mystic Shrine of Ali, he writes, "In about 1170 A.D. a fragile peace treaty was needed to attempt to stop the advancing waves of muslim armies in Jerusalem. The new Christian King, Baldwin II decided to make an alliance with the Persian leader, Bahram, who was the leader of the current Band of Assassins. It was this merger of the strange minds that would lead to the entire body of masonic work of which the 32nd degree alone still testifies to its origins. It will suffice to say that many other events took place, but later the templars would return to Europe and the assassins would merge back into secrecy. With a brief overview of historical events it quickly becomes apparent what happened. The Christian knights came into contact with hidden Islamic teachings, as well as insights into prophets in biblical scriptures that were common to both religions (i.e. Solomon, Jesus, Aaron, etc). These knights then took what they had learned, combined it with European perspectives and grew their own form of Islamic doctrine in the heart of Europe and look at the results of this eventful mish- mash."

However, it should be noted how "the Gnostic sects of Europe drew heavily on the wisdom of the Arabs, Alchemists, Templars thus forming a chain transmitting ancient wisdom to the West." This explains why within the ritual of freemasonry there is an admission "we came from the East and proceeded to the West." The plain fact that much of what we look upon almost entirely as freemasonry has been practiced as part and remnants of the religions of the Middle East for many thousands of years, lies open for anyone who cares to stop and read, instead of running by. But it is frequently and scornfully rejected by the average masonic student... so we find that just as Europe borrowed considerably from the learning of the Moors; European freemasonry took its "secret wisdom" from Muslim East.

This explains why the 32nd degree and the degree of knights templar are essential requirements upon entering the shrine. Because both degrees can trace its origins to the chivalry of medieval Europe. To fully understand this relationship I must note; as vast and complex as the mysteries of freemasonry I could never understand how such relationships could be established, namely the combination of Islam and Christianity, taking into consideration that these two groups are usually at odds against each other. Yet freemasonry has a way of combining even the most extreme religions into one harmonious system of learning, where by all men, regardless of race, color or creed can enjoy its abundance of knowledge. So the Shriners degree is considered by and for the most part, the last and final key to the completion of the masonic degree system.

"Although a few items are easily noticed in the lower masonic degrees, much of the intermediate degrees are merely works of pure allegory and ethnocentrism incorporated with Christian mythology, the last formal degrees in the York and Scottish rites. It wasn't until the late 1800's that the final cornerstone was placed to show a revealing light on masonry true origins, The Shrine." --Faison 19X Moamin

Such an unusual relationship between Christianity and Al Islam, and this relationship could only have been established through the inner workings of the mysteries of freemasonry. As I have mentioned throughout this chapter, freemasonry is so universal that any religious dogma that has ever been created, regardless of what conflicts that it has with any other faith, will find total peace and harmony within its vast body of religious and esoteric doctrine. In freemasonry words and thoughts are displayed be way of symbols, so in order to honor the relationship between both the Christian and muslim faiths, a symbol was created. This symbol is known as a scimitar with the crescent shielding a sphinx-head and a star. In freemasonry the sphinx-head and star represent a combination of the two religions, Islam and Christianity. The scimitar was given to Ishmael and until this day his hand has been against every man and every man's hand against him. The star has an origin in both Islam and the Christian faith. In Islam it represents Allah, which at one time was a name of a moon deity among the Arabs, and in Christianity is was the same star that lead the three wise men to the nativity of jesus Christ. So I hope this explains the relationship between the two religions but also it teaches us that we can live on this earth in unity without any disrespect to any one's faith.

One unknown author writes, "By the time freemasonry made its way through Europe and across the water to the shores of America, certain european freemasons became bored with the rituals of freemasonry that they created and were looking for another fraternal brotherhood; strictly for entertainment. These freemasons were not concerned with the true purpose of Islam for they only took pieces that interested them and made up european shrinery as it is today."

"The Shriners representations of Islam were simultaneously mockery and a celebration. The orders members presented themselves as authentic carriers of eastern culture received from muslims themselves. many masons believed audiences read the extravagant, unruly shriner parades as a mockery of the craft. However, being highly experienced masons who had invested substantial energy and money in obtaining a place in the shrine order. Shriners were by and large serious about the masonic wisdom.

They nonetheless seemed to make light of it in there flamboyant parades and fantastic foundational history. In fact, many Shriners understood their orders parades, regalia and rituals to communicate in a light-hearted, accessible way. Non- sectarian moral teachings shriner parades also often employed comic entertainment by men dressed, not simply in a fez, but as mock arabs or persians." --Author Susan Nance

All this exposure to freemasonry would play a vital role in the establishing of the Moorish Science temple. The mysteries of freemasonry would have influenced Noble Drew Ali because of his specific interest in the middle east and the ancient holy land and Egypt. All this would create a key to a lost knowledge; a knowledge which Noble Drew Ali was said to have found, and with this knowledge he established his movement.

1930 A.D. - Present - After the death of Noble Drew Ali the Moorish Science temple declined for a number of reasons. Prior to Noble Drew Ali's death, he appointed several members to the title of Grand Sheik to oversee the various Moorish science temples. When Ali died these high ranking members decided to form their own branch of the Moorish science temple, thus breaking into various sects and offshoots of the original movement. One such group is the nation of Islam, founded in Detroit in 1930 by W.D. Fard, who was a member of Ali's Moorish science temple. Over time, the nation of Islam membership increased due to the leadership of Elijah Muhammad who took over after W.D. Fard's disappearance. Elijah Muhammad was also a member of the Moorish science temple. Prior to changing his name to Muhammad, he was known as Elijah Poole Bey, a name taken from Moorish science temple. In the 1950's, the N.O.I. was moved from Detroit to Chicago where it stands today. The teachings of N.O.I. at the time were geared toward racism and separation of the races. The groups sole purpose of existence was to convert blacks to islam and reject Christianity. Just like the Moorish science temple, the nation of Islam introduced a watered down form of Islam, not revealing its true doctrines. In the 1940's and 1950's a new charismatic leader came to power within the N.O.I. and his name was malcolm X. The leadership of Malcolm X allowed the nation of Islam to flourish. Its membership increased and it gained nationwide attention with malcolm X being the spokesman. Malcolm X continued preaching N.O.I. teachings until corruption within forced him to break away and find his own calling. Now considered an outcast, malcolm began researching the religion of Islam and found that it was far different than the N.O.I.'s version of the religion. When he traveled abroad and discovered that there were white muslims, and other white people who were against racism and stood for righteousness. He began teaching that righteousness, rather than race should be the standard for judging others. Malcolm discovered that the doctrines which formed the basis of the nation of Islam were different than those of orthodox Islam as practiced in the Middle East. He was suspended indefinitely from the nation in 1963, after which he turned away from the doctrines of hatred and racism and sought to bring forth a new vision through a purer form of Islam. He founded a new organization, The Muslim Mosque in 1963, and in 1964 he converted to Islam as practiced by the muslims in Mecca. In any case, the nation of Islam is recognized as an altered version of the Islam that is practiced in the Arab world. One of the most famous practitioners to make this realization was Malcolm X himself when he visited Mecca. It was adjusted to serve the needs of the people of African descent in the United States of America, who were in, and in many ways continue to face a variety of social, political, and economic issues. These humble beginnings were history of things to come. The Americanization and institution of the Islamic faith among blacks in America. But it did not stop with the nation of Islam. There are countless other offshoots that were established from Ali's Moorish science temple. it seems that the religion of Islam is extremely rich in history and every one who has embraced its doctrines have done so because it offers something that is particular to their individual needs. It serves as a religious calling to his/her god.

"The relationship between Islam and freemasonry is indeed indisputable, but rarely acknowledged, largely due to the large base of masonic writings and works all having been done by Christians for Christians, and prior to this age of instant inter-global access to information. Why has not the general public, or even those Christians whom are Shriners, and 32 degree masons sought out the historical implications of the cultural/religiously borrowed symbology and terminology, in something they consider to be strictly Christian? Is it that the acknowledgement of these things might lead to a re-evaluation of their own standards of truth and knowledge? It is the ostrich-with-its head-in-the-sand syndrome, I suspect the noble ideologies that are the foundation and mortar of freemasonry, (of which I do not seek to dishonor) do rightly and exactly represent Great Light form the Grand Master Architect of the Universe: but as a student of pure Masonic virtues and morals and dogma, I must agree with a wise man whom said, "Great light shall have no lampshade." --Faison 19x Moamin

A Reflection of History

Before I begin my next topic, I would like to quote a passage from the writings of Dr. Muata Ashby on his reflection of the universality of religion. This entire book has been based on the study and analyzing of Islam's various relationships with other doctrines as well as new age teachings. Religion seems to be the basis for all thinking. No matter how scientific one individual may view the world it seems religion has influenced what one may and should think it is. If a scientist says a man can trace his origins to apes, then religion will speak otherwise. The beginning of creation according to religion begins with man and nature. For example, in Christianity's version of creation, God is seen in the image of a man, we know this because he created us in the likeness of his image. All this at some point was influenced by man in the form of intellectuals and biblical scholars. Scholars tend to rewrite biblical history to fit the needs of the people who are funding their research. Dr. Ashby writes, "All civilizations have created a form of religion throughout history as well as practices and philosophies to aid in the advancement of its practitioners. Some religions concentrate on certain aspects of religion while others excel in other areas. Some religions are mostly philosophical, while others are mostly ritualistic, and some are a more balanced mixture of ritual and philosophy. Some religions are orthodox, while others are more mystically oriented. Religions serve a purpose, to support those who need the particular type of emphasis they offer at a given point in their spiritual evolution. Ultimately, all beings in a family, with different desires, personalities and tendencies need to accept, cooperate, recognize, and even appreciate each other, as a florist appreciates how different flowers augment a bouquet. When the universality of the human need for religious movement is not accepted, a situation can develop in which the practice of religion is degraded to such an extent that conflict between the religious issues."

For this section, I would like to discuss how Islam was introduced into the African continent. In section 2 of this research book, I cover in depth the presence of African blood in the foundation of Islam, but since we know for a fact that Islam started in Arabia, it has spread throughout the world. Islam entered Africa shortly after its creation in the seventh century. After the death of Muhammad in 632, the first Caliph of Islam, Abu Bakr, ambitiously undertook a series of military conquests to spread the new faith across the world. Although he died two years later, his nephew, Umar, continued the ambitious program. By 636 the muslims occupied Jerusalem, Damascus, and Antioch. In 651 they had conquered all of persia. But they also moved west into Africa, for Arabic culture saw itself as continuous not only with the middle eastern culture, but with northern African culture as well.

When the muslims invaded Africa they found a weakened continent ripe for the picking. Before the arrival of Islam, Africa was already weakened by the Christian empires of Europe through heavy taxes, conversion and slavery. So with little defenses, the muslims marched right in to victory. In 646 the muslims conquered Egypt and quickly spread across northern africa. From northern Africa, they invade Spain in 711. Look at the dates: Islam is founded in 610, when Muhammad had the first of his revelations in the caves above the city of Qumrah. In 711, one hundred years later the muslims occupied the middle east, persia, the Arabian peninsula, Northern Africa, and had just entered Europe. The initial spread of Islam is the single most dramatic cultural change in the history of the world, and it flourishes large in the subsequent history of African civilizations. However, the spread of Islam was not all bad for people of African descent. Beyond religion, there are several important cultural practices that the Arabic culture of Islam gave to Africa. The first is literacy-the egyptians of old kingdoms and the ancient nubians had a long tradition of writing, and the Ethiopians had acquired the skill through their ties to the Semitic peoples of Southern Arabia. But these writing systems did not spread throughout Africa. Islam however, as a religion of the book spread writing and literacy everywhere it went. Many Africans deal with more than one language with Arabic being the center piece of learning. This is why there are several African muslim centers of learning. Let us not forget the accomplishments of the Moors of Spain. So with literacy, the Arabs brought a formal educational system. This system and learning institutions would produce a great system of African thought and science. In fact, the city of Timbuktu had perhaps the greatest university in the world. Islam continued to flourish throughout the world and its followers increased in numbers by converting all who crossed its path. Again, I reference the glory of the Moors. Most people are not aware that the peoples whom the classical greek and roman historians called, berber, were black and affiliated with the then contemporary people of East African areas. The word, berber, in fact was used to refer to peoples of the Red Sea area in Africa as well as North Africa. It was such populations that in large measure comprised the Moorish people, but because of the attribute of blackness, which sharply distinguished them from the bulk of the european people, the word came to be generally used by europeans to describe persons of black complexion in general. The word, moor, was used for people basically berber in origin but then came to include, during the Islamic period, the early Arabians. Both of these populations belonged to a physical type or types of men commonly referred to by early scholars as Hamitic, brown or Mediterranean. Throughout the Middle Ages and previous to the Atlantic slave trade other men of black or nearly black pigmentation, particularly muslim, came to be commonly referred to as Moors.

Now I wish to explore another Islamic impact on the world, the crusades. When people think of the crusades they think of a war between the Christians and Muslims. This may be somewhat true, but it was much more than just a series of war campaigns. In most cases, the crusades were generally portrayed as a series of holy wars against islam led by power hungry popes and fought by religious fanatics. They are supposed to have been the epitome of self-righteousness and intolerance, a black stain on the history of the Catholic church and western civilization in general. The crusaders introduced western aggression to the peaceful middle east and then deformed the enlightened muslim culture which was already established more than 500 years before and left it in ruins. It is obvious war was destined between the two religions. "In the last 500 years especially, European historians have inferred, or said outright, that the world waited in darkness for the Europeans to bring the light. In fact, the Europeans destroyed more civilization than they ever created. They destroyed civilizations that were already old before Europe was born." --John Henrik Clarke

As a reflection, Christians and jews can be tolerated within a muslim state under muslim rule, but in traditional islam, Christian and Jewish states must be destroyed and their lands conquered. When Muhammad was raging war against Mecca in the 7th century, Christianity was the dominant world religion of power and wealth. As the faith of the roman empire, it spanned the entire Mediterranean including the Middle East where it was born. The Christian world, therefore was a prime target for the early leaders of Islam and it would remain so for the next thousand years.

"With enormous energy, the warriors of Islam struck out against the Christians shortly after Muhammad's death. They were extremely successful. Palestine and Syria and Egypt, once the most heavily Christian areas in the world quickly succumbed. By the 8th century, muslim armies had conquered Asia Minor, which had been Christian since the time of St. Paul. The old roman empire, known to modern historians as the Byzantine Empire, was reduced to little more than Greece. In desperation, the emperor in Constantinople sent word to the Christians of western europe asking them to aid their brothers and sisters in the east. This is what gave birth to the crusades. They were no the ideas of ambitious popes or knights, but a response to more than four centuries of conquest in which muslims had already captured two=thirds of the Christian world. At some point, Christianity as a faith and a culture had to defend itself or be consumed by Islam.

The crusades were that defense. What happens next is that Pope Urban II called upon the knights of Christendom to push back the conquests of

Islam at the council of Clermont in 1095. Urban II gave the crusaders two primary goals, both of which would remain central to the eastern crusades for centuries. The first was to rescue the Byzantine Empire of the east. The second goal was the liberation of the holy city of Jerusalem and the other places made holy by the life of Christ. To my knowledge, their were five crusades in all and in religious terms, the crusades, hardened muslim attitudes towards Christians at the same time that doubts were raised among Christians about God's will, the church's authority, and the role of the papacy. Religious commitment halted to disinterest and skepticism. On the other hand, the crusades stimulated religious enthusiasm on a broad scale. The crusades helped some religions but they had to destroy and oppress others. So, did they further advance religion?

The results of the crusades for the Christians was a complete failure. They could not accomplish the given task of reclaiming the lost holy lands. The muslims would remain in control until the 19th century. Today, we can observe the story of the crusades being played out in the fraternal societies. The knight templar, for example, was at one time an elite religious order. Today, it serves as fraternal order of charity and allegory knighthood. It is a branch of freemasonry and is one of the requirements for entering into the Shriners order. The story of the knights templar began in year 1118 A.D. Formed by Christian knights, their job was to patrol the various roads and protect pilgrims on their journey to the holy lands. During their existence, the knight templar would gain power and wealth in their 200 years of existence until the order was disbanded by Philip IV and Pope Clement. It is still a mystery on why this order perished because the templars were crucial in the various crusades. This ends my reflection of history and the purpose of this section was to gain a more in-depth look on the world impact of Islam. From its eastern beginning to its establishment in the western world. This impact would last for several centuries from its holy jihad of the middle ages to its world impact of the 21st century.

17. *William J Florence and Dr Walter M Fleming*
founders of European shrinedom

JOHN G. JONES
Founder of Prince Hall Affiliated
Shrinedom
Expelled from Prince Hall Masonry
in 1903 for Clandestine activities

18. *John G Jones founder of Prince hall Negro shrinedom. Source*
history of the prince hall grand of Illinois from 1867 to 1983

Chapter 4

Overview of Islam in America:
From its Beginnings to its Involvement
in the Black National Movement

Islam in America; it brings to most minds the politically motivated extreme muslim groups of the early 1940's thru the 1970's. These groups were extreme in terms of expressing their political and religious beliefs. However, we must reflect on the times of trouble in America where muslims were not accepted by the predominantly Christian society. These early Islamic groups came into existence because in the eyes of some African Americans there was a need for change. First, we must understand the critical thinking of the African Americans at the time. In America, we observe among African Americans the impact of racism, which in turn created other internal problems within the community. Perhaps Islam was a way to create change and in some ways it did. But, why did some of our African American men and women decide to leave Christianity and embrace Islam? The answer to this question is change. Some black muslims believed that Christianity was a way to oppress African slaves since it was bestowed upon them during the times of slavery. This is the belief of all black muslims that are living in the United States, but why should we refer to African American muslims as black muslims. In fact, there is as diverse a presence of African Americans in Christianity as there is in the religion of Islam. I would like to change the stereotype that people have of muslims. If somehow we could tell the world that muslims are no different than anyone else, and that there good muslims and bad muslims. In America, there should never be a difference between black muslims and orthodox muslims.

African American muslims represent about one-third of North American muslims or about 1-2 million people. It is a small group and in most cases they are extremely political in terms of stressing their opinions on various racial issues. This explains why some branches of American Islam tend to partake in various forms on nationalism. The development of African American Islam dates back to the awakening self-consciousness of American blacks. That awakening was represented by movements such as the Universal Negro Improvement Association of Marcus Garvey (1887-1940). This had nothing to do with earlier forms of Islam directly, though some of his teachings were incorporated into mainstream Islam. However, it raised up the problems of blacks that eventually led to the consideration of Islam. Individuals, like Garvey, aroused black pride and interest in African culture. He called for an independent black economy and proclaimed the values of racial separation. All this can be acknowledged in such groups like the Nation of Islam. I can remember driving by their national headquarters and observing people trying to promote black business, but in their case black Islamic business. The Nation of Islam was setting up small store fronts and selling merchandise. Both the Nation of Islam and the Moorish science temple shared the same ideas. All this I observed in Chicago, but it can observed in other major metropolitan cities nationwide. The rise of Islam in America is a saga that has continued to flourish among people of African descent. As long as African Americans continue to face any forms of hardships there will always be a need for new ideas and new ways to change the situations of their communities and environments. The need for a black economy is essential and most Africans who believed in nationalism understood that this was needed in order to change the economic situations within the communities. All this was shaped into many forms of ideas and these ideas were manifested into black nationalism and Islam. Both of these ideas were combined for the sole purpose of enlightening people of African descent. When I study the works of Marcus garvey, I begin to fully understand his total disregard for what I call "the ruling elite." Because of their greed and oppression, blacks suffered not only in America but in other countries as well. Garvey's idea was to unite all blacks together for the purpose of creating a centralized black nation with a black economy. It was the foundation and philosophies of marcus garvey that gave forth the establishments of the various black movements in America. One such movement was the Moorish science temple of America. Within its abundance of literature, Moorish science contains the remnants of Garvey's works and ideas and this is a known fact because Noble Drew Ali acknowledges him as his forerunner. What the prophet borrowed from Garvey was the establishment of an identity. Ali gave his followers a new sense of identity. Most of them wore a fez, which set them apart from the typical urban black. Many were also bearded, and each one carried a membership card. Having a different religion from that of a typical ghetto black contributed further to their special sense of identity including Ali's heritage of which they could be proud. His emphasis on separatism instead of integration struck a harmonious note with their disillusionment. Instead of leaving them in despair, it permitted them to face white America boldly. Noble Drew Ali and Marcus Garvey both shared the same ideas in terms of what was best for black people in America. Realistically, neither man personally knew the other, and Marcus Garvey vaguely knew of Noble Drew Ali's existence, although he did speak of him vaguely in some interviews. Noble Drew Ali did not preach separatism as marcus garvey did, instead Ali placed great emphasis on the black people recognizing their true way of life. I think Ali's main intentions were to only preserve the American moor and his rich culture. The Moorish science temple played a vital role in the establishment of black nationalism. These two men were the co-founders of black nationalism. The only difference is the Moors followed a religious approach to nationalism.

20. The Honorable Marcus Garvey

"NATIONHOOD IS THE ONLY MEANS BY
WHICH MODERN CIVILIZATIONS CAN
COMPLETELY PROTECT ITSELF...
NATIONHOOD IS THE HIGHEST IDEAL
OF ALL PEOPLES!"
— The Honorable Marcus M. Garvey

Dear People:

During the month of August, many aware
brothers and sisters thru-out the Western Hemisphere
and in Africa will be commemorating the birth
of Africa's noble son, the Honorable Marcus Mosiah
Garvey.

Born August 17, 1887 on the island of Jamaica,
brother Garvey was very mature for a young man.
This maturity prompted him to take an interest in
the politics of Jamaica; and upon seeing the in-
justices done to Africanoid people, he began to
travel. He traveled to South & Central America;
to other parts of the "West Indies" observing the
same miserable conditions.

At the same time, he was also reading things,
and was inspired by Booker T. Washington in the
U.S.A. In his own words, Garvey began to ask,
"Where is the Blackmans Government?" "Where is
his President, his country?, his ambassadors?,
his army, navy, and men of big affairs?"
And after he could not find these things among our victimized people, brother Garvey declared,
"I will help to make them!" And this ushered in a glorious period of Black resistance to
European domination on an international scale.

MARCUS GARVEY
(1887-1940)

Our brother began to translate his thoughts into action when on July 20, 1914 he
founded the UNIVERSAL NEGRO IMPROVEMENT ASSOCIATION, and THE AFRICAN
COMMUNITIES LEAGUE. His program was that of, "Uniting all the Negro peoples of the
World into one great body to establish a country and government absolutely their own."

After establishing the organization in Jamaica, Mr. Garvey went to the U.S.A. upon an in-
vitation from Booker T. Washington, (whom had unfortunately died before Mr. Garvey could meet
him). In Garvey's own words, "I immediately visited some of the then so-called Negro leaders
only to discover, after a close study of them, that they had no program, but were mere oppor-
tunists..." This prompted him to establish the organization, (U.N.I.A.) in New York, and from
there thru his writings, great speeches, and organizing ability...built the U.N.I.A. into a
mass organization of over 6 millions of our people...with 900 branches thru-out the world!
This was the only movement of this magnitude at that time among our people in the world!
Marcus Garvey started THE NEGRO WORLD...an international Black-oriented
newspaper printed in several languages! He also established the BLACK STAR LINE fleet of
ships to help facilitate international trade for Africanoid people. The U.N.I.A. had developed
many other programs of an economic, social, & political nature, to uplift the African Race!
All of the U.N.I.A.'s programs were based on Garvey's belief that, "Black people should
have a country of their own, where they should be given the fullest opportunity to develop
politic lly, socially, and industrially. Black people should not be encouraged to remain in
White people's countries, and expect to be Presidents, Governors, Mayors, Senators,
Congressmen, Judges, & social and industrial leaders!"
***Learn about Mr. Garvey thru his books, THE PHILOSOPHY & OPINIONS OF MARCUS GARVEY (3 Volumes

21. Biography of Marcus Garvey

**Duse Muhammad Ali
Wearing The Fez (Tarbush) Also
(1866-1945 A.D.)**

*22. Duse Muhammad Ali a close friend of Marcus Garvey.
Source sheikh daoud vs, W.D Fard by M.Z York EL.*

Chapter 5

Islam in the African American Community: The Beginning of the Moorish Science Temple

There have never been more diversity among a group of people than the multi-cultural groups in America. Every race, culture and ethnic background is found in America's vast body of land and people. Every ethnic group has somehow found a way to establish a community for its masses of people, and through these established communities there lie remnants of old world ideas. Combining these old world ideas with new ideas forms the Americanization of these groups. It is amazing to see how such groups remain loyal to their point of origin and yet acknowledge America and the American way of life. Every ethnic community in America has its own ways of keeping their history, customs, families, and most importantly their own way of educating their youth intact. This chapter will focus on the situations of the African American communities. America is a great country because it gives its citizens the freedom to live without oppression and enjoy certain rights as an American citizen. Within the African American communities there are a variety of diverse groups. They are different by their skin color, by their country of origin and the religion they practice. In the African communities, there are black Jewish as well as black Islamic communities. Additionally, there are immigrants from the African continent such as Nigerians, Ethiopians, etc. Among these groups, black muslims are calculated as the fastest growing group. Muslims comprise approximately 6% of the population in the United States. The majority of the conversions to this growing religion are within the African American community. The idea for a community is to stand together and have a strong voice in political issues and this is why there are politicians lobbying for votes in these various communities. However, the African Americans have a history of not banding together and this has caused a multitude of problems. They tend to form several small groups instead of one large group. Nevertheless, communities in general are designed to follow their own ideas and visions.

One such community is the African Islamic community. In order to explain the primary objective of this community I must reflect on the old and ancient ways of our ancestors. In ancient times, the people of Africa had a high system of family and community and these communities were in the form of small villages and even small kingdoms. Today, we see this in the African Islamic communities. They are bonded together by their religious beliefs. Even within the African Islamic communities there are several groups that define themselves as muslims. This entire book is based on the Moorish American muslims and the group they have formed in America. Whether I am discussing Moorish Americans or orthodox muslims, the religion of Islam seems to bestow upon its followers a sense of pride and unity. In this country, muslims have adopted their religious practices to the requirements of the American society in varying ways. Most muslims tend to settle with fellow muslims, and if possible with those of similar ethnic backgrounds. It is rare to see an American muslim living next to an Arab muslim. However, Arab businesses are opening up in African American communities.

Let's focus on the rise of Islam in modern America. The first recognized establishment of Islam among blacks in America was the Moorish science temple of America. This organization was founded in 1913 by Noble Drew Ali. The prophet had a vision to uplift blacks in America. He felt that blacks were being suppressed because they were not identified as an ethnic group. His primary mission was to uplift African humanity.

Imam Isa writes, "Throughout the ages, there have been illuminated souls who have provided extraordinary leadership to the black nation. These great men such as Noble Drew Ali were endowed with wisdom and knowledge that they carefully utilized to guide blacks closer to the truth, Islam. They gave inspiration and guidance to those who were ready to unite as a nation. The prophet taught the black man and woman to be proud of their African descent and to trade in the culture of America for culture of the moor. He referred to blacks as Moors because of his belief that slaves in America were taken from Morocco in Northwest Africa."

This was the beginning foundations of the Moorish science temple, which when first established was known as the canaanite temple and it was located in Newark, New Jersey. Why the canaanite temple? The prophet believed that according to all true and divine records of the human race, there is no negro, black or colored race attached to the human family. That is because all inhabitants of Africa were of the human race and descendants of the ancient canaanite nation from the holy land of Canaan. It is obvious that the prophet possessed certain biblical knowledge to come to this conclusion. This was the beginning foundations of the restoration of an identity. Perhaps through the eyes of Noble Drew Ali there was a vision to awaken the black man in America. Blacks should no longer have to settle for what was given to them in terms of name calling, poverty and any other forms of mental oppression. 1913 was the year it all started and this was the year the prophet began his call:

"Come all ye Moors of America and hear the truth about your nationality and birthright. Come and link yourselves back with the families of the nation."

This was the beginning of his dream and that dream was turned into reality at the time the prophet was very influential in getting across his thoughts and ideas. Noble Drew Ali is rarely mentioned in history books and the most you will hear of him is that he is acknowledged as the father of the American black Islamic movement. The Moorish science temple gave birth to several off-shoot Islamic groups. It was Noble Drew Ali's ideas that started the American Islamic movement.

Imam Isa, in his book, Who was Noble Drew Ali? writes, "It is important that you recognize your great men; for whenever a leader is truly an aid to his people, he is either assassinated. labeled as crazy or not given any exposure by the media. It is no coincidence that many people have never heard of Noble Drew Ali and the role that he played as the founder of the Moorish science temple of America, for his accomplishments outshine the majority of the black men whom the ruling class labels your heroes and other black spokesman of his time. He was successful in uniting thousands of blacks under the banner of the Moorish science temple throughout the United States. Noble Drew Ali was a key figure in the establishment of Islam in America. He first began his teachings at a time when blacks were just beginning to be socially awakened. Although slavery had officially ended with the Emancipation Proclamation fifty-one years earlier (1863 A.D.) very little had changed for the black man in America."

The passage above sheds some light on black leaders and anyone who decides to speak up against the norm. This is usually the situation and as a result these leaders ar usually deemed an outcast and alienated from society. So the vision of the prophet was to seek citizenship of all blacks so they would receive their divine rights as citizens according to the free national constitution that was prepared for all free national beings. There were two important documents pertaining to the people of Moorish descent. The first was the Peace Treaty of 1787 and the revision of the treaty in 1836. The United States and the kingdom of Morocco had shared a long friendship and political relationship. If the prophet is correct that all blacks in America are of Moorish descent then this treaty would free all African slaves. Let us examine an article of this treaty.

"If any moor shall bring citizens of the United or their effects to his majesty, the citizens shall immediately be set a liberty and the effects restored, and in like manner, if any moor not a subject of these Dominions shall make prize of any of the citizens of America or their effects and bring them into any of the ports of his majesty, they shall be immediately released, as they will then be considered as under his majesty's protection."

This article would stand as a foundation point for freedom of all people of Moorish descent during the times of slavery. Of course, this article would not be recognized because slavery was established long before this article was ratified by the United States government. But as Moorish Americans this article would acknowledge us as citizens of Morocco, thus giving all Moors the American carpet treatment. For a man who has been acknowledged as being literate the prophet was well learned and well versed in the history of American government and the history of the Moors. There are stories of the prophet addressing the government in Washington, D.C. and asking them to acknowledge the Moors of America. There is one such event recorded in the Moorish voice magazine in March 1943. It states that Noble Drew Ali went to Washington, D.C. around 1913 and demanded the breaking of the seven seals which sealed the book of knowledge of the descendants of the dark people of this country and the Europeans present at this meeting fell to the floor like dead meat and the seven seals were broken. Then he went forth and began to teach Islam to the dark nation in this country and to claim their ancient tribes, BEY and EL. I do not know if this is true, but my guess is that perhaps he spent time in the library of congress learning more about the history of the Moors. Every event that has taken place in the history of the Moorish science temple brought forth many documents and historical events. From the canaanite temple of new Jersey to the Incorporated Moorish science temple in Chicago. I will address this in following chapters.

"You who doubt whether my principles are right for the redemption of my people. Go to those that know law in city hall among officials in your government, and ask under intelligent tone and they will be glad to render you a favorable reply. For they are glad to see me bring you out of the darkness into light."   --Noble Drew Ali

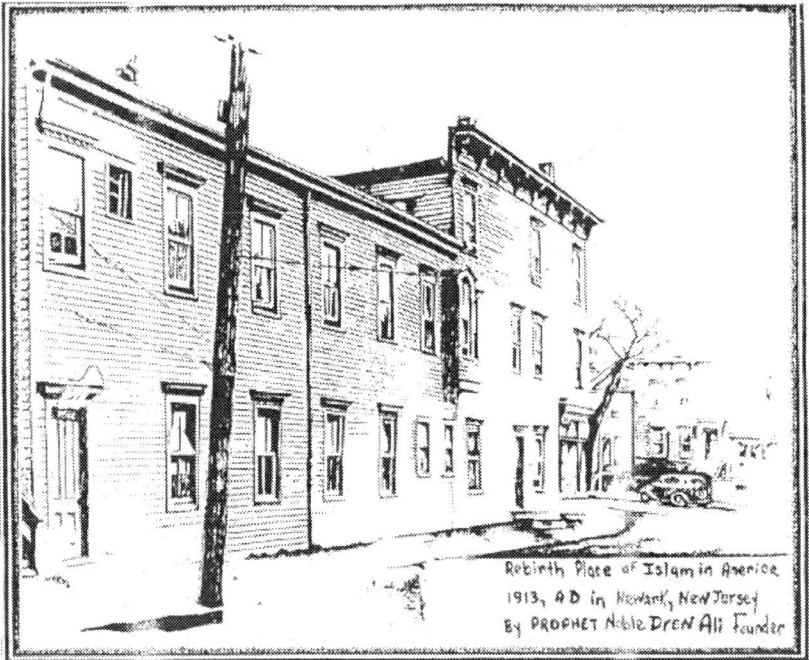

23. Post card rebirth place of Islam. Source Moorish literature

Don't Miss the Great Moorish Drama
Look!   Look!

COME YE EVERYONE AND SEE

THE SEVENTH WONDER OF THE WORLD

The Great Moorish Drama, which constitutes

"Events in The Last Days Among the Inhabitants of North America"

In this Moorish Drama the need of a nationality will be made know to you through the acts, of men, women and children. There will be great lectures and this Nationalistic topic by the Prophet Noble Drew Ali, and many of the Sheiks of the Grand Body of the Moorish Holy Temple of Science. You will also hear one of the greatest Moorish female songstress of the day—MME. LOMAX-BEY.

THE PROPHET NOBLE DREW ALI, WILL BE BOUND WITH SEVERAL YARDS OF ROPE, AS JESUS WAS BOUND IN THE THE TEMPLE AT JERUSALEM

And escaped before the authorities could take charge of Him; so will the Prophet Drew Ali, peform the same act, after being bound by anyone in the audience and will escape in a few seconds.

He also will heal many in the audience without touching them, free of charge, as they stand in front of their seats manifesting his divine power.

COME ONE. COME ALL TO

THE MOORISH HOLY TEMPLE OF SCIENCE

AT COMMUNITY CENTRE
3140 INDIANA AVE.

8 to 11 p. m.   Refreshments Served.

ADMISSION: ADULTS 50c   CHILDREN 25c

NOBLE DREW ALI

On Monday Evening, May 16th, 1927

24. The great Moorish Drama Source Moorish literature

75

Chapter 6

A Biography of Prophet Noble Drew Ali:
His Aims and his Mission to
Uplift Asiatics in America

Everywhere human life is a great and solemn dispensation. Man. Suffering, enjoying, loving, hating, hoping, and feeling chained to the earth and yet exploring the far recesses of the universe and some how man has the power to commune with God and his angels. Around this great action of existence the curtain of time are drawn; but there are openings through them which gives us glimpses of eternity. Throughout the writing of this book, I have attempted to try exploring every aspect of what is define as Moorish science and yet everything centers around the trials and lifetimes of Noble Drew Ali. Never before have I encountered such an individual who is vaguely known throughout the world but his past presence have impacted African Americans in such a way that his accomplishments are usually overlooked by negative publicity from the local media. In this case, it was The Chicago Defender. During the 1920-1930's the Defender recorded every event of the Moorish Americans and their activities from their uprising to their downfall. My intentions for this passage are to explore the early life of Noble Drew Ali. In order to gather together a biography of the prophet I researched the various documents of Moorish literature. Timothy Drew, who later changed his name to Noble Drew Ali, was born on January 8, 1886 in North Carolina. Some Moors would say that their was an earthquake during the arrival of his birth. This was to have symbolized the so-called prophet's spirit hitting the earth. Little if known of his early childhood nor of his father and mother's true character. His father was a Moabite and his mother a Canaanite; both soon passed out of his life. Born amongst the Cherokee Indian tribes of North Carolina, young Timothy was put in the care of his aunt after the death of his mother. Next he was raised by an aunt who would often physically abuse him. There are stories of him receiving mental abuse and one such story of him being thrown into a furnace leaving him to die, but Allah glorified and exalted in his unrelenting mercy saved the child from the burning furnace. From that point on, he was prepared for the great work that he was to perform for his people. One elder moor describes this story, "The permanent scars on Noble Drew Ali's hands and faces were evidence of the abuse he endured as a child. There are tales of his young life having been spent with gypsies and how, one day, when he was walking alone the voice of Allah said, 'if you go, I will follow.'" The so-called prophet did not accept the job at first, but the voice kept saying, "if you go, I will follow." He accepted the mission, left the gypsy camp and never returned.

During his childhood, in the early 1900's he was a victim of racial discrimination, poverty and suffering. As he grew older he was interested in eastern cultures and religion, so one he reached manhood he left home and began travelling. He went to Egypt and learned of his heritage. he observed the various egyptian monuments and artifacts. While in Egypt he realized that the African race had a glorious past and this is where he laid the foundation for establishing Islam. He went to Egypt as Timothy Drew and he returned to America with the Arabic name, Ali.

Imam Isa writes, "In Egypt he had the opportunity to visit the great universities, sit with the Egyptian sages, travel through the inner chambers of the pyramids and also to learn the origin of the slave trade that took place from the northern coast of Africa to America. He was able to see and believe that the true way of life was Islam, and Allah is the creator of the original black man. By being in Egypt, he could see for himself that the black man had laws, science, math, art, dignity, citizenship and power over his land."

All this the prophet understood and he digested this information and brought it back to America. In some ways this exposure to African history gave birth to fields of African studies, African American history and egyptology. We must understand that prior to this movement black people in America had very little knowledge of their past and history. Most European historians have written about Africa as having no history and its people having no civilization. Noble Drew Ali, with his newly found knowledge, returned to America and began teaching what he had learned from his travels.

"Noble Drew Ali was inspired with his origin and returned to America to claim his people to raise them up as clean self-respectable, upright citizens who descended from a glorious race of people after he returned to the United States, he began his mission. --Imam Isa

25. Picture of the prophet's early life and his family in North Carolina courtesy of bro Rochon bey

26. Noble Drew Ali in Mexico courtesy of bro Rochon bey

27. Moorish Guide newspaper of noble drew Ali

28. Post card noble drew Ali and secretary. Source Moorish literature

29. *Noble drew Ali in Havana Cuba 1928 at the pan America conference*

30. *Post card of the Moorish Science temple first annual convention*

31. Noble Drew Ali blesses the Moors, source news paper the Moorish guide

32. Members of the Moorish science temple

Moorish Leader Attends Inauguration of Governor

The Moorish Science Temple of America was represented at the inauguration of Governor Louis L. Emmerson in Springfield, Ill., Monday, Jan. 14, by Prophet Noble Drew Ali. It was a busy day for the distinguished Moorish leader in Springfield, beginning with breakfast aboard one of the special trains of the Illinois Central railroad, attending the inaugural ceremonies of the State Arsenal building and ending with interviews with many distinguished citizens from Chicago, who greeted him on every hand. The prophet expressed himself as being highly pleased with the trip and the many courtesies extended him by the military and state officials.

Noble Drew Ali

Mrs. Drew Ali Organizes Young Moorish People

Mrs. Pearl Drew Ali, national secretary treasurer of the Moorish Science Temple of America, has organized the Young People's Moorish league, composed of the young men and women of all Moorish Science temples. Its purpose is to create interest in educational pursuits and to awaken and cultivate an appreciation for the arts, a greater attendance at the literary and trade schools is also sought.

Mrs. Pearl Drew Ali

Mrs. Ali sees this movement as a constructive gesture toward a general uplifting of standards among the young people and she has secured the hearty cooperation of the entire membership as well as other fellow citizens not affiliated. She is being assisted in the organization work by Miss Juanita Richardson Bey, a graduate of Wendell Phillips high school and city editor of the Moorish Guide. Meetings of the Young People's Moorish league will be held in the club rooms on the second floor of Unity hall 3140 Indiana Ave.

It is the intention of the leaders of the Moorish movement to train the youth in every step of the work so that they may be able to carry on the policies of the organization when the pioneers have gone. To do this they must be better educated and superiorly trained. Mrs. Ali and her assistants are receiving hearty support and are being congratulated for their foresight.

Moors to Celebrate Birthday of Founder

On the evening of Jan. 8 members of the Moorish Science Temple of America will celebrate Prophet Noble Drew Ali's birthday with a grand Moorish costume ball in the main auditorium of Unity hall, 3140, Indiana Ave. The occasion will also be celebrated by all subordinate temples in other sections of the United States. The occasion will be the first of its kind in America, in that all members participating will wear native Moroccan costumes. A number of prominent men, both in the business and public life of Chicago, will join the members in honoring the Moorish leader's birthday.

Noble Drew Ali

83

MOORISH LEADER ON TOUR VISITS SUBORDINATE BODIES

Prophet Noble Drew Ali, founder and leader of the Moorish Science Temple of America, left Saturday to visit the members of the 17 different subordinate Moorish science temples, which are organized in 15 different states. He is accompanied by Rich-ard Ross Bey, editor of the Moorish Guide, a bi-weekly publication of the organization. Up-to-date Detroit, Newark and Philadelphia have been visited. During this tour special emphasis is being put on the importance of strict observance by the members and officers of the constitution and by-laws recommended by the prophet and unanimously adopted during the first annual convention of the Moors at Chicago in October, 1928.

Prophet Ali

The message of the prophet, published in the Moorish Guide issue of Nov. 10, has created very favorable comment. It was directed to the nations as well as the Moors of the United States. Two prominent visitors from an eastern country called at the prophet's private study, 3140 Indiana Ave., to personally compliment him on the article. According to information from Mrs. Pearl D.

Richard Ross Bey

urer of the Moors organization, members are responding encouragingly to the per capita tax system adopted at the convention. It is believed that in conjunction with his other plans, upon his return to Chicago, Prophet Ali, in all probability will interview Governor Len Small of the state of Illinois.

MOORISH HEAD MAKES PLANS FOR CONCLAVE

Beginning Oct. 15 and continuing through the entire week the Moorish Science Temple of America, of which Mr. Drew Ali is founder and president, will hold its first general conference at Unity hall, 3140 Indiana Ave., Chicago, Ill. President Ali began definite plans to this end upon his recent return from Pine Bluff, Ark., where he spent several days lecturing at the local Moorish temple. This organization is playing a useful and definite part in advancing the sacred obligations of American citizenship. Indications are that this convention will be one of the most interesting ever held in the city. It will be featured by delegates attending in pilgrimages from 15 different states where local temples have been established. There will be an interesting parade, in which men and women members will wear regalia similar to that worn in eastern countries. A camel will be used. During the sessions specific reports of the general work and civic accomplishments of local temples will be made. Reports also of the business enterprises that have been established in connection with these temples, such as two grocery and market stores in Detroit, a laundry in Pittsburgh, Pa., and moving and express business and grocery in Chicago.

Drew Ali

These examples of collective effort show that the members of the Moorish temple and their leader have a sound economic program and are blazing the trail and marking the pathway over which our posterity may travel unhampered and unafraid. "It must be kept in mind that no great movement can take definite shape in two or three years so as to be error proof," said President Ali. "However, through accumulating experience each annual convention ought to witness a more perfect and wider functioning organization, representing the organized experience of men and women members throughout the country and possibly in time the world over." And, continuing, President Ali said: "Constructive criticism from sympathetic friends in and outside of our ranks is welcome."

HOLD SESSION OF MOORISH SCIENCE BODY

Many Delegates From Temples Attend

The annual convention of the Moorish Science Temples of America opened Oct. 14 at Unity hall, 3140 Indiana Ave. Prophet Noble Drew Ali, founder and head of the body, will preside over the sessions, with close Saturday evening. More than one thousand delegates from the 15 temples in America were reported present during the meetings.

Following the registration at headquarters Monday reports were read from the two grand governors, T. Crumby Bey, Pittsburgh, Pa., and Lomax-Bey of Detroit, Mich. Tuesday evening the welcome address was delivered by Alderman Louis B. Anderson. Other speakers were Oscar DePriest, Third ward committeeman; Dr. Roman, of Memory Medical college, Nashville, Tenn.; Attorney George W. Blackwell and Aaron Payne. Richard Ross was master of ceremonies, and Claude D. Green, managing editor of the Moorish Guide, is chairman of the arrangement committee, who has worked hard to get everything in splendid order for the reception of the visitors. Wednesday a parade was held.

Teach Koran

The Moorish Science Temple was founded by Prophet Drew Ali at Newark, N. J., in 1913. Their belief of his followers are that their forefathers were Asiatics brought to America along with all other persons of dark skin. They bar the name Negro, African origin and such in color. They follow the teaching of the Koran, and seek its movement toward free thinking in a powerful step toward the solution of racial problems. They teach strict cooperation and reciprocity toward each other.

The Chicago temple was organized in 1925 and has a membership of more than three thousand. The many-hued turbans of the women and children, and the red fez and sashes worn by the men attract much attention. Saturday a public reception will be given in honor of the prophet and the visitors.

Moorish delegates and visitors were served wholesome meals in the Unity hall grill room by the members of the Chicago temple.

Sister Pearl Drew Ali, the distinguished wife of the prophet, wore the costume of a native Moroccan princess. Other very beautiful Moroccan costumes were worn by Sister Lomax Bey, wife of the grand governor, of Detroit; Sister Whitehead El, Chicago; Sister Loop Bey, Chicago; Sister Cliff Bey, Indianapolis; Sister Watts Bey, Chicago and others. Prophet Noble Drew Ali wore a native Moroccan prince's costume. Grand Governor Lomax Bey and Grand Governor Crumby wore native Moroccan sheik costumes.

Because of certain incidents in some of the branch temples' prices to the convention, far-reaching changes for betterment in the administration announced by Noble Drew Ali and enforced by the supreme grand council in future to the letter.

To Make Changes

It is reported that the prophet, the supreme executive authority will appoint a supreme grand council, of which he will be the supreme grand chairman. The Supreme Grand council will have power and duty to control and supervise all the affairs and properties of the Moorish Science temples of America, and he will be the sole judge of what constitutes conduct injurious to the order peace, interest or welfare of the organization or at variance with its constitution and by-laws, also the rules and regulations made by the prophet, and shall be the sole judge of the sufficiency of the evidence by which such conduct is shown.

Prophet Noble Drew Ali is being congratulated by Chicagoans on the success of the Moors' first annual convention and for his splendid work in promoting the cause of human

Chapter 7

Morocco: The History of the Moors and Their Accomplishments

"Noble Drew Ali led his congregation to the history of the Moors because the slaves of 1779 A.D., who reached the shores of America, were of the Moorish nation. The British won the battle against the Moors in 1774 A.D. They captured some Moors and bound them into slavery. They were sent to North America and given degrading names such as negro, black or colored Ethiopians, darkies and coons." --Excerpts from the Moorish guide

Morocco is a small country in Northwest Africa. It lies only nine miles from Spain across the Strait of Gibraltar. Moroccans call the country Al Maghrib which means the farthest west in Arabic. Rabaat is the capital of Morocco and Casablanca is the largest city. Morocco is a monarch controlled government whose powers are restricted to those granted under the laws of the nation with the king as the head of state. 98% of the country is muslim and the other 2% is a mixture of Jewish and coptic Christians. Europeans, French and Spanish live nearby cities. The official language of Morocco is Arabic. However, they do speak various berber languages The name Moors has most often been used as the equivalent of Moroccan and sometimes to describe the muslims of Spain that were mixed Arab, Spanish and berber origins. Approximately 50% of Moroccans are Arab and 25% are berbers and 20% are Moors. In most cases, the term moor has been related to the country of Morocco, when in fact it served as a universal term for people of dark color. According to the Sidjul Moors, the term moor has three common meanings; muslim, Maghribi (person on Northwest Africa) and Melano (person whose skin is melanin rich). A

Moorish American typically is a melano American muslim of Maghribi descent. A moor might be a muslim, but not all Moors are muslims. Medieval Spaniards and Portuguese stereotyped Moors (Melanos) as muslims because the Moors they encountered usually were muslim. A moor is a moor regardless of his religion, cultural orientation or assumed ethnic identity. The term Maghrib refers to a Phenotype or geographic region. In reference to Phenotype it refers to a racial phenotype, a type possessing a dark complexion like the realm of the setting sun. Phenotypically speaking, Maghrib is synonymous with moor and refers to the melano race. The geographic Maghrib is Northwest Africa. Persona of northwest African descent are often referred to as maghribi. A geographically defined Maghribi can be a moor, but not all Maghribi's are Moors. The term moor is a generic term referring to the Melano race. Moors are not Arabs, but are phenotrypically different due to the hybridization of the latter. When we speak of Arabs we are usually referring to modern Arabs (Arab Hybridia).

If we focus on the ethnicity of Morocco we find two types of Moors; light skinned and dark skinned. They are only different in skin color and yet they are defined as Moors. The light skinned moor is a mixture of African, Arabic and European blood. Perhaps when the Moors were established in Spain there were interracial relationships between the existing groups.

The Moors were the light of the Spanish civilization and this civilization was fueled by the technologies of the African, Arab and Jewish communities. For example, there were great cities in Spain that were the homes of great universities. It is no wonder that it was called the city of light. The glory of the Moors went south to Seville, Cordova, Granada, Malaga and Valencia. The sunny south was the natural home of the Moors because it was closer to the continent of Africa. Cordova was their chief city and it is singular how few people know, in spite of its recent date, that it rivaled Babylon, Rome and Baghdad in magnificence and importance. The dark skinned moor on the other hand has a different story. Their history can be connected by their point of origin and the conquest of north Africa by the Arabs. All the northern countries of Africa are dominated by Arabic muslims. The primary origin of the dark skinned moor can be traced to ancient moabites of biblical times. The prophet Noble Drew Ali writes in chapter XLV, 2nd verse of his holy koran circle 7, "The key to civilization was and is in the hands of the Asiatic nations. The Moors, who were the ancient moabites, and the founders of the city of Mecca." In chapter XLVII he writes, "The inhabitants of Africa are the descendants of the ancient Canaanites from the land of Canaan." In Verse 6 he states, "The moabites from the land of Moab, who received permission from the pharaohs of Egypt to settle and inhabit North-West Africa, they were the founders and are the true possessors of the present Moroccan empire with the Canaanite, Hittite and Amorite brethren who sojourned from the land of Canaan seeking new homes."

The moabites were the originators of the Moors and also were the descendants of Moab. The story of Moab is a unique one, not because it is a biblical story but the story of his birth is what invokes the curiosity of scholars. Scholars have learned that the Moabites and Jews are related by way of Abraham's brother, Lot. So the Moabites would also be deemed God's chosen people just as the Jews proclaim.

There is an ancient nation located in the uplands east of the Dead Sea and now a part of Jordan. The area is unprotected from the east, hence its history is a chain of raids by the bedouins. The Moabites were close kin to the hebrews and the language of the Moabite stone is practically the same as biblical hebrew. The relations of Moab with Judah and Israel are continually mentioned in the bible. As a political entity, Moab came to an end after the invasion of the Assyrians. Its people were later absorbed by the Nabataeans. The Moabite religion was much like that of Canaan. Archaeological exploration in Moab has shown that settlements first occurred in the 13th century B.C. The holy bible speaks of Moab's birth from a union between Lot and one of his daughters. We must remember that Lot had lost his wife in the fall of Sodom and Gammorah. In order to preserve the seed of Lot, his daughters conspired to lay with him. This event is in the Book of Genesis, chapter 19:

"And it came to pass when God destroyed the cities of the Plain that God remembered Abraham and sent Lot out of the midst of the overthrow when he overthrew the cities in which Lot dwelt. And Lot went up out of Zoar and dwelt in the mountain and his two daughters with him, for he feared to dwell in Zoar; and he dwelt in a cave, he and his two daughters.

And the firstborn said unto the younger, our father is old and there is not a man in the earth to come in unto us after the manner of all the earth. Come, let us make our father drink wine and we will lie with him that we may preserve seed of our father. And they made their father drink wine that night; and the firstborn went in and lay with her father and he perceived not when she lay down nor when she arose.

And it came to pass on the morrow that the firstborn said unto the younger; behold I lay yesternight with my father; let us make him drink wine this night also and go thou in and lie with him that we may preserve the seed of our father. And they made their father drink wine that night also; and the younger arose and lay with him and he perceived not when she lay down nor when she arose.

Thus were both the daughters of Lot with child by their father, and the firstborn bore a son and called his name Moab; the same is the father of the Moabites unto this day...

This is the origin of the Moabites and according to the prophet, the Moabites gave birth to the dark skinned Moors of Spain and Morocco. Overall the knowledge and civilization of the Moors was renown throughout both Europe and Africa. Somewhere along the line the religion of Islam was bestowed upon them by way of the east and the conquering Arabs. Perhaps I can further acknowledge the advance civilizations of both the Moors and the Arabs by observing other African and Islamic countries they were to advance in civilizations and technology.

Prophet Noble Drew Ali writes in his historical message to America, "The Moors, or Mohammedans, added to the beauty and grandeur of Spain. For centuries, art, science, literature and chivalry flourished among them while the rest of Europe was still sunk in the gloom of the dark ages. The Moors were the most ingenious and industrious of the subjects of Spain. Their expulsion from Spain in 1610 was one of the chief causes of decadence of that country for both agriculture and industry fell into decay after their departure."

Spain was the only multi-racial and multi-religious country in western Europe and much of the development of Spanish civilization in religion, literature, art and architecture during the later Middle Ages stemmed from the moor's presence in Spain.

"The spread of Mohammedanism included the whole of North Africa and, in time penetrated Spain. It found Spain a desert and a wilderness and turned her into a garden of beauty. Never before nor since has she seen such glory as was hers when the Moors reached Toledo, Seville and Granada, the most beautiful cities of Europe. Cordova became the educational metropolis of civilization, Seville became the literary center of the world, and Granada was the triumph of wonderful architecture. Spain was never anything until these Africans, Negroes if you will, made her a land of flowers, wines, music, art, beauty and love." ---George Wells Parker

33. Moors playing chess

Chapter 8
Teachings of the Moorish Science Temple

"Those who live today will die tomorrow. Those who die tomorrow will be born again; those who live will not die. The reality of a thing is its relation to the creator, not that which we see. It was created by the word of the creator, this word is its true name; to know a things true name is to know its true power, to pronounce it exactly is to release its energy. Truth is but one; thy doubts are of thine own raising. It that made virtues what they are, planted also in thee a knowledge of their pre-eminence. Act as soul dictates to thee, and the end shall be always right." --Egyptian proverb.

Everyday in life we are given a specific path to follow. Some people choose the right while others may choose a path that is not. Man is traveling an endless path into the unknown; not knowing where to go, not knowing where it will lead or if it will lead anywhere. But we do know that life is sacred and beautiful as it is will continue to exist; for man is immortal, constantly being born and eventually dying only to be resurrected again and again. Throughout this book, I have approached the study of Moorish science from a religious standpoint not truly revealing the spiritual side of this sacred science. Manly P. Hall writes, "Religions are a group of people gathered together in the labor of learning. The world is a school. We are here to learn, and our presence here proves our need of instruction. Every living creature is struggling to break the strangling bonds of limitation-- that pressing narrowness which inhabits vision and leaves the life without an idea." Hall continues, "every soul is engaged in a great work the labor of personal liberation from the state of ignorance. The world is a great prison; its bars are the unknown."

In spite of what Mr. Hall is saying, there is another side of this material world; the spiritual realm. In the material world we are limited only to this ball of mud, air and water that we call the earth. The spiritual realm on the other hand, allows us to travel beyond this world exploring and obtaining as much wisdom as one can absorb. This chapter explores the spiritual aspects of the philosophy of Moorish science. We know from the previous chapters that Moorish science is a mixture of religious doctrines but it is not limited to just these doctrines. Here lies a much deeper thought that can only be revealed to those who want to embrace it. Moorish science is a much more spiritual form of learning. To acknowledge it is to embrace the spiritual realm of pure thought. Any man or woman who undertakes a task should personally reflect upon himself and all that he truly believes in. Perhaps a more intimate reflection is needed to accomplish this. For the following passage I drew heavily on the ancient wisdom of the east because it is a place of knowledge and it is the foundations of the eastern civilizations that gave birth to the now powerful western world.

To understand the true meaning of the study of Moorish science we must create a link between the world we live in and the world that lies outside the existing boundaries of life. It is through this contact that we can now fully understand the presence of Allah within ourselves, and this presence is what molds us out of the clay of ignorance to the mold of perfection. To the material man, Allah has bestowed upon him attributes of spirit life. All true Moors recognize the spirit of Allah as he journeys through the unknowns of the world. Each attribute is a step to an elevation of higher learning. Observe the following attributes.

1. Allah, as creator of the universe, transcends it.
2. Allah cannot be expressed in words.
3. The inner light (one's own soul-spirit) is a sufficient source of religious guidance.
4. The universe and Allah are actually one.
5. Since humans are part of creation, a human being can, through mystical discipline, become one with God. Therefore the soul is immortal and at death, the soul passes into the body of a newborn child. We are all descendants from the supreme being.
6. Moorish Science is described as a tool for learning and following a path of seven principles: Love, truth, peace, freedom, justice, righteousness and consciousness.
7. Allah and man are one.

These 7 attributes present a sense of understanding of the sacred wisdom. There is nothing more beautiful in this world than pure transcendent knowledge. All this is designed to fuel the spirit. Your spirit is that part of you which is the direct creation of Allah. Your spirit is the highest aspect of who and what you are. Your spirit is devoid of all elements of human personality and character. it is a direct fragment of the divine life of Allah. The spirit is one with all and understand fully that oneness, as well as Allah, its creator. The spirit is perfect and universal in all aspects save one; the spirit is not Allah. The spirit is the highest expression of universal individuality for it contains many keys to truth and has its roots with Allah and with all the spirits, within the highest realm of creation; a realm which we cannot even begin to comprehend here on the material plane. As spirit, we were created and we live in Allah's image of spirit. Thus, within us, we have all the attributes of Allah. We are all part of Allah and Allah's spirit, and we are created of the embodiment of Allah. There is only one supreme master. It is said that in ancient days he walked in the light of pure knowledge and this knowledge was placed in the hearts of every living thing that he created. The world itself is considered the central point of this knowledge. Allah is infinity and the world is a symbol of the permanence of Allah. Life is a symbol of the presence of Allah. To those who are able to sense the inner life of things and read into forms even a small part of that great agency which actually ensoul them, all that is in harmony is part of the universal good and it is pure perfection.

To those individuals who lack sufficient knowledge of Allah they are to be swallowed up in darkness, but Allah is all forgiving and all compassionate. He embraces those who acknowledge him and he opens his heart to all men because Allah is love.

"An inherent aim is in the soul of man, that it must seek and go after its destiny. God has given the soul destiny; Allah has created man with an excellence, that excellence is in his soul is in him when he is born. Some people look at the fallacies in man, at the problem of man, the clumsiness of man, the lack of skills on the part of man, the ignorance of man; they look at all of the shortcomings in man, and they judge him by his errors and not by his purpose." --Wraith Deen Muhammad

Man cannot die; the spirit-man is one with Allah, and while Allah lives man cannot die. When man has conquered every foe upon the plane of the soul the seed will have fully opened out, will have unfolded in the holy breath. The garb of soul will then have served its purpose well, and man will it never more, and it will pass and be no more and man will then attain unto the blessedness of perfectness and be at one with Allah.

Exclusion of the knowledge of God seems to me the greatest injustice to anyone. There are many different paths to knowledge and yet it is an endless path. Some paths are more complex than others and these various paths can take on many different forms. In this particular situation there is one path that I must explore and that is Moorish Science. There are two subjects that need to be explored; the first is the physical Moorish science that we may learn by way of stories and history books. The second is a hidden esoteric science that was produced from the wisdom and the mind of Noble Drew Ali. This is the wisdom that I plan to explore. When Noble Drew Ali established the Moorish science temple he incorporated numerous sources from other religious doctrines. Moorish Science can be defined as a divine movement and a divine science. It is composed of five categories.

1. Teaching the divine origin of man. Every one has a point of origin and a right to exist. Moorish Science serves only as a tool of explanation.
2. Teaching that we must claim our divine rights. Perhaps that is why the prophet labored so long to establish us as Moorish Americans. Then and only then would we receive the same equal rights as other Americans of different nationalities in this country.
3. Teaching our divine relationships. We are Moorish descendants and the Moorish people were the ancient Moabites and the founders of the holy city of Mecca.
4. Teaching that our descendant nature (Moabite) connects us to known divine prophets, such as Jesus who was one of the true blood of the ancient Canaanites and Moabites an the inhabitants of Africa.
5. Teaching that the national principles of our forefathers was divine and that we have proclaimed and are practicing the same principles as members of the Moorish science temple of America.

All five principles are what constitutes Moorish science and are the very core of this science. Next we find that the prophet renamed his movement from the Canaanite temple to the Moorish holy temple of science, and finally the Moorish science temple of America. The origin of the name, Moorish Science Temple, in defined in three ways. Author Imam Isa, in his book, Who was Noble Drew Ali? writes, "Noble Drew Ali being the first Islamic pioneer in the west signed the first charter making the Moorish science temple of America a legally incorporated organization."

Where did Noble Drew Ali get the name for the Moorish science temple? Ali identified himself with the Moors of North Africa who were brought to America as slaves. Knowing that the history of the black man in America was as an African slave, he believed that we were descendants of the Moors. For this reason, he called us Moorish American. The word, science, represents Noble Drew Ali's Islam is a science and through this science the black man can be independent in solving his problems. Moorish

Science is a divine science. In divine science all true branches of science interlock, for it is the study of Allah and creation and the development of related technologies and skills. The use of the word science is based upon the belief that everything finds its roots in mathematics. All the questions in the universe can be answered through the application of the 360 degrees of knowledge contained in the universe. The use of the word temple is based upon the knowledge he acquired in his travels through Egypt. He understood that a mosque is a place of prostration and a temple is a place of knowledge. The prophet did not possess the knowledge of the scriptures to guide the people religiously; however, he had the knowledge of the fundamentals of Islam to teach and guide the people to the truth. Thus, the name Moorish science temple is based upon;

    a.   what he thought was our nationality -- Moors

    b.   our way of life -- Islam a science, and

    c.   the manner in which it would be presented to the teaching within a temple.

This lays the foundation for future topics to be explored. We will explore the various teachings of the Moorish doctrines and shed light on its inner meanings ranging from the Moorish American prayer to the constitutions and bylaws. All of these are essential to the overall teachings of Moorish science. Moorish American Prayer Allah the father of the universe. The father of love, truth, peace, freedom and justice. Allah is my protector, my guide, and my salvation by night and by through his holy prophet, Drew Ali. (Amen)

This is a prayer that is always spoken when any Moorish science meeting is open. Meetings usually start at 8 p.m. on Friday. members will stand up, raise their arms with 7 fingers facing the east just as other devout muslims do. The only difference is that Moorish Americans stand up and pray. "What is Islam?" From Moorish literature as published in the "Moorish Guide National Edition"

Islam is a very simple faith. It requires man to recognize his duties toward God Allah, his creator and his fellow creatures. It teaches the supreme duty of living at peace with one's surroundings. It is preeminently the religion of peace. The very name, Islam, means peace. The goal of a man's life, according to Islam, is peace with everything. peace with Allah and peace with man. The Koran, the holy book of Islam, tells us that the final abode of man is the "House of Peace," where no vain word or sinful;l discourse will be heard." The holy prophet, Noble Drew Ali, says that a follower of Islam in the true sense of the word is one whose hands, tongue and thoughts do not hurt others. The object of man's life, according to Islam, is its complete unfoldment. Islam teaches that man is born with unlimited capacities for progress. Islam does not support the idea that man is born in sin. It teaches that every one has within him the seed of perfect development and it rests solely with himself to make or mar his fortune. The cardinal doctrine of Islam is the unity of the Father-Allah. We believe in one God. Allah who is All God, All Mercy and All Power. He is perfect and holy. All Wisdom, All Knowledge, and All Truth. These are some of His great attributes so far as we can understand. His is free from all defects, holy and transcendent. He is personal to us in so far as we can see His attributes working for us; but He is, nevertheless, impersonal. Because He is infinite, perfect, and holy, we do not believe that death, decay or sleep overtake Him, neither do we believe that He is helplessly inactive and inert force. Nothing happens without His knowledge and will. He neither begets nor is He begotten, because these are the traits of frail and weak humanity. This unity of Allah is the first and foremost pillar of Islam and every other belief hangs upon it. --By, Noble Drew Ali, The Prophet

This is the prophet's interpretation of the religion of Islam and he writes passionately about this religion. Nevertheless, we must acknowledge the differences between Orthodox Islam and Moorish Science. Orthodox muslims acknowledge Islam in its true and ancient form, but Moorish Americans have a far different concept of God and Islam. The Moorish nation has faith in Allah as our protector, guide and savior. We rely upon him, seek His forgiveness and thrive in the light of His love. Surely there is no God but Allah, for He has no partner. Moorish America believes in the oneness of Allah. Allah is eternal. He begats not, nor is He begotten, and none is like Him. The Holy Creed The holy covenant of the Asiatic nation. Ye are the children of one father provided for by his care and the breast of one mother has ye such. So let the bond of affection therefore unite with thy brother that peace and happiness may dwell in thy father's house. And when ye separate into the world remember the relationship that bindeth you to love and unity. And prefer not a stranger before thy own blood. If thy brother's in adversity assist him, if thy sister's in trouble forsake her not. So shall the fortune of thy father be contributed to the support of his whole race. And his care be continued to you all your love to each other.

Perhaps this creed was written for the sole purpose of acknowledging the unity of all Moorish Americans. I am not certain whether this creed was written by the prophet or by other prominent members of the order, however, this creed was adopted by the Moorish science temple a symbol of the birth right.

The Moorish Flag and the Five Pillars This flag is displayed at every Moorish meeting along with the American flag. To the Moorish American it is a symbol of our Asiatic roots and it links us to a country of origin along with a religious foundation. The use of the flag in Morocco as a symbol of the state dates back to the Almoraviole dynasty (1062-1125 A.D.). Prior to this time, white silk banners were often carried in battle sometimes with Koranic inscriptions written on them. The Almoravioles institutionalized this practice. They gave one banner to every unit of 100 soldiers. The leaders carried one inscribed, "There is no god but god, and Muhammad is his prophet." The following dynasties (The Marinades and the Saadiens) continued the use of the white flag as the symbol of the state. The Alaouites beginning in the 17th century, which are the ruling dynasties and the ancestors of his majesty King Hassan II, were the first to introduce the red flag. It was raised every morning and lowered every evening on the fortresses at Rabat and Sale. The green Sulayman star on the flag was introduced in 1912 when Morocco was under French protectorate, in order to distinguish the nation's flag from the others. The description of the flag is red with a green fice-pointed, linear star known as Solomon's seal in the center of the flag. Green is the traditional color of Islam and some Moorish Americans would state that it is the true symbolism of the Moorish flag. The flag is blood red to symbolize the blood that was shed by all Asiatics. At first it was white, but because of the blood that was shed by our people at the hands of Europeans when the Asiatic nation fell from the ruling status, the flag was dyed red. The five-pointed star in the center in the center of the flag represents the five pillars of Moorish science; love, truth, peace, freedom and justice.

The five-pointed Pentagon star. Shall it stay most mighty and merciful. Love - for the love of Allah, yourself and your nation. Truth - If there is no love or truth there is no nation. Peace - Our main goal, and Freedom - What we strive to maintain.

If the first four points have not been followed, justice will uphold. We are justice seeking people and it is the eye of Allah watching over his people. There is a sword of justice and its colors are red and green.

The five-pointed star can represent a variety of topics; for example: The masonic blazing star; the five-pointed star is a symbol of creation, note the five points, which represent the five limbs of man, one head, two arms and two legs. Combine these limbs and they form the human body. They also represent the five senses of hearing, seeing, feeling, smelling and tasting. The star is a symbol of guidance and infinite light. it was a star that guided the three wise men to the nativity of the Lord Jesus Christ. If you are a muslim, like all other believers of the Islamic religion, you would follow a flag containing the star and crescent moon. This is the most commonly used symbol in the religion of Islam.

"The founders of the American republic, as high-degree freemasons, were aware of the importance of Moorish wisdom and culture to the birth of western civilization. This may explain why Morocco was the first nation in history to recognize the United States, and what's really behind the story of george Washington being presented with a Moorish flag? Some researchers believe this flag consisted of a red background with a green five-pointed star in the center of it. The star or pentagram, which the Moors called the Seal of Sulaiyman and colored green to honor Islam, also figures prominently in Masonic art and architecture. The layout of the city of Washington D.C. - designed by freemasons, incorporates the pentagram." --Author Mehmet Sabehdolin, The Masons and the Moors.

Dr. C.M. Bey writes, "The banner of the star and crescent or the flag with the moon and five-pointed star in the center, is the insignia of the Asiatic Moorish nation and it is the mother of all national banners of the world today. The Moorish flag namely the star crescent represents the entire human family; some two billion and one hundred sixty million upon the ball of mud that we call Earth. The Moorish flag is not limited to the citizens of Morocco. Its boundaries cover not only the country of Morocco but Asiatics worldwide. The Moorish flag is further strengthened by the five pillars of Moorish science, love, truth, peace, freedom and justice."

Bey explains the five pillars of Moorish science: (Love) Love is the strongest force in the universe. it cannot be described in words but in deeds. It cannot be measured nor weighed, yet it is that which bonds all living things to all other living things. We say that Our love is Allah made manifest. (Truth) Truth is the opposite of falsehood; it never had a beginning, thus it can have no ending. Truth is Allah. It always was, is and evermore will be. Amen. (Peace) Peace according to Islam is man's goal of life. Peace with everything, peace with Allah, peace with man. Peace is that state which one finds in one's self that is to know thyself, but not only to know but be able to control ones own anger and lower self when one is able to accomplish this, then one will have peace within himself or herself. (Freedom) Freedom is the state of being free to exercise one's will to choose. If one has harnessed love, truth, and peace one will be able to gain freedom within one's self and will be able to love in harmony. (Justice) Justice we say is a reward or punishment regarding one's conduct in accordance to laws and principles. In the universal sense, justice will take its course. Therefore, love is the key and justice is the lock; Islam is the peace be still! The Moorish Names Bey and El When an individual becomes a member of the Moorish Science temple they are asked to take a name for themselves. In order to become a member, the candidate has to write a statement addressing why he or she wants to become a part of the uplifting. When they are accepted they swear an allegiance to prophet Noble Drew Ali and are issued a nationality care which announces his or her new ethnic identity. The names Bey and El. according to the prophet were the original names of various Moorish indian tribes. Over time the names were taken from them and the prophet restored the name of the native American moor. Dr. C. M. Bey, in his book Clock of Destiny, writes, "The Moorish nation Latin Sir names (Bey and El), are the Moorish descendants of America. Without legal due process your Moorish nationality and name Bey and El comprise your birthright, which will change you from being a United States negro slave to a respected citizen. Bey means Lord of the earth - meaning subdue the earth and make it yield all of the necessities of livelihood. Thus the earth obeys. Islam means I am the great. I am, namely you and me, woman and sons. El means the center of wisdom or gravity - the law of attraction and the power of the human mind and education. In the southern European countries the El was used as a title of a name, usually in Spain, Portugal and Morocco or any countries that spoke the Spanish language. El is also found in Arabic names and countries. Holy Koran Circle 7: Its Origins, Its Teachings Every religion that is known to man has a series of truths and hidden knowledge contained within its body. In most case these truths and knowledge are somehow manifested into holy and sacred scriptures for each member of that religion to practice and study. In most religions the holy scriptures are a way to reveal the words and laws of that deity. They reveal events that are designed to show man's trials and errors and we should learn from them and apply this knowledge to our daily lives. We should not only apply them but live them. To Christians, we have the holy bible, to the jews and muslims we have both the torah and holy quran. All of these serve as a learning tool to enlighten the mind which desires light or knowledge. But in this day and age, there is a new scripture. To the devout Moorish american it is a book called the Holy Koran Circle 7. This book in no way resembles that of the holy quran of Mecca. They both speak of different paths of knowledge and yet truth is displayed in one way or another. To my knowledge, the holy quran of Mecca is a mixture of Judaism, Christianity, Paganism and finally the sayings of Muhammad. It gives various details of the lives of the biblical patriarch; from the teachings of Jesus Christ and the pagan philosophies of ancient Arabia. Like all major prophets of old, the sayings and beliefs are written down and passed on for future generations to come. The Holy Koran, on the other hand, speaks of a different path. it deals primarily with Jesus' travels through Africa, Asia and Europe, There are stories of him studying under buddhist monks, egyptian sages and greek philosophers. But where did all of this come from? There are theories that the prophet plagiarized the early section of the holy koran from a book called the Aquarian Gospels of Jesus. This is a book written by Levi Dowling in the early part of the 20th century. Just like other new age books it is said to be another testament of Jesus Christ. We can find other stories of Jesus in various other sources, for example the book of Mormon. This book speaks of Jesus Christ and His dealings with the ancient Americans, and it is said to be another testament of Jesus' life. Needless to say, the Aquarian Gospels are just one of many books that speaks of different journeys of Jesus. Whether Noble Drew Ali plagiarized the holy koran is a mystery, though there are similarities in the scriptures. Noble Drew Ali designed the holy koran for all Moorish americans to read and learn from.

Author Jose Pimenta-Bey writes, "When discussing the Moorish koran some imply that Ali knowingly plagiarized much of it from the Aquarian Gospels of Jesus Christ, but Ali never claimed to have written the Moorish koran, he only states that he prepared it. The Aquarian Gospels is a text which is said to have been spiritually revealed to Levi Dowling, a Scot-Welshman living in 19th century Ohio. Levi's Aquarian Gospel and Ali's Moorish koran were both part of a continuum of more ancient sources. Dowling himself had most likely drawn from an earlier written source and that is precisely what Irish-American researcher Peter Lamborn Wilson found in his research. In his more contemporary work of the early 1990's, Wilson traces much of the Aquarian Gospels and Moorish koran text back to manuscripts found by Nicolas Notovich in a tibetan monastery. Notovich was a Russian Jew who had converted to the Russian Orthodox faith. Notovich published the manuscript in 1894 after having acquired them from tibetan monks who had compiled them as the works of Saint Issa."

Now that we have covered the origins of the holy koran circle 7, we must explore its contents. The book itself is 45 chapters long and contains a variety of information all of which has been borrowed from other religious doctrines.The book can be divided into three sections. The first part is the travels and teachings of jesus in Africa., Asia and Europe. The second part is based on moral character. In this section, the prophet gives instruction on how to live and conduct oneself as Moorish citizens. The third part is the acknowledgement of Asiatic origins. We know the first part of the book came from the Aquarian Gospels. This work is one in a long tradition of Apocrypha describing Jesus as a mystical figure, only one of a number of Christ's in world history. The Aquarian Gospels were very influential in the first three decades of the 20th century among black spiritualists and white believers in gnostic spirituality, or new thought, who understood Jesus' miracles not as the work of a god but as evidence of his ability to tap into his own divine essence. Many perceived Jesus as a profound example of a degree of perfection that all men and women could strive for through examination of wisdom of mystical brotherhoods which dated to the ancient holy land of Egypt. This can be defined as metaphysics; the ability to somehow tap into spiritual energies that all human souls possess. What makes the Aquarian Gospels so unique is that it allegedly cover the missing years of Jesus' life between the ages of 12 and 30. The holy koran circle 7 and the Aquarian Gospels give us an idea of Jesus' early life that the new testaments do not. So it gives us an alternative history whereby jesus travels during these lost years through Egypt India and Tibet gaining invaluable spiritual wisdom from Buddhists, Hindus and scholars of Egyptian mystery schools. All of this is in the Christian doctrines. For example; all the pictures displaying Jesus depicting Him with His hand clasped together in prayer; the clasping of hands can be found all throughout Asia. We can observe this practice among the Hindus with brahmin priest and this can also be observed among the buddhist monks of Tibet. This means that Jesus had to have learned the ways of the Buddha and Lord Krishna like clasped hand meditation. Another example of Asiatic influence is what the prophet defines as the holy breath. The art of breathing is also found in both Asia and Egypt. In modern times this art is manifested into a study called yoga. The holy breath symbolizes the beginning of life in man. "This age will be an age of splendor and of light, because it is the home age of the holy breath; and the holy breath will testify a new for Christ, the logos of eternal love. At first of every age this logos is made manifest in flesh so man can see and know and comprehend a love that is not narrow and circumscribed." --Excerpts from Levi Dowling's cusp of the ages.

All this is proof that jesus may have studied and learned from other religious sources. Upon discovering how to overcome his human self Jesus returns to the holy land where He is persecuted, then crucified. Afterward, He appears in Asia and Africa to revisit His teachers and disciples in his spiritual form and promises that each human will someday discover his or her own divinity and be reborn as spirit, one with God.

The second parts of the koran deal with what is called holy instructions from the prophet. They are composed of a series of conduct rules and instruction that are designed for Moorish Americans to live by. Finally, the third section defines the overall chronology of the Asiatic origins, their history and their points of origin. In addition, this section also lays the foundation of Moorish science, its aims, its teachings and the coming of the prophet.

SALVATION ALLAH UNITY

The Moorish Science Temple
of America
The Divine Constitution and By-Laws

ACT 1. - The Grand Sheik and the chairman of the Moorish Science Temple of America is in power to make law and enforce laws with the assistance of the Prophet and the Grand Body of the Moorish Science Temple of America. The assistant Grand Sheik is to assist the Grand Sheik in all affairs if he lives according to Love, Truth, Peace, Freedom and Justice, and it is known before the members of the Moorish Science Temple of America.

ACT 2. - All meetings are to be opened and closed promptly according to the circle seven and Love, Truth, Peace, Freedom and Justice. Friday is our Holy Day of rest, because on a Friday the first man was formed in flesh and on a Friday the first man departed out of flesh and ascended unto his father God Allah, for that cause Friday is the Holy Day for all Moslems all over the world.

ACT 3. - Love, Truth, Peace, Freedom and Justice must be proclaimed and practiced by all members of the Moorish Science Temple of America. No member is to put in danger or accuse falsely his brother or sister on any occasion at all that may harm his brother or sister, because Allah is Love.

ACT 4. - All members must preserve these Holy and Divine laws, and all members must obey the laws of the government, because by being a Moorish American, you are a part and partial of the government, and must live the life accordingly.

ACT 5. - This organization of the Moorish Science Temple of America is not to cause any confusion or to overthrow the laws and constitution of the said government but to obey hereby.

ACT 6. - With us all members must proclaim their nationality and we are teaching our people their nationality and their Divine Creed that they may know that they are a part and a partial of this said government, and know that they are not Negroes, Colored Folks, Black People or Ethiopians, because these names were given to slaves by slave holders in 1779 and lasted until 1865 during the time of slavery, but this is a new era of time now, and all men now must proclaim their free national name to be recognized by the government is which they live and the nations of the earth, this is the reason why Allah the Great God of the universe ordained Noble Drew Ali, the Prophet to redeem his people from their sinful ways. The Moorish Americans are the descendants of the ancient Moabites whom inhabited the North Western and South Western shores of Africa.

ACT 7. - All members must promptly attend their meetings and become a part and a partial of all uplifting acts of the Moorish Science Temple of America. Members must pay their dues and keep in line with all necessities of the Moorish Science Temple of America, then your are entitled to the name of, "Faithful". Husband, you must support your wife and children; wife you must obey your husband and take care of your children and look after the duties of your household. Sons and daughters must obey father and mother and be industrious and become a part of the uplifting of fallen humanity. All Moorish Americans must keep their hearts and minds pure with love, and their bodies clean with water. This Divine Covenant is from your Holy Prophet Noble Drew Ali, through the guidance of his Father God Allah.

NOBLE DREW ALI
Founder

MOORISH AMERICAN PRAYER

Allah the Father of the universe, the Father of Love, Truth, Peace, Freedom and Justice. Allah is my protector, my guide and my salvation by night and by day, thru his Holy Prophet Drew Ali. "Amen."

THE MOORISH SCIENCE TEMPLE OF AMERICA
Home Office of Noble Drew Ali

Home Office: Chicago, Ill., U.S.A.

34. The Moorish Divine Constitution and by laws. Source Moorish literature

35. The Moorish flag

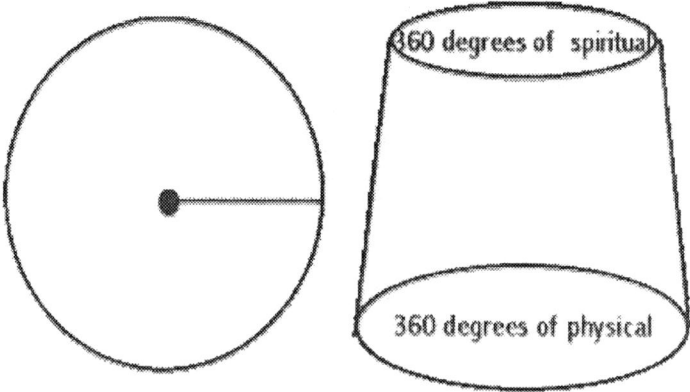

360 degrees of spiritual

360 degrees of physical

36. Symbolism of the Fez. Source Moorish literature

Chapter 9

The Aquarian Teachings of the Moorish Science Temple

Recently, I acquired a copy of Levi Dowling's version of Gospels and began comparing his works with the various scriptures of the Holy Koran Circle 7. I noticed similarities between the two books. It seems that Noble Drew Ali sourced various chapters from the Aquarian Gospels and added them to his own research, and this very research is what laid the foundations of Ali's Moorish Aquarian teachings. Supposedly, the Aquarian Gospels are said to replace the missing or hidden years in the bible. This book is an extensive reworking of the Jesus story with strong theosophical and spiritual influences. Of interest it is an attempt to fill in the two decade gap in the traditional biblical Jesus biography. According to Levi Dowling, Jesus spent a lot of time in the mystical east where he learned esoteric methods from the various masters, while rebelling against the well established caste systems of Asia. The narrative, unfortunately, has numerous historical inconsistencies involving Jesus meeting historical figures who lived hundreds of years before or after his birth. Re-examining the Aquarian Gospels, it is said that Jesus traveled throughout Africa, Asia and Europe and in these places he studied under various religious scholars and learned from them. In the book we find several stories of his travels; first He arrives in India where He meets prince Ravanna who exposes Him to the ideas of Karma and the Holy Breath.

This is the same Holy Breath that is referenced in the Holy Koran Circle 7. This is where Noble Drew Ali learned of the Holy Breath. I will compare the discussion of the the Holy Breath in Ali's Koran with that of the Aquarian Gospels. The Holy Koran states, "Teach that the holy breath would make them one again, restoring harmony and peace." Chapter 2, 19 verse.

In the Aquarian Gospels Section VI, Chapter 10, it reads, "The holy breath is truth, is that which was and is and ever more shall be; it cannot change nor pass away."

Chapter 13 of the Aquarian Gospels reads, "Man is the breath made flesh so truth and falsehood are conjoined in him; and then they strife, and naught goes down and man truth abides." There is no doubt in my mind of where Ali received his doctrines. I must emphasize what is the main purpose of the holy breath. In the holy scriptures it states that a birth God grants the breath of life in all life. So perhaps that is why the holy breath is so sacred in both Moorish and aquarian teachings. Proper breathing and meditation practices are very common in the eastern religious beliefs Today, we know it as yoga.

The number of the holy breath is seven, and God holds in His hands the sevens of time. In forming worlds He rested on the seventh day and every seventh day is set apart as sabbath day for men, God said. In the Aquarian Gospels it states that while in India, Jesus learned the knowledge of the Hindu religion. It was here where the concept of the trinity was borrowed from the Hindus and added to the newly established Christian faith. Instead of the trinity of the Brahmin the Creator, Vishnu the Preserver and Shiva the Destroyer, it was replaced with The Father, the Son and the Holy Spirit, which is acknowledged by Christians worldwide. We must remember that Jesus was never a Christian and the establishment of Christianity was created by His followers. After leaving, Jesus next traveled to persia where He was introduced to the Magian priest and silent brotherhood. Here Jesus learned the knowledge of meditation and the magic of healing. While in meditation Jesus learned how to become one with His spirit through silence and prayer. Reflecting on Chapter 40, verse 9 and 10, it states, "And when life's heavy load is pressing hard, it is far better to go out and seek a quiet place to pray. The silence is the kingdom of the soul which is not seen by human eyes." Throughout the book, Jesus continues His travels by visiting Assyria, Greece and His visitation to these lands were limited. The Aquarian Gospels only speaks of Him teaching in Assyria and Greece. it is my opinion that He did not wish to remain in this area very long because of the hostility He was facing not to mention the inhabitant barbaric behavior. In Chapter 32 of section VI, Jesus takes on the buddhist doctrines. He tries to convince the Buddhist monks that their doctrines are false and to embrace His teachings. He receives opposition and is forced to leave India fearing for His life.

There are numerous contradictions in the various chapters of the Aquarian Gospels. For example, in Chapter 32, 2nd verse, it states, "Together Jesus and Barata read the Jewish Psalms and prophets; read the vedas, the Avesta and the wisdom of Gautama the buddha."

Barata is a priest that Jews had met during his travels. Now the verse states that they read several different sacred books. First they read the Jewish Psalms which is written entirely in the hebrew alphabet, next they read the vedas written in Sanscrit, the Avesta written in the Persian language, and finally the buddhist scriptures. At that time, this would have been difficult with the language barriers. It would have been nearly impossible for such a conversation to have taken place I have covered some of the stories in the Aquarian Gospels. The book is too vast to be explored any further. I recommend that any Moorish Americans who wishes to learn more of the origins of Ali's teachings should purchase a copy and read it themselves. The Aquarian Gospels are the key to understanding Ali's Moorish Aquarian connection.

"Let's practice what Christ taught, what Buddha taught, what krishna taught; love for God and for God in every being. We need to spread the universality of God's love, of God's light by our own example, by how we live our lives. Yes, there is darkness in this world. There is a great tug-of- war going on between good and evil and darkness and light. God will never permit His world, which He created, to be overtaken by evil. His goodness and love are a force. That divine love is the most powerful force in the universe." --- Author unknown.

Jesus found in Egypt I must point out that the Aquarian Gospels do speak of Jesus venturing into Egypt and it was there that Jesus received certain knowledge and mystical rites. The number 7 is so important to Moorish Science because according to the gospels, there were seven brotherhoods. Jesus was initiated into the Egyptian brotherhood. I have found examples of Moorish science teachings in each of the degrees of the brotherhood. In chapter 48 of the Aquarian Gospels Jesus receives the first degree.

Sincerity: In this degree Jesus learns the knowledge of the number seven and all of its properties. The circle is the symbol of the perfect man, and seven is the number of the perfect man. Chapter 49: Jesus passes the second brotherhood test and receives the second degree.

Justice: Remember justice is one of the five pillars of Islam. Love, truth, peace, freedom and justice. Chapter 50: Jesus passes the third brotherhood test and receives the third degree.

Faith: In this degree Jesus learns to have faith and trust in God almighty. Chapter 51: Jesus passes the fourth brotherhood test and receives the fourth degree.

Philanthropy: Chapter 52: Jesus passes the fifth brotherhood test and receives the fifth degree.

Heroism: Chapter 53: Jesus passes the sixth brotherhood test and receives the sixth degree.

Love Divine: Now the seventh and last degree is what makes all of this very interesting. Chapter 54: Jesus receives the seventh brotherhood test and in a sacred room of the temple receives the seventh and highest degree. The Christ: He leaves the temple a conqueror.

It is strange that he was bestowed the title of Christ in Egypt. So I would conclude that most devout Christians would deny this theory taking into consideration that it is mentioned in a book not recognized by any churches and that it goes against the very foundations of the Christian faith. To think that Jesus may have studied in Egypt and learned their knowledge only to bring it back to the holy land and preach its teachings. Now in the Christian teachings, Jesus is known by two titles; Messiah and Christ. However, what most people do not know is that both words have their origins in the ancient Egyptian mystery language. Therein you find the word, Messeh, meaning anoint, which is an egyptian ritual. The word, Christ, in Egypt is Karast, which means the Christ or anointed individual.

Author Muata Ashby writes, "The word Christ is not a name but a title, like vice-president is a title. Christ means he or she whose head is anointed with oil or "the anointed one." Christhood refers to the certain qualities exhibited by mythological or historical personalities as symbols representing the potential statehood of enlightenment of every sentiment. Christ is those persons who have attained complete purification of their psychological personality. They experience cosmic consciousness; the experience of being one identifying self with everything. This is a state of supreme bliss that comes from becoming one with one's essential nature. God, this is a state which cannot be achieved through earthly pleasures or relationships as explained in the Egyptian book of the dead."

"And while the hierophant yet spoke the temple bells rang out; a pure white dove descended from above and sat on Jesus' head and then a voice that shook the very temple said this is the Christ and every living creature said, Amen." --Aquarian Gospels, Chapter 55, verse 10,11,12

Jesus had been driven out of Judea in his early youth because of His initiation into the secret wisdom of Israel. During His stay in Egypt He had augmented this knowledge through his initiation into the Egyptian mysteries. This initiation had proved to Him that the secret wisdom of the Jews and the Egyptians were identical. He had divined the occult theology of Israel compared it with wisdom of Egypt and found thereby the reason for a universal synthesis. But as Jesus' mission was particular to the Jews, it became necessary for Him to return to His native land as soon as possible in order to carry on His chosen work. --Source unknown.

All this is overwhelming proof that Jesus was somehow connected to Egypt. The new testament gives us two examples; first it tells how Mary and Joseph fled to Egypt to escape the wrath of King Herod and second, the gospels of Matthew say He remained in Egypt until after the death of Herod, so that the prophecy might be fulfilled. While in Egypt it is only fitting that Jesus learned the knowledge of the Egyptians and it was this knowledge that not only gave birth to Christianity but also Judaism and Islam. Koran Questions for Moorish Children In addition to the Holy Koran Circle 7 the prophet also bestowed upon his members a series of questions for the purpose of study. They are known as the 101 questions for Moorish children. These questions are essential for every Moorish american and they are required to memorize them. To my knowledge the questions are drawn form a variety of sources ranging from biblical Quarnic to historical and finally the Holy Koran Circle 7. it is my intention to analyze and explore all 101 questions for Moorish children.

1. Who made you? Allah
2. Who is Allah? Allah is the father of the universe.
3. Can we see him? No.
4. Where is the nearest place we can find him? In the heart.

Questions 1-4 is the acknowledgement of god. It reveals to the Moorish American the omnipotence of his presence to man and the world. The presence of god cannot be seen by the human eye, but his presence can be in the heart for Allah is love. In the bible it states, "And the creator formed man of the dust of the ground and breathed into his nostrils the breath of life; and man became a living soul.

"Allah must be glorified and exalted as the creator of the heavens and the earth. He is one and the eternal, the living, the omnipotent, the omniscient who hears, sees and wills everything. Allah most glorified and exalted is neither form nor limits. Allah most glorified and exalted cannot be explained by what or how. Nothing escapes his knowledge and power. He speaks without the limitations of sounds and letters yet his speech is not silent, not subject to deficiency." -- Iman Isa

5. Who is Noble Drew Ali? He is Allah's prophet.
6. What is a prophet? A prophet is a thought of Allah manifested in flesh.

Again Noble Drew Ali acknowledges himself as a prophet of the ages. Now according to this definition of a prophet, anyone, man or woman can be considered a prophet. This is not to say that a prophet is a thought manifested in flesh, but not by the Arabic definition of the word. Perhaps a prophet is one who received direct inspiration by means of an angel, or by the inspiration of the heart, or has seen the things of god in a dream or by a messenger.

7.   What is the duty of a prophet? To save nations from the wrath of Allah.

In ancient times the biblical prophets were sent by god to warn the inhabitants of his wrath. The duty of a prophet was to reveal the message of god.

8. Who is the founder of the Moorish science Temple of America?

9. What year was the Moorish Science Temple of America founded? 1913 A.D.

10. Where was it founded? Newark, New Jersey

11. Where was Noble Drew Ali born? North Carolina in 1886.

12. What is his nationality? Moorish American

13. What is your nationality? Moorish American Reference: Islam in the African American Community and Morocco and the History of the Moors.

14. Why are we Moorish American? Because we are descendants of Moroccans and we are born in America.

During the slave trade, the majority of slaves taken from Africa were from the northern hemisphere around the west coast. These countries were predominantly Muslim and were Moorish inhabitants of Morocco, Ivory Coast, Tunduneia, etc...

15. For what purpose was the Moorish Science Temple of America founded? To uplift fallen humanity.

16. How did the prophet begin to uplift the Moorish Americans? By teaching them to be themselves.

The prophet Noble Drew Ali established the Moorish Science Temple for of uplifting African Americans from a slavery mentality. He taught them to be themselves by acknowledging their Moorish-Asiatic origins.

17.   What is our religion? Islamism

18. Is that a new or is it the old time religion? It is old time religion. In this question, the prophet acknowledges the religion of Islam as the religion of all Asiatics in America and he refers to Islam as the old time religion. Technically, Islam is not as old a religion as Christianity or Judaism.

19. What kind of flag is the Moorish flag? It is a red flag with a five-pointed green star in the center.
20. What do the five points represent? Love, truth, peace, freedom and justice.
21. How old is our flag? It is over 10,000 years old.

The five points on the star represent the five senses as well as the five wounds inflicted upon the body of Jesus. The combination represents Jesus Christ, the anointed one and Muhammad, the praised one. Answer 21 states that the flag is 10,000 years old. It is not so much the age of the flag, but the actual age of its primary symbol; the star, which represents man and yet man is older than 10,000 years.

22. Which is our holy day? Friday
23. Why is Friday holy? It is the day on which man was formed in flesh and it was when he departed out of flesh.

John Jackson writes, "The hypothetical first man of the bible is rightly named Adam, since the word Adam, which means "man" was reputedly made out of Adamah, which means the ground or earth. Similarly among the ancient romans, man was called Homo because he was supposedly made from Humus, the earth. According to an ancient Egyptian Myth, Knoumou, the father of the gods, moulded the earliest men out of clay on a potter's wheel. We are informed by the Chaldean priest, Berosus, that the great god Bel decapitated himself, and that the other gods mixed his blood with clay and out of it fashioned the first man. In the greek mythology, Prometheus is depicted as manufacturing men from clay at Panopeus."

According to Imam Isa, "For in six days the sustainer made heaven and earth. The sea, and all that is in them, and rested the seventh day; where fore the Lord blessed the Sabbath day and hallowed it." Friday is also the day that all Muslims come together in prayer and worship.

24. Who was Jesus? He was a prophet of Allah.
25. Where was He born? In Bethlehem of Judah, in the house of David.
26. Who were His father and mother? Joseph and Mary.
27. Will you give in brief the line (genealogy) through which Jesus came? Some of the great fathers through which jesus came are: Abraham, Boaz by Ruth, jesse, King David, Solomon, Hezekiah and Joseph and Mary.

Questions 24-27 deal with the origins of Jesus, His purpose for coming to earth and his family lineage. Most orthodox Muslims acknowledge Jesus as a major prophet but not the son of God as most Christians do.

28. Why did Allah send Jesus to this earth? To save the israelites from the iron-hand oppression of the pale skin nations of Europe who were governing a portion of Palestine at that time.

29. How long has that been? About two thousand years ago.

30. What was the nationality of Ruth? Ruth was a Moabite.

"And he (Boaz) said, Who art thou? and she answered, I am Ruth thine handmaid; spread therefore thy skirt over thine handmaid; for thou art a near kinsman. And he said, Blessed be thou of the LORD, my daughter... Fear not; I will do thee all that thou requirest." Ruth 3:9-11

I must reference the biblical matriarch Ruth. The stroy of Ruth is very complex. Naomi, Ruth and Boaz is one of the gems of sacred literature - so beautiful that it is not surpassed in writings of fiction or fact. The incidents of the story are among the most fascinating of the entire Bible, marked with poetic beauty and simplicity. The climax is reached in the romance and marriage between Ruth and Boaz. But the events of some years prior must be read for one to fully appreciate this beautiful and happy climax.

Ruth, the heroine of the story, was a lovely maiden of Moab, while Boaz was a nobleman and wealthy citizen of Israel. The Moabites were aliens to the Israelites, idolaters and inter mixture of the two races was forbidden by Jewish law. Mutual relationship between the two races.

For economic reasons Naomi, her husband Elimelech, and their two sons had migrated to the land of Moab from the little Hebrew town of Bethlehem. Some of the Moabite people were wholesomely influenced by the piety, devoutness and religious strictness of this family, Ruth became the wife of one of the sons, and quite evidently a proselyte to the Hebrew religion. Tragedy came to this Hebrew family in a strange land. Elimelech and the two sons died, and three lonely widows were left desolate. When Naomi decided to return to Israel and to her native town of Bethlehem, Ruth refused to sever her attachment to Naomi and accompanied her. The depth of her love for her mother-in-law and her devotion to the Hebrew religion were given expression in these immortal words:

'Entreat me not to leave thee,
Or to return from following after thee:
For whither thou goest, I will go:
And where thou lodgest, I will lodge;
Thy people shall be my people,
And thy God my God:
Where thou diest, I will die,
And there will I be buried:
The Lord do so to me, and more also,
If ought by death part thee and me.'

In providing for the material needs of herself and her mother-in-law, Ruth followed a law and well established custom in Israel which provided the privilege of gathering fragments of grain behind the reapers at harvest time. This was a humiliating and arduous form of employment followed only by the very poor and needy. The nobility, industrious disposition, and frugality of Ruth were impressively manifest in this menial engagement.

Through the strange workings of divine providence it happened that Ruth was gleaning scattered grain in the wheat fields of the nobleman Boaz, a distant relative of her deceased husband. While making the usual rounds among his reapers, Boaz was attracted to this young woman, and inquired about her identity and other information about her. He made himself known as the owner of the farm and extended unusual courtesies and favors to her. He invited her to have lunch with him and the acquaintance soon blossomed into an enchanting romance. Genuine love for each other throbbed in the hearts of both. According to the customs in Israel under the circumstances in which both Ruth and Boaz related, Ruth must take the lead in presenting her charms for marriage.She did this with timidity and modesty under the guidance of her mother-in-law Naomi. The love and esteem which Ruth manifested for Boaz was fully reciprocated and the nobility of his character shined in superb brilliance and glory. He took the necessary legal steps to remove all the barriers to marriage between himself and Ruth and she soon became his bride. There was born to them a son whom they named Obed, who was later the father of Jesse, who was the father of David. Boaz and Ruth became the ancestors of a long line of kings who ruled over Israel and Judah and of the Messiah-Saviour.

31. What is the modern name of the Moabites? Moroccans
32. Where is the Moroccan Empire? Northwest Amexem
33. What is the modern name Amexem? Africa
34. What is the title given to our ruler in Morocco? Sultan
35. Where do we get the name Jesus? From the East.
36. What does the name Jesus mean? Justice
37. Did the angel give to the child that was called Jesus a holy name? Yes, but it cannot be used by those who are slaves to sin.
38. What is an angel? An angel is a thought of Allah manifested in human flesh.

Their are seven primary archangels of God who preside, under the God, over all affairs of mankind. Michael: Ma-Ha-El. "The Great God." In sanskrit Maha means great and El stands for God (as it does in ancient Egyptian and Hebrew). Appropriately we find the suffix El in all the archangel names. Michael's light is red, in all its shades and he is the archangel of light and fire. Michael gives us the bodily warmth and warm red blood. Gabriel: Or in the ancient Egyptian language pronunciation, Kha-Vir-El. Ga or Ka denotes desire, sentiment and expressed love. Bir or Vir indicates element. Gabriel's light is sky-blue in many different shades and he is the ruler of water and the liquids. Gabriel is the steward of the entire physical kingdom and gives us the body's various fluids.

Raphael: Ra-Fa-El. In ancient Egyptian Ra stands for the sun, and Fa for vibration. "Sun- vibration-God." Raphael, the archangel if energy, is characterized by the shades of violet. This color derives from the mixture of red (Michael) and blue (Gabriel), and thus tallies with the role of Raphael as fellow worker with the other two. The planet in its entirety is within Raphel's domain who controls the electromagnetic forces, etheric vitality and plays an invaluable role in the maintenance of good health in each of us.

Uriel: Coordinates the work of all the archangels within the gross material body. U-Ra-El, as known to the Egyptian forefathers stands for space and sun. "Space-Sun-God." The great harmonizer of substance, Uriel keeps the Universal Law of Order and Harmony both within and between each body. Uriel is the great harmonizer and balancer of substance.

Raguel: Presides over those who have been lifted to worlds of light. He is the father of the faithful multitude and the prototype of that way of life that leads to unity with the elohim.

Phanuel: Saves the pertinent from darkness so that they can live among the elohim in realms of light.

Remiel: Leads mankind to the resurrection, preparing everything for the descent of the son of man in radiant light. He is the testator, who bears witness of the father and mother and their divine son. Through him, every thing will be restored before the end of time.

39. What are the angels for? To carry messages to the four corners of the world, to all nations.
40. What is our prophet to us? He is an angel of Allah who was sent to bring us the everlasting gospel of Allah.
41. What is the everlasting gospel? It is a saving power that comes from Allah through our ancient fathers by his prophet.
42. What is the covenant of the great god Allah? Honor thy father and thy mother that thy days may be long upon the earhtland which the Lord thy God-Allah hath given thee.
43. At what age did Jesus begin to preach? Twelve
44. Where did Jesus teach? India, Africa and Europe
45. How long did he teach? 18 years
46. What did Jesus say that would make you free? Truth
47. What is truth? Truth is Aught

48. What is aught? Aught is Allah
49. Can truth change? Truth cannot change or pass away.
50. What other name do we give truth? Holy Breath
51. What do you have to say about Holy Breath? All we can say is it is great. It is good. it was, it is and evermore to be. Amen.

At the birth of every human being the first breath is being given by the Holy Spirit or the Maha Chohan. The last breath at the end of our time span is taken by one of them. The breath can contain the qualities of the Holy Spirit when you concentrate upon them. The Holy Breath is composed of 4 parts:

1. The inbreath when you breathe the quality (for instance patience).
2. The absorption, when you hold the breathe in your body, absorb the quality into your four vehicles (physical, etheric, emotional and mental.)
3. The expansion when you breathe out, it increases the power and momentum of the Holy Breath.
4. As you hold your breath out of your body project those magnificent God qualities forth to all life.

"One is the Breath of the Living God. This is Holy Breath.

Breathe in. Be aware that you are alive because you breathe. This one breath of life is holy. It is holy because it is from God who is one. Every living thing breathes in this same one breath of the Living God. Ruah Hakodesh -Holy Breath - is about knowing that you are breathing in God every time you inhale, Be aware that being alive gives you incredible creative powers. We engrave and carve letters and words in the air with our voices, our speech - our breath. The letters that are formed by your breath tell your story, your unique Sippur. All the words that pour from your voice with your breath speak your truth out into the world.

We 'breathe' in One Breath as we live in God and we breathe out a second breath. Breath from breath, as we form letters with out breath. Ruah Hakodesh, Holy Breath, is also knowing how amazingly creative you are every time you exhale. Your breath and the letters of speech that flow from your mouth engrave and carve the story of your soul into the elastic tablet of space-time. As your breath continually flows in and out of your body, whether you are aware of it or not, every moment that you are alive your heart beats with the rhythm of Life, sending blood streaming through your arteries and veins to all the different parts of your body.

These are all paths for the wondrous wisdom of the living God to reveal itself through, exquisite living forms that are crafted with awesome artistry and creativity. Just as every cell in your body tells the unique story (Sippur) of your soul, everything in the universe writes its own book (Sepher), weaves its own unique pattern into the fabric of space-time. The flight of birds and the song of the whales, the structure of crystals, the patterns of storms, the spiral shapes of galaxies, the double-helix of DNA, the form of every living thing tell of the wondrous wisdom of the one God. There are countless paths for the one breath, countless creative expressions of the living God." -- Resource unknown

"Men call the thought of heaven the holy breath." --Aquarian Gospel Ch: 9:18

52. At what place on earth was the physical part of man formed? In the Garden of Eden.
53. Where is the Garden of Eden? In the land of Canaan, in the city of Mecca.
54. What is the modern name for the Garden of Eden? Mecca
55. What is the name of the first physical man? His name cannot be used, only by Executive rulers of the A.C. of the M.S.T. of A.
56. What are the words of A.C. of the M.S.T. of A.? Adept Chamber of the Moorish Science Temple of America. (3rd Heaven)
57. Who were Adam and Eve? They are the mother and father of the human family. Asiatics and Europeans.
58. Where did they go? They went into Asia.
59. What is the modern name given to the children? Asiatics
60. Who is guarding the holy city of Mecca today to keep away the unbelievers? Angels
61. What is the modern name for these angels? Asiatics
62. What is the shade of their skin? Olive
63. Are the Moorish Americans any relation to those angels? Yes, we all have the same father and mother.
64. Give five names that are given to the descendants of Adam and Eve: Lucifer, Satan, Devil, Dragon and Beast.
65. What is the devil sometimes called? The lower self.
66. How many selves are there? Two
67. Name them: Higher self and lower self
68. What people represent the higher self? The angels who protect the holy city of Mecca.
69. What people represent the lower self? Those who were cast out of the holy city and those who accept their teachings.
70. What is the higher self? The higher self is the mother of virtues and the harmonies of life and breeds justice, mercy, love and right.
71. Can the higher self pass away? No

72. Why? Because it is Allah in Man.
73. What does the lower-self breed? Hatred, Slander, Lewdness, Murders, Theft and everything that harms.
74. What did the higher-self say to the lower-self at one time when he met Satan? "Where are you going Satan?"
75. What was the answer the lower-self gave to the higher-self? "I am going to and fro the earth seeking whom I may devour." Questions 65-75

The higher self is the part of the person not directly concerned with his or her physical survival. It is concerned with maintaining a correct alignment and doing what is right. The aspect is an essential part of the higher self. The aspect is a tool used in pursuit of truth. So the higher self is the part of the person interested in creating a work unit. The higher self is usually less in the foreground of the person's mind than the lower part.

The lower self is the part of the person that is directly concerned with material existence. It is the part of the person that is working toward survival on the physical plane. It is thus more motivated by physical rewards and punishments. It is less interested in creating a work unit than surviving. Consequently, it often pushes the higher self out of the foreground.

At certain times the higher and lower selves of a person are out of agreement. As Abraham Lincoln said, "A house divided against itself cannot stand." A synthesis is needed between the two selves or stress will be created within the individual. The stress occurs within his or her mind, transferring to the body and finally outward to other people. If the relationship between the over and under part is skewed, then the synthesis will be incorrect between the higher and lower selves. If a person is focused too heavily on material existence and physical survival this may result in a swelled over part and a bad alignment or a swelled under part and an evil alignment. More often it will create both effects in the same person at different times. When he or she is confronted with a more powerful badly aligned person, he or she will use an evil alignment. Conversely if he or she is confronted with a weaker person, he or she will revert to a bad alignment.

There is an odd paradox with relation to the higher and lower selves. The more one strives to preserve oneself physically, the harder time the person has surviving, while the more energy is ut on creating work units, the better the survival is. Upon closer inspection this actually is not paradoxical since, as we have already discussed, positive work units help people keep better overall health.

76. Has he finished his task of devouring? Yes
77. When was his time declared out? When he nailed Jesus to the cross.
78. What were the last words Jesus uttered? It is fulfilled.

The seven sentences Jesus pronounced on the cross:

1. My God, my God, why have you forsaken me? (Mt 27, 46)
2. In truth I tell you, today you will be with me in paradise - to the good thief (Lk 23, 43)
3. Father, into your hands I commit my spirit. (Lk 23, 46)
4. Father, forgive them; they do not know what they are doing. (Lk 23, 43)
5. Woman, this is your son (to John): This is your mother. (Jn 19, 26)
6. I am thirsty. (Jn 19, 28)
7. It is fulfilled. (Jn 19, 30)

This further references the number 7 in Moorish Science.

79. What did He have reference to? He had reference to the end of Satan.
80. Did Jesus say the He would return to conquer him? Yes
81. What is the first name of the person into whom Jesus was first reincarnated? Prophet Mohammed, the Conqueror.
82. Was Satan to be bound then? Satan was bound in part.
83. When was the head of Satan taken off? 453 (Byzantine)
84. By whom? By Mohammed.
85. Name some of the marks that were put upon the Moors of Northwest by the European nations in 1774? Negro, Black, colored and Ethiopian.
86. Negro, a name given to a river in West Africa by Moors because it contained black water. This is reference to the Niger river located in the southern area of Africa.
87. What is meant by the word, black? Black according to science means death.
88. What does the word, colored mean? Colored means anything that has been painted, varnished or dyed.
89. What does Ethiopian mean? Ethiopia means something divided.
90. Can a man be a Negro, Black, Colored or Ethiopian? No.
91. Why? Because man is made in the image and after the likeness of God, Allah.
92. What title does Satan give himself? God
93. Will you define the word, white? White means purity, purity means God, and God means the ruler of the land.

94. To whom do we refer at times, as being the great God? Allah.
95. Is the devil made in the image and likeness of Allah? No, he is the shadow of our lower selves and will pass away.
96. Who made the devil? Elohim
97. Who is Elohim? Elohim is the seven creative spirits that created everything that ever was, is and evermore to be.
98. What is Elohim sometimes called? The seven eyes of Allah.

In the apocryphal book of Enoch, it speaks about the seven watchmen, the seven great mountains, the seven great rivers, the seven great islands. Biblical prophet Zechariah speaks about the seven eyes of God which supervise all the people of the earth.

99. How many days are in the Circle? Seven

Symbol of the totality of the created universe (3 the sky + 4 the earth), it expresses the creation within which the man evolves. The seven indicates the senses of change after an accomplished cycle and of a positive renewal. Symbol of eternal life for the Egyptians: it symbolizes a complete cycle, a dynamic perfection. The etheric body of the man is completely developed and installed only around the age of seven. The circle further alludes to the Masonic point within a circle which is represented of man within the boundary of God. The seven symbolizes the cross with its six directions plus the center - indefinite extents moving toward the top, the bottom, the right, the left, forwards and backwards. The holy family Mary, Joseph and Jesus remained seven years in Egypt, in Heliopolis to escape King Herod.

In the Islamic religion, the Koran has seven esoteric senses, according to Muslim mysticisms (sometimes they talk about seventy senses); there are seven consonants, called sawakit, that are not in the first verse of the Koran; there are seven towers at the Mecca; during the pilgrimage to Mecca, they have to take seven turns of the Kaba and seven courses between the mounts Cafa and Marmia; the soul of the dead remains seven days beside the tomb and the new born baby receives his name the 7th day; the cats and the dogs have seven lives; the Fatiha counts seven verses (opening the Koran); the seven gates that possess the Hell which are in relation with the various torments it contains, and there would be also seven hells: Gehennan, Ladha, Hatorna, Sair, Sakar, Jahim and Hawiyat; the Koran says that Allah has created seven skies and as much lands. (Koran 65, 12 and 41, 8-11.)

The ceremonies in the cult of Apollo were celebrated the seventh day of the mont. Apollo is referenced in the holy Koran circle 7.

100. How many days are in a creation?

Seven. The seven paths to the paradise, each one having to be traversed by the body, the heart, and the spirit in a unique communion.

- The number 7 is used 507 times in the bible.
- The number 7 is used 32 times in the Koran and it is used in 13 verses. 101. According to science how many days are in a year? Seven.

777 - Further reference to thee number 777 symbolizes the biblical age of the biblical patriarch Lamech who was the father of the founders of science. He was 777 years of age.

The Moorish American Fez Noble Drew Ali instructed his male followers to wear fezzes as an expression of the Moorish identity. Hence Moorish Americans of the old movement proudly wear their fezzes for all the world to see. -- Sidjul Moors.

From the 1920's to the present, the fez is worn by all Moorish Americans as a symbol of their allegiance to the country of Morocco. To my knowledge, the fez was normally worn by the Shiners Fraternity and somehow this headdress was incorporated in to the Moorish Science Temple. However, it was the Masonic Fraternity who brought this dress to the western world. The fez is named after the city of Fez, one of the four traditional capitals of Morocco and was a great Islamic center of learning. The fez, also known as tarboosh, was customarily worn by students of a great school in the city of Fez, Morocco. It has come to be known as a mark of learning. In addition to the country of Morocco, the fez is worn in other countries like Egypt, Turkey and several countries in North Africa.

In his book, Shrinedom, author A.Z. Plummer writes, "The fez gets its name from its original place of manufacture. Fez or Fes, in the empire of Morocco to which pilgrimages were made by muslims about 980 A.D. and those of the muslim faith living west of the Nile, journeyed to Fez as to the holy city. Until recent times the town of Fez had a monopoly on the manufacturing, for it was supposed the peculiar dull crimson hue of these skull caps could not be obtained elsewhere. The dye was taken from the juice of a small berry which grows in large quantities in the immediate neighborhood of the town. A manufacturer of that city supplied to the students of a great school there, a scarlet tarboosh, which was the insignia of the school, and the mean by which the students were readily recognized.

This is where the color and style of the fez come from. The headpiece today is upon nearly every male head in the orient. In the Moorish science temple the wearing of the fez has both a material and spiritual significance. It is material because of the identity that it possesses, a link to a culture or a way of life. The prophet wore a fez frequently, and this could be seen in the various photos of him. It is described as a conventional uniform of nobility and, in most cases, a title of distinction is usually presented with the wearing of the fez. Faas also fez, is a felt cap worn by men with a circular flat top, with a small circular extension connected with black tassels. It is not more than 5 inches in height and 6 inches in diameter at the top. -- Author unknown

On the spiritual side the terms are much more complex. To some of the Moors, the fez represents the pyramids of Egypt, an ancient tomb built to house the dead, and valuable treasures of both precious stones and inscriptions of wisdom. In short, the knowledge of the ages past. The pyramids were built with a large square base and inverted walls of perfect symmetry, therefore, the fez is to be worn straight and flat without any indentures to destroy its perfect likeness. The flat top of the fez represents the unfinished pyramid. The tassel suspended from the top represents the cable that will someday pull up the capstone to complete the unfinished pyramid when the trials and tribulations of this world have been completed.

Notice that the fez is shaped just like a cylinder and towards the end of the cylinder is a circle. In mathematics the circle represents 360 degrees, and this further alludes to 360 degrees of spiritual knowledge at the top and 360 degrees of physical knowledge at the bottom, equaling 720 degrees to perfect circles.

In his book, Clock of Destiny, author C.M. Bey writes, "The red fez of the Moorish nation represents Atlas the human head and earth. The tassel of the fez represents the center of the universe namely the human head and the force of gravity which attracts all objects and draws them to the center of the earth and human beings." Bey also says, "The head dress of our Moorish forefathers, the red fez with the symbol of the star and crescent or moon in this hemisphere. The Moorish fez represents the supreme height of wisdom and practical knowledge of the science of the 12 signs of the Zodiac, the universal law and constitution upon which civilization is founded."

Throughout this passage, I have explored the esoteric teachings of the Moorish science temple, secretive as they may be. Their symbols and their meanings all came from other mystical rites of learning and it was the prophet's exposure to these various rites that allowed him to create this science. Nevertheless, these are the teachings of the Moorish Americans and these teachings were designed by the prophet in order to spread the ideas of Islam in America.

Chapter 10

The Decline of the Moorish Science Temple: The Various Religious Sects that Sprung from the Original Movement

By the late 1920's, the Moorish science temple has accumulated more than 100,000 followers with the prophet Noble Drew Ali being the supreme head and leader. All was well until strife began among the leaders of the various temples. It seems the prophet being as powerful as he was could not control the mass numbers of members. This started the decline of the Moorish Science Temple. it was not that the prophet was not strong enough to hold it together. My theory is that every individual at some point in his life develops a desire, and that desire is to want to accumulate. Then it becomes an ambition to the point that it manifests itself in to greed. This was the downfall of the Moorish science Temple of America. Of all the chapters that I have written within this book, this by far is the most complicated and difficult. It is not difficult because of the history of this organization. The research materials that I have accumulated allows me to give a precise detailed view of events that occurred. The difficulty comes form the personal feelings I have developed from the study of this science. To understand my reasoning I reflect on the reasons why this organization fell into disarray.

In the beginning, the prophet had a vision to uplift, and although in some cases his vision and his teachings were corrupted by other higher ranking members of his organization. Now I must unravel the mysteries of this event. According to Imam Isa, Noble Drew Ali was no longer able to personally supervise the inner workings of each individual temple. So he designated more power to his subordinate leaders. These men were known as Grand Sheiks. They were put in charge of the temples. The so called sheiks that Noble Drew Ali shared power and authority with, abused their responsibilities and began exploiting the temple members. A power struggle began with Ali caught in the middle. The leaders became rich from their positions in the temple and saw Ali as a threat and they wanted him out of the way.

One such case was the conflict between Ali and Sheik Claude Greene. One source states that that Ali's leadership was soon contested. In 1929, he became embroiled in a quarrel with Claude Greene, a politician and former butler who had joined the organization. One day Ali arrived at his office to find that Greene had moved all the furniture outside and had declared himself Grand Sheik. A civil war ensued, each faction enlisting support from temple in other cities. A few days later, a crew of gun and knife wielding men burst into the south side offices of Sheik Claude Greene and shot and stabbed him to death. Greene, a well liked black civic leader was also the former business manager of the Moorish Science Temple of America. Rumor had it that Ali was behind the assassination. Ali and a number of his followers were engaged in celebrations at his home when police arrived to take Ali and forty rank and file Moors into custody. Ali was released on bail and defended by attorneys Aaron Payne and William L. Dawson, both members who later gained political prominence.

The prophet, from prison issued a message to his members. An edict that said, "To the heads of all temples, Islam, I your prophet do hereby and now write you a letter as a warning and appeal to your good judgement for the present and future. Though I am now in custody for you and the cause, it is all right and it is well for all who still believe in me and my father-God Allah. I have redeemed all of you and you shall be saved, all of you, even with me. I go to bat Monday, May 20, before the grand jury. If you are with me, be there. Hold on and keep the faith, and great shall be your reward. Remember, my laws and love ye one another, prefer not a stranger to your brother. Love and truth and peace I leave all. Peace from your prophet." Noble Drew Ali.

This was the last statement that the prophet wrote. Son after he was released from prison and died suddenly in his apartment. The news media never identified the cause of death. Some say that he was beaten by police officers, and other rumors state that he was accosted by opposing Moors and stabbed to death. This marked the end of the original Moorish Science Temple. After the death of the prophet, the group splintered into many different sects.

Author Susan nance writes, "On the day of Noble Drew Ali's funeral, one would inhabit his chosen successor, attorney Aaron Payne. Another believer told the paper, 'The prophet was not ill. His work was done and he laid his head upon the lap on one of his followers and passed out.' Ali's public image never managed to convey the deep respect many Moorish Americans had for him as a religious leader."

What Nance stated is what now has come to pass. Two members of the organization eventually came forth and acknowledged themselves as the reincarnate of the prophet. All this will play a major part in explaining the next section.

The Rise of the Various Religious Sects

After the death of the prophet, there were several attempts to hold the group together. Several of the prophet's disciples announced that they alone were the rightful inheritor of Ali's leadership. Of these leaders there were three that stood out as the stronger of the group. They were John Givens El, E Mealy El, and Ira Johnson Bey. John Givens El

Shortly after the prophet's death, John Givens El appeared before a large crowd of Moors and announced that he was the prophet Ali reincarnated, and he was the rightful successor to the temple leadership. To my knowledge, Givens El was said to be the former chauffer of the prophet and somehow he felt that the earned the right to lead the temple. Givens was arrested by the police and sent to an insane asylum, but was released several years later. In 1941, he was heading a Chicago temple on East 40th Street and still asserting his claim to the title of Grand Sheik of all Moorish temples. Givens was one of six contestants, each a temple leader and each designating his own temple as temple number one. As for Ira Johnson Bey, he was committed to the state hospital for the criminally insane where he eventually died. E Mealy El

E Mealy El also claimed the right to the head leadership of the temple. As far as I know, the prophet was said to acknowledge him as his successor in the case of his own demise. But, because of his claim to the leadership he was attacked by opposing Moors and received injuries. Mealy El survived and established his own Moorish Science Temple as temple number one.

After the collapse of the temple, a new organization called the Nation of Islam was formed. The organization was founded by Wallace D. Fard who was a follower of Ali, though some would later say otherwise. Fard founded the temple of Islam in Detroit, Michigan around 1930. At least one source notes that both he and his protege, Elijah Muhammad were members of the Moorish Science Temple and exposed to the teachings of Ali. Originally

Muhammad was known as Elijah Poole Bey, a Moorish name. In 1934, Fard disappeared and Muhammad took control. Muhammad moved the organization to Chicago and established its national headquarters. The Nation of Islam operated pretty much the same way as the Moorish Science Temple did with the exception of being more militant. Eventually the Nation of islam became a powerful force nationwide through both political and social programs. Muhammad's power began to unravel when his protege, Malcolm X discovered that the Nation of Islam leader had not only committed adultery but had fathered illegitimate children. Malcolm X was assassinated in 1965.

Following X's assassination, Muhammad remained in power until his death in 1975. A power struggle divided the groups into two different branches. One led by Elijah's son Wallace Muhammad and the other by Minister Louis Farakhan. Both branches share a common point of origin and a mission to spread Islam. However, they have different philosophies.

There were many different sects that branched off from the Nation of Islam. One such group was lead by Yahweh Ben Yahweh, once known as Moses israel whose real name is Hulon Mitchell Jr. Ben Yahweh received his teachings from the NOI and formed the hebrew Israelites. Their doctrine is a mixture of Hebrew and Islamic beliefs. As far as I know, this organization is still in existence and their leader is now serving a life sentence for murder. There is also the nation of 5%. Located within the deep ghetto's of harlem, new York, this organization is a product of Moorish Science and NOI doctrines. This sect was founded by Clarence Edward Smith in 1964. Unlike the Nation of Islam, the 5% philosophies were based on the science of numbers. Smith who later changed his name to Father Allah, took the original lost and found muslim lessons from NOI and put them into the hands of the youth in the streets.

In his article, Black Gods of the Inner City, author Prince A. Cuba writes, "Father Allah borrowed Fard's initiation ritual and related a mathematical formula for the human society, which was broken down into percentages. The 5% were those who taught righteousness, freedom, justice and equality to all humans. They taught that the god of righteousness was not a spirit or a spook but the black man of Asia." (Moorish Science origin)

The 5% teachings were broken down into three aspects. The eighty five percent, the ten percent and the five percent. The eighty five percent, the masses, believed in a mystery God and worshipped that which did not exist. They believed in a spirit deity rather than a material man as God. They function on a mentally dead level and are easy to lead in the wrong direction but hard to lead in the right direction. The ten percent were the bloodsuckers of the poor who taught the eighty five percent that a mystery god existed. They kept the masses asleep with myths and lies, catering to their superstitious nature and living in luxury from the earnings of the poor. The five percent were destined to be poor righteous teachers and to struggle successfully against the ten percent. Their job was to lead the eighty five percent to freedom, justice and equality.

The membership of the 5% continued to grow under the leadership of Farther Allah. His primary membership was composed of inner city youths. He set up picnics and opened a school to teach his doctrines. On Friday June 13, 1969, he was assassinated by three unknown men. His murder remains an unsolved mystery.

The Washitaw Nation

I am not certain that this particular group has any connection with the original Moorish Science Temple movement. However, according to their own history, this group traces its origins to a group of indigenous American Indians. This particular group exist almost as a cult and is led by Empress Verdiacee Washitaw Turner Gaston El-bey. According to Washitaw literature, she is said to be a descendant of a great washitaw chieftress who reigned during the second half of the 1700's. Empress Verdiacee claims that the washitaw are descended from the ancient Olmecs of Mexico who are said to be the original migrants who came to America form the lost continent of Atlantis. The empress received her information of her heritage from her grandmother and has spent more than 30 years researching the history of her tribe. Over the years she has been subjected to attacks because of her claims. Additional information can be found on this group in a book called, Return of the Ancient Ones. This group is connected to the Moorish Science Temple by way of acknowledging and tracing their origins to the native American moor. Another name for this group is the washitaw Moors. This group is based out of Louisiana because they lay claim to the Louisiana Purchase of 1803. This was land taken away from them by the French and sold to the United States. The washitaw established itself as a sovereign independent nation and seceded from the union with empress as supreme ruler. To my knowledge, they are recognized by the United Nations and several native american groups as being legitimate American Indians.

Nuwaubian Nation of Moors

This group is another offshoot of the Moorish Science Temple. Founded by Malachi Z York-El in the late eighties. This group is based in Georgia with York as the supreme leader. I know very little about this particular sect. They incorporate a variety of religious teachings into their beliefs ranging from native American folklore, freemasonry, egyptology and Moorish science. As far as I know, this sect is still in existence. Another aspect of this group is that Malachi Z York claims to have traced his lineage to the great leader of Sudan, Muhammad Ahmad Ibn Abd Allah. Born in 1844, he is known as the divinely guided one and the Mahdi of the Sudan. He said that God had given him the mission of purifying Islam and to fight all those who were against the religion. He managed to wage a successful holy war against British colonization. he created an islamic state that extended from regions in central Africa all the way to the coast of the Red Sea. He died in 1885 after becoming ill. Today, he has a large following known as the Ansaru Allah community, which was another community fostered by Malachi Z York. This group has a very dark history and have been constantly monitored by law enforcement for their practices of fraud and prostitution. As far as I know, this group is stationed in Eaton, Georgia and the FBI classified them as a cult. Currently, Dr. York is serving a jail sentence.

Old Time Revision A Movement called NUWAUPU by: Jeffrey Johnson

People of African descent have remained deeply connected to spirituality for thousands of years. As an African people, our connection to our belief in a Higher Power is vital and integral to the development of our cultures. Even after enduring centuries of torturous slavery in the United States and in many other parts of the Westernized world, this remains an unshakable element of our reality. In the African-American experience, we have endured being force-fed religion, being born-again into religion, and converting to other religions. What we classify as religion i being challenged by a movement that has similarities to the spiritual and Black nationalist movements of the past and present, such as the Nation of Islam and the original African Hebrew Israelites. This movement is called Nuwaupu.

Nabi Me-Lek Ye-huda Ben Ma'at Yisra-El-Bey, referred to by most simply as Yisrael, is a Nuwaupian or adherent to the Nuwaupian faith. Not only was he born a Pentecostal Christian, but also, his grandfather founded the Pentecostal Assemblies of the World Church in Cleveland. Later, he became a part of the 5% Nation of Gods and Earths. But now, Yisrael is a studying Nuwaupian, an adherent to a spiritual system that is much more of a philosophical system than a religion. Yisrael states, "All religions are correct, but they have bits and pieces of the puzzle. Bits and pieces of truth are in every one. Each one is like stair steps to knowledge."

Nuwaupian, according to Yisrael, means "New-Being." It also means "New-Nubian" and most Nuwaupians are black. Nuwaupu as a spiritual or philosophical system is a vast body of information and is difficult to limit to a set of core beliefs. But, a minor familiarity with Hermetic Philosophy, Hebrewism, Islam, and the beliefs of the 5% Nation of Gods and Earths is a healthy start. When asked what his core beliefs were he answered, "The word was with God, now here's the word, brother. I am a god. Not the God, but a god. If God created you, doesn't that make you part of him?"

Nuwaupu is reminiscent of the race conscious beliefs of the Nation of Islam and the 5% Nation of Gods and Earths. This is because it descends from the same root as those movements, a root called Moorish Science, brought to the U.S. by a man named Timothy Drew, later known as Noble Drew Ali. The beliefs of this spiritual system were that black people were Moors, who ruled Spain from 711 A.D. to 1492 A.D. And, that Moorish Science was the spiritual system practiced by those Moors. "I'm Moorish. The biggest threat is that you (Black people) would find out you were Moors. The United States used to pay taxes to Morocco." Morocco was named for the Moors of antiquity who occupied the area centuries ago.

An example of their race conscious beliefs is the emphasis placed on identifying Biblical, Toriac, and Qur'anic figures as black. When asked about Jesus Christ, Yisrael responded, "God sent down a Hebrew. You can call him a Jew or a Nazarene or whatever. But, God didn't send down no Greek." This is quick reference to famed Pan-American studies teacher, Dr. Yosef ben-Jochannon, which Yisrael used to validate his claims.

In fact, Yisrael says that everything he teaches can be validated by research and much of the information he teaches. It can easily be authenticated in classes taken in the department of Pan-American studies. Yisrael says, "We (black people) are too lazy to do the investigation. You can alchemy your mind. You can be resurrected. Your worst death is your mental death. Mental death leads to spiritual death. If you are not spiritually well, you can't even be physically well."

The Nuwaupian information that was once available at small African book stores is no longer there. Nuwaupians have removed public access to the teachings of the spiritual leader, Dr. Malachi Z. York. When asked about how one could access this restricted information, which ranges form explanations of Biblical verses (according to Yisrael, the word bible is an acronym that stands for Biological Instruction Before Leaving Earth) to incorporating ancient Kemetic (Egyptian) rituals into daily practices to extraterrestrial visitors (most call them angels.) Yisrael said, "They can see me, that's a start. We make Xerox copies. I live to teach."

Islam, Hebrewism, Hermetic philosophy, Freemasonry and conspiracy theories of every type are taught in the lessons of Nuwaupu. A general philosophy of Nuwaupu is to never stop learning. This Islamic saying, : Ye should learn from the cradle to the grave." Adopted by the Nuwaupian community and should be adopted by anyone calling themselves a "Believer." But as Yisrael asks, "What is belief? Belief is not knowing. When your child comes inside in the summer and you ask him, 'Is the door closed?' is it sufficient for him to respond with 'I believe so?' You'd have to know the door was closed to be safe. The same should go for our understanding of God."

Moorish Orthodox Church of America

Founded in the early 1950's this group is somewhat new age. This sect approaches he study of Moorish science through an Eastern Christian theme. It is set up as an orthodox church calling itself the Diocese of New Jersey and combines Christian gnostism with Moorish Science. I believe this group was founded by whites who some how were exposed to Moorish literature. In the Baltimore/ Washington DC area, white poets and jazz musicians came into contact with the science temple and acquired nationality cards. They formed another offshoot of Moorish Science, the Moorish Orthodox church of America. At that early stage the church was seen as partly Moorish and partly eastern orthodox, and governed by a head bishop. Over time they abandoned the eastern orthodox part of the church and focused more in depth on the doctrine of sufism. As far as I know, this group is till in existence and remains true to the original teachings of the Moorish Science Temple.

The teachings of the Moorish Science doctrines are to universal to be just kept within one organization. What makes Moorish Science so universal is that it incorporates teachings of other religions and political doctrines.

All of these named groups are but mere shadows of the original Moorish Science Temple. After the death of the prophet, members of the original group decided to form their own subgroups with the exception of bringing with them the original teachings of the prophet. Yet incorporating additional information into an already complicated series of dogmas.

Needless to say, nothing could ever replace the original divine movement and this one original group became the mother of things to come. I have named only a few offshoot groups of the original movement, but there are countless others. There are too many to name and too complicated to discuss their beliefs. The teachings of the Moorish Americans spread through the black community like wild fire. Whether it is the Moorish science Temple, The Nation of Islam, The 5%, or any other Moorish related group, all of them have displayed bits and pieces of the teachings of Noble Drew Ali. When the prophet left this world he left an impact on African Americans in such a way that it lingers throughout the community impressing those individuals who yearn for a different way of understanding the world around them.

37. Father Allah Clarence 13x

38. Father Allah Clarence 13x

39. The Moorish Zionist Temple of the Moorish Jews

40. E Mealy El

John Givens El

41. John Givens EL

42. *WD Fard and Elijah Muhammad*

Most Noble Drew Ali Is Laid to Rest

Followers Mourn at Bier of Leader

Shrouded with the royal raiment of the "prophet" and encased in a $1,000 full-couch metallic casket, the body of Noble Drew Ali, late leader of the Moorish Science Temple of America, lay in state at Frank Edwards' undertaking parlor, 4135 Michigan Ave., from Monday until Friday.

During that period thousands of persons—members of the temples from other cities and citizens of Chicago—passed the bier to take a final look at the dead "prophet." Many of the Chicagoans were taking their first as well as their last look at Drew.

At 1 o'clock Friday the body was taken to the Pythian temple, 37th Pl. and State St., where funeral services were held. The services, which included singing, the burial ritual of the cult, resolutions and an oration, lasted one hour. A solo was sung by Edna Mae Robinson, and other songs, led by the choir, were sung by the audience. The eastern burial ritual was led by Kirkman Bey. Whatever he was saying in connection with the ceremony was as foreign to the audience as Caesar is to a fourth grade pupil, at least in that part of the audience not affiliated with the cult. It was evident that he was lamenting the passing of the "prophet" and praying for blessing from Allah. [illegible] Kirkman circled the casket three times. He made three more trips around the casket, this time he was followed by 19 men, the grand sheiks of the branch temples.

"Prophet's" Work Done

The obituary was read by William Mealy and resolutions from temples in Philadelphia, Pittsburgh, Detroit, Richmond and other cities were read by representatives from those cities. Attorney Aaron Payne, assistant city protector, business manager for the Moorish Science temple, and said to be a candidate to succeed Noble Drew Ali, delivered the principal oration.

Lay members of the cult were not averse to talking about their dead leader, his work and his position or each, Allah is their god, Islam, their religion, and Drew Ali, their prophet. One elderly woman whispered to a friend, "The 'Prophet' was not ill! his work was done and he laid his head upon the lap of one of his followers and passed out."

In reference to a successor to Drew, another remarked, that the "prophet's" spirit will come back and enter the body of one of the governors. Others report that Drew Ali's dying act was so throw the mantle to Adept Aaron Payne, who, consequently, may become the "prophet."

Noble Drew Ali was set upon his last journey as the two-mile long funeral procession moved south on State St. en route to Burr Oak cemetery, where the interment was made. Drew died at his home, 3603 Indiana Ave., July 20, after an illness of three months. He came to Chicago from North Carolina. His real name was Timothy Drew. Drew could scarcely read and write.

DREW ALI LAID TO REST—Hundreds of Chicagoans attended the funeral last week of Noble Drew Ali, founder of the Moorish Temple, who died at his home after a long illness. Services were held from the Pythian temple and the "prophet" was buried at Burr Oak cemetery. Attorney Aaron Payne Ali (wearing white gloves at left) becomes the new head of the society.

Greene Heads Chicago Boosters Civic Club

Claude D. Greene, manager of Unity hall, 3446 Indiana Ave., was elected president of the Chicago Boosters at the recent annual election. Mr. Greene has been executive secretary of the club ever since it was organized in 1925 and is widely known here and in other cities for his civic, political and railroad excursion activities in the Booster's organization. He is a product of the St. Paul church school of Shreveport, La., his native home, and of the Tuskegee institute. His wife is Dr. Agnes Ateman

Claude Greene

Greene, daughter of Luke Ateman, who conducted the largest moving and express business in New Orleans in earlier years. Mr. Greene, a staunch supporter of Alderman Louis B. Anderson, holds that the alderman of the Second ward has, by his ability, intelligence and experience, demonstrated the highest type of representative, and that the Race needs able and purely representative men in public office if it is to be credited with being a factor in municipal affairs. Mr. Greene further holds that no apologies have ever had to be made for Alderman Anderson's ability and intelligence as a member of the city council of Chicago.

For a number of years Mr. Greene held responsible positions in several departments of the United States government.

Mr. Greene is business manager of the Moorish Science Temple of America and is a close personal friend of the distinguished Moorish leader, Prophet Noble Drew Ali.

CLAUDE GREENE SLAIN BY LODGE MEMBERS

(Continued from Page 1)

of the secret meeting Sunday and the reason for the appearance of Cumby Bey in the city. They found out, however, that another powerful member of the order. Lomax Bey, who is head of the Detroit temple, was also a marked man because he was allied with Greene to establish a rival organization.

Greene was formerly business manager for Timothy Drew, the prophet, and knew his innermost secrets. When the split came Greene notified Drew that he would have to hold his meetings elsewhere than Unity hall. Monday Drew moved his office equipment.

Greene was well-known throughout the city. He came to Chicago 20 years ago following his graduation from Tuskegee institute. He was an interior decorator by trade. For several years he was employed in the home of Julius Rosenwald, noted philanthropist, as a butler. He gave up this position to go into the real estate business. Four years ago he took over Unity hall on a lease from Daniel M. Jackson, committeeman of the Second ward, and has conducted it as a community center ever since. He was captain of the 59th precinct in the Second ward and took an active part in the recent Aldermanic campaign. Mr. Greene was also president of the Illinois Boosters club, which ran excursions to southern cities during the summer months. He is survived by his widow, Mrs. Agnes Greene, formerly of New Orleans, La., and two children, Dorothy and Ashton Greene.

The inquest was held Friday morning at the Bell Undertaking company, 3115 Indiana Ave. but continued to give police time to work on several valuable clews.

Cult Leader Lured Girls to His Harem

Government authorities have been called in to make an investigation into the activities of the Moorish Temple of America following disclosures made by policemen that young girls in the teen ages were being immorally used by the head of the cult.

Fourteen-year-old Mary Foreman, 3365 Indiana Ave., is now in custody of the juvenile authorities where she gave the information that Timothy Drew, who styles himself "Prophet Noble Drew Ali," is the father of her unborn child.

The Foreman girl named two other girls of tender age who were given over to the alleged prophet by their mothers after he had persuaded them that it was holy to have their daughters receive the affections of "Mohammed's representative here on earth." In the event that Drew has transported the girls out of the state he will be held on violating the Mann act. If the government fails to make a case the juvenile authorities have asked the state's attorneys office to place a charge of statutory rape against him.

Jail Drew, Nine Others

Drew is now in jail with nine of his followers pending the outcome of the inquest over Claude Greene, who died at the hands of assassins last Thursday night at Unity hall, 3446 Indiana Ave. So far Drew has failed to give the police any information regarding the shooting, but it is their belief that he knew of the plot to kill Greene. One of his ardent followers, George Johnson, who is known in the cult as "Johnson Bey," disappeared on the night of the slaying and was seen in Detroit, Mich., two days later. He has been identified as the man who accompanied Greene to the second floor of Unity hall, where the murder occurred. Johnson, according to a witness, ran out of Unity hall with a gun in his hand a few minutes after Greene was shot down.

Information came from Detroit that Johnson's appearance in the city was occasioned by the fact that Timothy Drew, the alleged prophet, had ousted Edward Lomax as head of that temple and the latter refused to abdicate his throne, but took the prophet's followers into a new camp under a new name. Johnson is thought to have come to Detroit to kill Lomax, who was allied with Greene in the formation of a new organization.

Mysterious Call

A long distance telephone call from Detroit to Unity hall two days after the slaying of Greene was investigated by police, and it was revealed that it was made from a drug store and a description given by a clerk of the man who made it tallied with that of Johnson. He inquired if Greene was dead and seemed pleased when given the news.

An examination of Drew's records revealed that he had collected $35,000 last year from his followers, who believed him to be a prophet. He can scarcely read and write. In addition to duping his followers with religious hokum, Drew sells medicine made by himself and alleges that it is blessed by the Prophet Mohammed. The ignorance of the crowd following him is appalling, the police probe brought out.

Chapter 11

Moorish Science's Connection with the Mysteries of Freemasonry

Freemasonry is a system of ethics and religion in which there are hidden truths about how one should conduct his life. In addition, it is composed of a variety of teachings that have been borrowed from other sources. Contained within its body are the mystical thoughts of the ancients. I must note that the ancients are the creators and the keepers of this wisdom, and masonry draws from it like the earth absorbs light from the sun. It is a system held and defended by many men; men of learning, of wealth, of social influence; men of strong and magnetic personality; men of kindly and liberal tendencies; men who have piety in their peculiar religious consciousness; men who have taste for the artistic, the beautiful, the sublime, men who in the eyes of the world see it as one beautiful and harmonious entity. It is only fitting that Noble Drew Ali would some how be exposed to the mysteries of freemasonry. However, general Moorish science teachings would not accept this theory. It seems the way Moorish science is structured, it is a design to justify Ali's teachings as being of his origination, when in fact they were borrowed from other sources. I must now try to explain why I feel that freemasonry some how found its way into Ali's teachings.

As I sat down and read through the pages of the various Moorish doctrines, I could not help but notice the presence of various masonic terms and masonic symbols. It is obvious that the prophet traveled through the mysteries of freemasonry. Whether or not prophet Noble Drew Ali was ever a mason is yet to be proven. However, it is self-explanatory when he writes the various doctrines of the Moorish science temple. My guess is some how the prophet received certain knowledge of an auxiliary branch of freemasonry known as the Ancient Arabic Order of Nobles of the Mystic Shrine. I would say that 80% of the symbols found in the Moorish science doctrines can be traced to wither the mysteries of freemasonry or the Shriners rituals. Perhaps, masonic symbols were a way for the prophet to express his ideas so his points could come across clearly to his members. In the mysteries of freemasonry, symbols are a way to present knowledge in a hidden form so the outside world could not view its meanings. Needless to say, Moorish science is a product of freemasonry, but Moorish science is not the only new age religion with masonic influences.

Joseph Smith, the founder of the Mormon church of Utah was a mason and he incorporated masonic teachings into the religion. If you have noticed any of the numerous portraits of Noble Drew Ali, his stance is a masonic stance with both of his feet forming an oblong square and his right hand is in the place of his heart. This symbolized fidelity and his allegiance to the American flag and country. In almost every known picture of the prophet there are some remnants of the mysteries of freemasonry, from the clothing that he wore to the position that he took in the picture. I find several references to the square in Moorish science literature including in the Moorish science journal of 1943 and also in the holy Koran Circle 7. The square is not just a masonic aspect but can be viewed as a universal symbol, and masonry like all other doctrines, borrowed from the universal symbols. Physically, the square as an emblem is geometrical and not mechanical in its origin; according to authorities, who trace it back to the ancient egyptians. They carried the cubit of justice in solemn processions, by which perpendiculars, right angles, and squares were laid, its form being that of one arm of a square, with the inner end cut to an angle of 45 degrees. The close analogy between justice and that which is perfectly upright is so obvious as to have become universal. The terms, "an upright man and a just man" are spoken of in nearly all languages. (Note, justice is one of the pillars of the Moorish science doctrines.) Hence the scriptural phrases: The way of the just is uprightness; Thou, most upright dost weigh the path of the just; He that walketh uprightly, and the admonition to walk uprightly before God and man.

Besides this, the square was used in Egypt to re-determine he boundaries of each man's possessions when, as frequently happened, the land marks were swept away by the inundation of the Nile River, thus recovering to every man his just rights. The Egyptian land measure itself was an aura or a square, containing one hundred cubits. The square represented the fourth part of a circle, has a direct allusion to division of the ecliptic and celestial equator into four equal parts. Indicative of the solstitial and equinoctial points, and the division of the year into four seasons.

"We use the square to measure all our lines to straighten out the crooked places of the way and make the corners of our conduct square." -- Moorish Science Voice, March 1943

All these are just some of the maternal views of the sacred tool. However, there is more to learn about the tool that we know as a square. First allow me to clarify something else about the square. It has been used symbolically for thousand of years in virtually all the ancient cultures whenever the building of large structures were taken place. If we focused on a particular group it would be the ancient Egyptians. perhaps, it is through the Egyptians that we find the practice of ancient masonry by just studying the science of the pyramids. Focusing on its beauty and its structure it is that of both a square and a triangle. It is obvious that the science of freemasonry can trace its roots to the land of Egypt. The pyramids and its structures are represented in all the symbols of freemasonry. In the study of geometry, we know for a fact that the triangle has three sides and three angles. Dr. C.M. Bey writes on the science of geometry pertaining to the Moors. He writes, "Geometry is the universal law of perfection, the science of the cultured Moors, which has, and always will be in the hands of the kinky-haired Moors of North America. Thus, the Moorish nation of North America referred to as negroes cannot be destroyed."

What Dr. Bey has discovered is the link between the science of the Moors and both the negroes and the Moorish Indians of America. This can be seen in the ancient pyramids of Central America. The strength of the negro slaves is what helped build this country through slave labor and hardships. In addition to the square, it further alludes to the number 3, which symbolizes the science. I will explain he manifestation of 1 under 3 forms. The triad presented in almost every religion, the elements that make up man; spirit, soul, and body. The three stages of life; youth, manhood, and old age. The triangle represents one in three individuals or the points that are combined together. The square represents the four directions. Now there is formed a cross, consisting of four 90 degree angles, which total 360 degrees. In ancient times 360 degrees represented 360 days a year. In pre-Islamic culture, there were 360 different idols of worship in Mecca. They were placed around a black cubed box called the Kaaba, a square shaped black box that is composed of 4 right angles, and during a typical pilgrimage to Mecca, they walked around a circle performing circumambulation around the Kaaba seven times. This is where the prophet created the symbol of the Circle 7. So we must be reminded that the square as an emblem is geometrical and not mechanical, and yet it has been used in mechanical structures.

The second aspect of the relationship between Moorish science and freemasonry is shrinedom. To the elevated mason, the Shriners were considered to be the playhouse of masonry. They are known throughout the world for their charity work and contributions to education. Just like the Moorish Americans, the Shriners wore lavish costumes displaying oriental and Arabic themes. Perhaps, this is where the prophet furthered contrived his wisdom of the east, and the knowledge of the mystic shrine did nothing but fuel his desires of the Arabic culture. To focus more n depth on the shrine literature, there are symbols that used in shrine masonry as well as Moorish science. For example, the symbols of the Moorish charter. Every Moorish science temple must have a charter in order to exist. Just as every masonic lodge is required to display a charter or warrant. The symbols of the Moorish charter display 10 different symbols that can be found in both masonry and the shrinedom. They are the crescent and moon, pyramids, lion and lamb. a camel, the fez, the sphinx, the grip, Islam, and the prophet Noble Drew Ali. With the exception of the prophet, all of these have some form of relationship with the symbols of freemasonry.

Author Iman Isa writes, "Noble Drew Ali accepted many customs and symbols from the masonic lodge, a secret pseudo-religious fraternity. Certain parts of Noble Drew Ali's uniform as well as the names El and Bey were taken from the masons. Noble Drew Ali also borrowed the Noble and other customs and symbols from the Shriners which is a secret fraternity that was designed for the Amorite in Mockery of Islam. This is one of the major attributes to the doctrines of Moorish Science. The various teachings of the Shriners. All this proves that Noble Drew Ali was a mason. In fact, a mason at an elevated level of learning. because Noble Drew Ali was a mason of such a high degree, it was only natural that the symbols of masonry were so heavily incorporated into his teachings."

43. Noble Drew Ali in Masonic stance

44. Two moors giving each other the Masonic Grip

45. Shiners Emblem

Chapter 12

Symbols of the Moorish Science Temple: Islamic and Universal Symbols and its Relation to the Moorish Doctrines

Every known recorded religious doctrine is in some form represented by a symbol of that belief. To the Christians, its primary symbol is the cross because it represents the teachings of Jesus, his trials, and his everlasting spirit. To the islamic faith, it is the crescent and moon.

In previous chapters, I have explored some of the symbols of the Moorish doctrine. However, there are additional symbols that need to be explored. To my knowledge, the Moorish science doctrine has three primary symbols which acknowledge its existence. The Circle 7, the handshake, and the crescent moon and star. All three symbols are placed together as a symbol of perfect unity. Again, I mention that the prophet Noble Drew Ali calls this uniting of Asia, and perhaps this three symbols represent this calling. In addition to the Moorish symbols there are other non-Moorish or Islamic symbols that were incorporated within its doctrine.

According to C. M. Bey, "You are what you know, now what do you believe? One never knows by being told or preached to. One will have to acquire applied knowledge by way of study, and prove that which they know by practical scientific demonstration minus mystery, mystic phrases, signs and mythology, and mystic passwordism, and secret clanism. Symbols are an object of expression. So it is only fitting that they are displayed in Moorish science."

Again, for the prophet, symbols were used as a learning tool to teach his followers. This chapter will focus on various different sets of symbols either incorporated or related to the Moorish science doctrines.

The Circle 7

This is a symbol that is deeply rooted in esoterism as well as mystical thought. The Circle 7 serve as a symbol of perfect unity. Its circle represents pure completeness and the seven represents the life of man in his environment. These two symbols combine to represent the ultimate union between man and nature. However, before I explore their combined creative powers, I must analyze them separately.

The circle represents the embodiment of God. His infinite wisdom strengthens man in all his trials and error. it is the harmony of His presence that allows us to exist. The world alone is controlled by God. Knowing this we shall be mindful of the mind of God; conscious of God's conscious; sensible of His sentiments, and our own existence will be in the infinite being of God. The circle represents the world is a whole, which has its harmony; for a God who is one, could make none but a complete and harmonious work.

Masonic author Albert Pike writes, "The harmony of the universe responds to the unity of God, as the indefinite quantity is the defective sign of the infinitude of God. To say that the universe is God, is to admit the world only and not acknowledge its creator."

Again the circle alone had several different meanings but more importantly it is deep rooted in the science of geometry ad I will continue from this point. The circle is the result of 4- 90 degree angles combined in unity. They represent the regenerative powers of man. It is the cycle of life that is mentioned in the Hindu doctrines. To the hindus, man is born, he lives, and then he dies only to repeat the cycle numerous times, in an endless circle.

The seven has a different interpretation. Originally, the circle 7, in its original form was borrowed from the masonic symbol; the point within circle. Somewhere down the line the prophet incorporated his own ideas thus creating the Circle 7. During his lifetime, the prophet taught his followers many different ideas on the meaning of symbolism. To interpret these symbols would only bring you closer to the key of learning Moorish science in the fullest. The prophet expresses his teachings of the circle 7 in numerous ways and perhaps each time he explained the symbol he brought new ideas to add on to the existing ideas.

Islamic scholar Iman Isa writes, "Noble Drew Ali taught his followers that seven is the number which centers around universal ideas, such as there are seven days in creation, seven days in a year, and seven days in a circle. He also gave his followers the surname, El, which stands for Elohim. Elohim is sometimes called the seven eyes of Allah. In hebrew, Elohim means Allah and his angels. The mystic number seven was held sacred by our ancient brethren for reasons which had a purely astronomical origin."

The reason for this will lead us to inquire into the origin of the division of time into days, weeks, months, and years. We were naturally induced to divide our time into periods called days, because the sun makes its apparent diurnal revolution in that time. All our divisions of time, whether of days, weeks, months, or years, have therefore an astronomical origin, and perhaps the prophet was a student of the number 7. This has an esoteric property.

Author Robert Hewitt Brown, in his book, Stellar Theology, writes, "It is, however, probable that, like the zodiacal and planetary sign, they were originally hieroglyphs. Now, as each seventh day, when the moon assumes a new phase, she has traversed just one quarter of her orbit, we might naturally expect that the hieroglyphic representing the word seven would, in harmony with the ancient method of writing be a right angle 90 degrees, or one-fourth part of a circle."

"The circle is the symbol of the perfect man, and seven is the number of the perfect man; the logos is the perfect word which creates, that which destroys, and that which saves. This hebrew master is the logos of the holy one, the circle of the human race, the seven of time, and in the record book the scribe wrote down, the logos circle-seven; and thus was Jesus known." --Aquarian Gospels, Chapter 48, verses 2-5.

"And when the divine God breathed forth, 10, seven spirits stood before the throne. These are the Elohim, creative spirits of the universe." --Aquarian Gospels, chapter 19, verse 19.

The Lion and the Lamb

The lamb is the poor people, the lion is the rulers and the rich, and through love, truth, peace, freedom, and justice all men are one and equal to seek their own destiny; and to worship under their own vine and fig tree. After the principles of the holy and divine laws of their forefathers. This excerpt was from the holy koran circle 7.

In Moorish science doctrine the lion and the lamb is mentioned in the holy koran circle 7 and it is also present as one of the symbols of the Moorish charter. The prophet borrowed this symbol from the teachings of the holy bible and we can find references of the lion and the lamb throughout both the old and new testaments. For example, the lion and the lamb represented both David and Solomon. Next, the Lord Jesus Christ was also represented as being the Lamb of God.

"And one of the elders saith unto me, weep not: behold, the lion of the tribe of Judah, the root of David, hath prevailed to open the book, and to loose the seven seals thereof.

"And I beheld, and, lo, in the midst of the throne and of the four beasts, and in the midst of the elders, stood a lamb as it had been slain." -- Revelation 5:5, 6

"Behold the Lamb of God, which taketh away the sin of the world." John 1:29

We must remember that in ancient times the lamb was often sacrificed as a symbol of worship in the book of Genesis. Abraham sacrificed a lamb instead of sacrificing his son Isaac, and there are several other stories that are mentioned in the bible referencing the lamb. Scholars state that John wrote the book of Revelation before his gospel and epistles. it is not likely that anyone had a question as to which the slain lamb was, but with John's gospel record of John the Baptist speaking, as Jesus came toward him, all discussion certainly would have been settled. And perhaps the most beautiful of all religious concepts takes on a deeper meaning; the lion is also a lamb. Think about that. We long for the time when the lion and the lamb shall lie down together. truthfully, until the fullness of the lion and the lamb are reproduced in a final generation, until a balance is developed in us of all that is strong and noble, meek and lowly, Jesus cannot come, for the world has yet to have that witness manifested.

"Judah is a lion's whelp; from the prey, my son, thou art gone up; he stooped down, he couched as a lion, and as an old lion; who shall rouse him up? The scepter shall not depart from Judah, nor a lawgiver from between his feet, until Shiloh come; and unto him shall the gathering of the people be." Genesis, 49:9, 10.

Characteristics of the Lion

Let us take a look at some of the characteristics of our lion in scripture. Whether as the young lion ready to pounce or the old lion lying in his regal nobility, who shall rouse him? He holds the scepter; the kingship, the royalty, the nature of rule is unmistakable.

"We are supposed to be children of a King, brethren of a King, espoused to a King. It is stated in different ways throughout the bible. As such, we are to exemplify the highest traits of nobility and the welfare of a king would bestow upon his children, his family, and his bride. As a people, have we not been given the finest counsels and opportunities in regard to doctrine, health, clothing, education and service in the King's world? Unless we are living up to the privileges and responsibilities of all the counsel of God, we cannot possibly be fit representatives to complete His work on earth; a lion roars, and everything around pays attention. I heard a lion roar at a zoo once. I not only felt it in my stomach but amazingly enough, it seemed to reverberate right through my feet and into the ground. It was an awesome experience indeed. And mind you, the lion was lying down. He was not angry. He was not shouting. He just had something to say, and you definitely paid attention. So it was with Jesus. People were enthralled with His teachings, because they could see and perceive that He truly meant what He said. There was no equivocation in His voice. He knew what He believed, why He believed it, and how He needed to get His points across to the people. Oh, to have that perfect balance of authority in our own witnessing, that the world around us should know that we KNOW what we believe and why we believe it. It is God's quest for our lives. The world will know, when God has a balanced, authoritative people." Unknown author.

Characteristics of the Lamb

"How dependent is the lamb? How dependent was Jesus upon His father? How dependent should we be in all things heard, believed, taught and lived? Without that dependence, failure is at the door. Without that dependence, self rises up; self tries to rule, and self corrupts the soul. The innocent lamb of God. Not guilty of any wrong, nothing in Him or corruption, nothing in Him of sinful practice and perpetuation, tempted in all points like as we are yet without sin.

Make no mistake, sheep are not robots. They must eat where the Good Shepard leads them, drink at the waters He provides, rest where He stops, and follow His voice wherever it leads. They have their part to do, and without it, they will die. Our dependence upon God's power does not lessen the use of it in our lives. A gift is a gift. But a gift on a back shelf, or in a closet, is of no benefit to anyone. Though salvation by grace through faith is a gift from God, let no one deceive themselves that so prized a gift is to collect dust. It is anything but an ornament or knick-knack. Depending on His Father certainly did not lessen Jesus' use of that connection. He is an example in all things.

Sheep are not necessarily busy. They lead fairly quiet lives. Like all illustrations using earthly things, it has its limitations. O the other hand, it is very possible to become so busy that all hearing of the Shepard's voice gets lost in the shuffles of life. Dependency on God is replace by dependency on an employer, a paycheck, insurance companies, government, husbands, wives, preachers and leaders. The chain is only as strong as the weakest link. Everyone agrees, yet so much improper dependency exists in the church is keeps us in this world. We are not living it until complete dependency and cooperation with God becomes a daily habit." Author unknown.

The Handshake

The symbol of the handshake represents unity. This is another symbol borrowed from the mysteries of freemasonry. The prophet often said that where there is unity, there is strength. In freemasonry, the handshake represents the strength of man and this is further represented by the strong grip of an lion, which can be referenced in the bible. To my knowledge, this symbol is found in two places within the Moorish science temple. The first place is on the nationality card and the second is the Moorish charter.

The Sphinx

Focusing on the mysteries of Egypt, I can only approach this subject with a curiosity and enthusiasm about trying to solve the abundance of mysteries surrounding it. It is obvious that the prophet had this vision when the explored the ruins of the pyramids. Though I have visited the country of Egypt, I can feel its mystical presence in the abundance of literature that has been written on this sacred land of ancient wisdom. Egypt is located in Africa, which in the past has been referred to as the dark continent, a place of savagery. All this is the least description of what really is. Its beauty is its hidden knowledge. This section explores the mystery of the sphinx. In Moorish science, the sphinx is one of the symbols of the Moorish charter. The prophet incorporated this symbol and perhaps through his visits to the large monument he unlocked its mysteries and embraced its wisdom. This he proclaimed himself an adept of Egyptian wisdom. In the mysteries, the sphinx, a human-headed lion, symbolizes strength and intelligence. The monument is usually displayed in pairs at the entrance of temples or palaces. The rising and setting of the sun was guarded by these deities. The greatest of these is the Great Egyptian Sphinx, Gezeh. Notice the position of the body of the sphinx. The feet and claws point downward for esoteric reasons. This represents the setting of the moon of the old faith, at the moment of the rising of the sun the faith in brotherhood of all mankind. The essential unity of humanity is of one blood, the children of our fatherhood. The great Egyptian sphinx is the watcher of the desert because of its massive size. The next excerpt is taken from the Moorish voice of february 1943.

Written by brother G. Cook Bey it states, "No one knows just how old the sphinx is, nor why is was created. It is an enormous figure and appears like a crouching rock. It is as high as a five- story house and so large that is would cover the ordinary city lot. Its body is one hundred and forty feet long and its fore-logo measures fifty feet. The head of the sphinx is so large that it would fill an ordinary school-room. A man standing on the tip of his own feet could not reach to the crown of its head. The bars are each four feet long and the nose measures more than five and one half feet, while the mouth is so large that if it were open, an ox or a camel could be put inside it. The face of the sphinx is now somewhat mutilated, for it has been damaged by the Arab soldiers and has born away the sands of the desert. As you climb upon the great body, you wish you could whisper in its ear and ask it to tell you the riddle of its existence and something about the strange people who moulded it out of rock. All about the sphinx and throughout the desert near Cairo, are the remains of ancient monuments of great ancient Egypt, the pyramids and the sphinx."

The sphinx is taken from an ancient Egyptian divinity, personifying wisdom and the fertility of nature. The sphinx, a being with the body of a lion and the head of a woman, the wings of a bird, and a serpent's tail represents the solar deity, Ra, and was originally placed in paris at the entrances of the temples and palaces, not for ornamental purposes only, but mainly for an acknowledgement of a deity.

The sphinx is composed of four creatures; lion, bull, man and fowl. This confirms the four beasts in Revelation 4:7 came from Egyptian supreme being. This is where they copied their concept of the four horsemen of the apocalypse in the new testament, and Daniel 7:4-6 of the old testament. According to Revelation, the face of a man represents humanity, the eagle represents the fowl of the earth, the calf represents the wild beast, and the lion represents the tribe of Judah.

The Egyptians called the sphinx Hu or Neb (Lord). Its present name is derived from the greek sphinx, "the binder." The great sphinx of Egypt is a representation of the sphinx hewn from solid rock, with a body of 172 feet in length rising about 66 feet above the surface. The structure, being near the pyramids of Gezeh, is thought to have been built around the same time, about 2700 B.C. In Greek mythology, there is knowledge of a sphinx who had her seat near the city of Thebes, commanding a pass that the

Thebians were compelled to traverse. There the sphinx gave a riddle to all travellers and tore to pieces those who failed to solve it. And is stated that the sphinx could not be destroyed if her riddle was not solved. The riddle: What creature goes in the morning on four legs, at noon on two and in the evening on three? This interpretation is easy. The creature is a human being. In childhood he crawls on hands and knees, when he grows into manhood he stands upright on two feet, and in old age he brings a staff to his assistance, and thus balances on three legs. This represents the three stages of a man's life; youth, manhood, and old age. This is the true meaning of the legendary sphinx the prophet Noble Drew Ali incorporated this symbol into Moorish doctrines as an explanation to the riddle of life.

The Pyramid

In addition to the sphinx, we also focus on another of Egypt's most prized mysteries, the pyramid. To my knowledge, the primary purpose of the pyramids were to house treasures and the tombs of the great pharaohs of ancient times, and they served as both a house of eternal rest and a mystery school for the neophyte. In the Moorish science doctrine, the pyramid is recognized as one of the symbols of the Moorish charter. These great pyramids were built over a period of time dating back as far as 5000 B.C. Such old and ancient monuments, and yet they have withstood the sands of time. It is obvious that the pyramids contain many mysteries that have yet to be solved. So perhaps through strict examination, I can unlock some of there secrets. The pyramid is shaped in a triangular position. At the base are four corners and each connected corner forms a square or angle of ninety degrees. The four angles give us the circumference of a circle, 360 degrees. This alone speaks to the in depth knowledge of geometry that the great builders of the pyramid must have had. This is known as squaring the circle.

In his book, Freemasonry Ancient Egyptian, author Mustafa El-Amin writes, "we find that the great pyramid is located in the exact center of the earths surface. Researchers tell us that a close study of the pyramids reveals such information as the distance of the earth from the sun, the weight of the earth, and that its weight per square yard is related to the weight of water, as is the average weight of the earth to the same substance. The pyramids display a great wealth of knowledge and science that appears to be beyond modern man's comprehension. It not only reflects the keen understanding and appreciation that the great builder had for the physical material environment, but it also reveals their vast knowledge of the human sciences. Further investigation and discussion will show that the ancient wise men of Egypt were greatly concerned with the mental and spiritual progression of man towards enlightenment. They understood the correlation between the macrocosm and the microcosm. History tells us that in ancient Egypt there existed various mystery systems that were designed to introduce and educate its elects into the higher knowledge of human sciences, immortality of the soul, and the monotheistic concept of the the creator."

W. Deen Muhammad writes, "Nothing grows out of space down from air. Everything grows out of the ground upwards. Our ancient fathers had this knowledge of the natural world and their sign was the pyramid. This kind of knowledge was known to the people of ancient Egypt. Ancient Egypt built great pyramids and they knew the psychological nature and composition of man."

Mustafa El-Amin writes, "The ancient Egyptians built the pyramids for several reasons. The pyramids embody the concepts and ideas of the wise. Some say they were used to instruct and initiate those who were found worthy to received the higher knowledge. Others say that only certain men were taken through the pyramids where they experienced certain things which were symbolic of man's growth and development."

Crescent Moon and Star

This symbol represents the very foundation of Islam and is displayed in every muslim country and every muslim organization. In the Moorish science doctrines, this symbol is displayed in all Moorish doctrines so its presence strengthens the Islamic faith in all Moorish Americans. The crescent moon and star are representations of the celestial heavens. Together they remind us of the beauty of the night sky, another of God's creation. In the religion of Islam, the crescent moon represents the deity, Allah. Originally this is no the Allah of today's Islamic faith. The crescent moon represents the ancient moon goddess Allah of the Quarish tribe. The symbol represents the ancient moon goddess of the Arabians, and it was later manifest into a male principle in which all muslims worship today.

The crescent moon is symbol of infinite hope at night. it gives us a light of direction to our destination, not to mention that it represent the beauty of the sky. The star, on the other hand, has a totally different meaning. Imagine looking out your window at night and observing the sky with its many constellations. Each star is connected to form an individual of mythology, whether it be of greek or roman origin. The studying of the heavens did not begin with either the greeks or the romans. It actually was the prodigy of the known earlier cultures of the Egyptians and in some cases, the Mesopotamians. The Egyptians were counting the stars long before there was even a greek civilization.

There are three examples of how stars are formed into constellations. I will focus more in depth of ursa minor, which takes you into the ancient zodiac studies of the Moors of mapping the constellations and tracking the stars, which they learned from the Egyptians.

Ursa minor: The constellation having the shape of a ladle, with polaris at the tip of its handle, also called little bear, from latin. Minor means, lessor, and usa, means, bear. Ladle is a long handled spoon with a deep bowl for stirring liquid.

Polaris: A star of the second magnitude. At the end of the handle of the little dipper and almost at the north celestial pole. It is also called the North Star, the Polar Star, the Polestar, latin Stellar, for po-laris (star). Old latin polus meaning, pole.

North Star: In a previous chapter, I stated that Columbus studied the maps of the Moorish seafaring navigators. From this was the prodigy of those Moors who studied the stars and the heavens. Perhaps from the study of astronomy, the Moors were able to create maps to navigate about the seas. The stars were used as a guide, but most notably, the north star. This star was used by the Moors for navigation to sail back and forth from Africa to America, originally called the land of the frogs because of its various swamp regions. The Moors of Timbuktu were known to be the greatest seafarers and taught the vikings how to build ships and sail the seas.

The Religion of the Moon God

This section is designed to give more detail of the true origins of crescent moon and star. Have you ever wondered why this crescent moon and star is a symbol of Islam? Why do muslims put a crescent moon on top of their mosques and minarets? Why do flags of Islamic nations bear the crescent moon? The worshiping of the moon goes back into antiquity. Throughout the fertile crescent from Egypt to Turkey, archeologists have dug up hundreds of little idols with a crescent moon sitting on their head. In ancient pagan temples, there are walls with pictures of a God sitting on a throne with a crescent moon over his head, and at times there are several stars placed near the moon to symbolize the daughters of the moon god. Obviously, there is a connection between the ancient pagan religion of the worship of the god and Islam. Before prophet Muhammad was born, the Arabs worshiped 360 pagan gods housed in the Kabah in Mecca. One of the pagan gods they worshiped was the moon god who was married to the sun goddess. The stars were their children.

The Rituals of the Moon

People worshiped the moon god by bowing in prayer toward mecca several times a day. The made pilgrimages to mecca and ran around a pagan stone temple called the Kaaba seven times; slit the throat of a sheep; and threw stones at the devil. They gave alms to the poor in honor of the moon god. They fasted during the month, which began with the appearance of the crescent moon in the sky, and closed when the crescent moon reappeared. They put the symbol of the crescent moon on the walls of their homes and on their clothing. This moon religion was the pagan religion in which Muhammad was reared. We must remember that Muhammad's tribe worshiped the moon god. So the ancient religious ritual of the moon are what muslims are still practicing today. Somehow these rituals were manifested into Islamic practices still used today.

The Camel

This symbol is represented on the Moorish charter. The camel is used to travel the across the desert hot sands because of its ability to store large quantities of water within the two humps on its back. Camels are very durable animals when it comes to traveling for long periods of time. Just imagine what life was like in ancient Arabia and Africa. Even today, the history books gives precise details of the use of the camel; a beast of burden.

The Black Stone

A meteorite was said to have fallen from the sky. The Arabians took this stone and began worshiping it. H.Z. Plummer writes, "The black stone is really a number of fragments, twelve to be exact, united by dark cement and held together by a silver band. The whole is oval and about seven inches in diameter. What these stones or fragments are made of, no one seems ever to have established. Tradition asserts that the original stone came from paradise and was handed by the angel Gabriel to Abraham and Ishmael when they were building the Kaaba. In the beginning, the stone was white. its present color is the outcome of having been kissed by the millions who annually make the pilgrimage to mecca. In ancient times, the stone was whole until a great war caused damage to the structure.

The structure was rebuilt and has been worshiped ever since. The stone is further housed on the northeast corner of the Kaaba. Since the black stone is worshiped by all muslims, it is acknowledged by all Moorish Americans."

Mustafa El-Amin writes, "According to the history of Abraham and the black stone in mecca, it is reported that the black stone was originally a light in the heaven. Some reported that when it fell to the earth it turned black, as it was burned while entering the earth's atmosphere. The falling of this light from the sky served as a sign to Abraham as to where to build the Kaaba, the first house erected by a man for the glory of Allah. There was a connection or union made between the heavenly object and the earth."

These are the primary symbols of the Moorish Science Temple of America. Like any organization these symbols are the visual pictures behind the hidden lessons of the Moorish science doctrines. Symbols have great psychological significance because without them there would be no possibility for the mind to exist, function, and interact with the environment. A deeper examination of symbols reveals that they are more than just a representation of images and ideas. The human mind understands things first by making a mental picture of it, and then associating that mental concept with other ideas and thoughts. Symbols like the circle 7, the pyramid, and the sphinx are all tools of knowledge to any moor who understands them. These symbols and others like them are vital keys to understanding the workings of the mind and the spirit.

*59. The Circle 7 Theory seven is the number which centers around universal
ideas it is a symbol of the totality of the universe (3the sky + 4the earth)
it expresses the creation within which man evolves. The circle represents
perfection which further represents the almighty god may it be most merciful.*

47. Moorish Symbols

48. The Great Sphinx

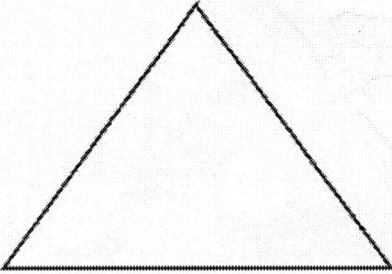

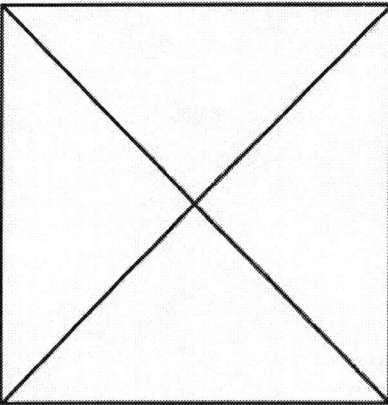

There are 3 visible
Points on a Pyramid with
its Triangular shape and
4 Sides each side
contributing 90° degrees
90° x 4 = 360
A circle is 360 degrees
Or 4 90 degree Angles

3 + 4 = 7

Moorish Science mathematics
7 + 360 degrees =

⑦

50. *Pyramid 4 sides there are 3 visible points on a pyramid with
it's triangular shape and 4 sides each side contributing 90 degrees
90x 4 = 360 a circle is 360 degree or four 90 degree angles 3 + 4 =
7 Moorish science mathematics 7 + 360 degrees = a circle 7.*

155

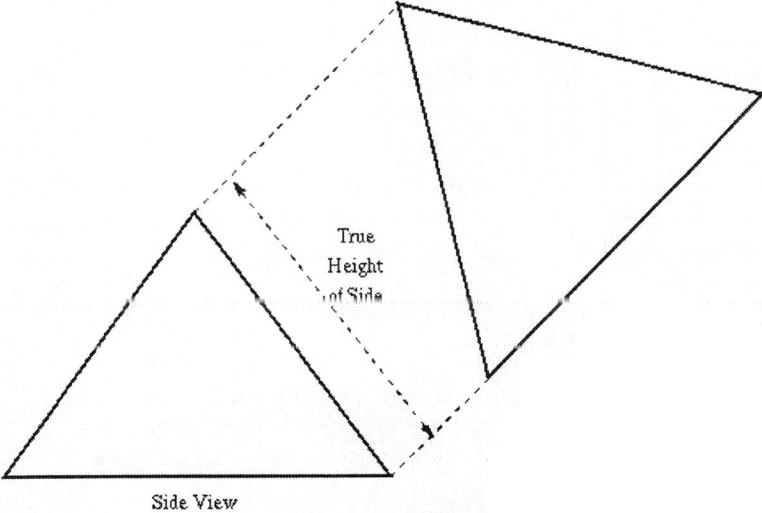

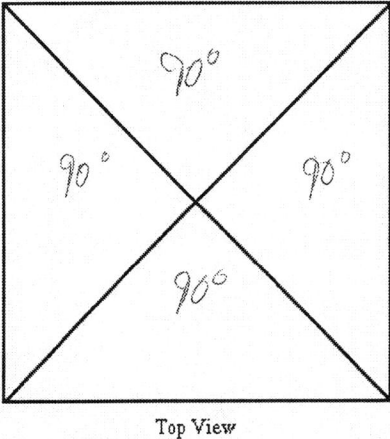

51. *Situations of the pyramid notice the two pyramids. Combine them together and you have the Star of David this is where the Hebrews adopted their symbol from. The pyramid it self is a symbol of perfection fours 90 degree squares equals 360 degrees.*

The Great Pyramid of Egypt with the Mystical Constellations (view from the East).

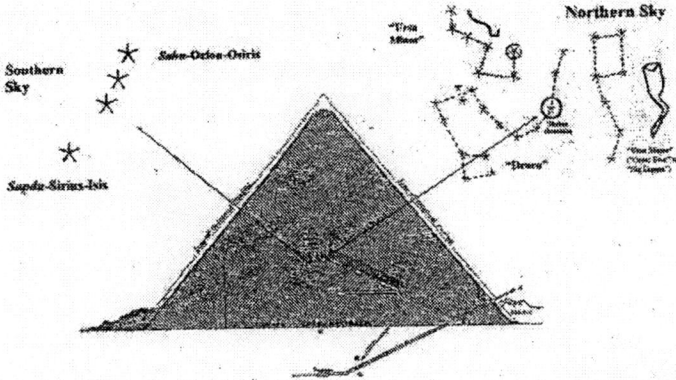

53. The Great Pyramid sky constellations. Source
The African Origins by Muata Ashby

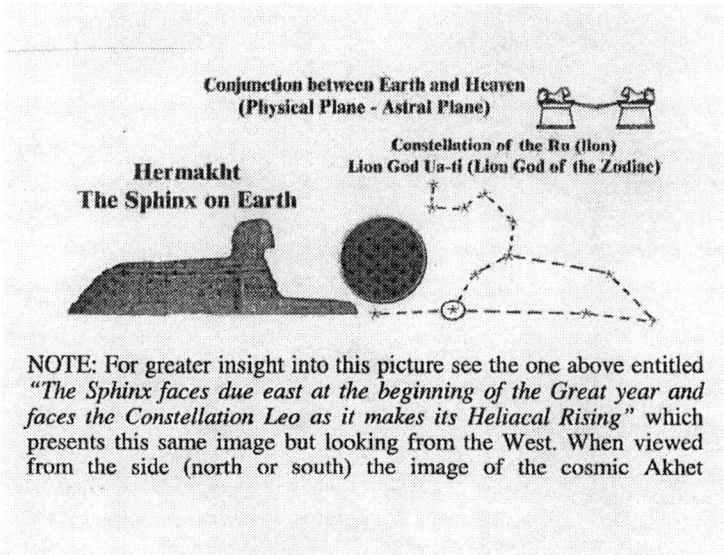

NOTE: For greater insight into this picture see the one above entitled *"The Sphinx faces due east at the beginning of the Great year and faces the Constellation Leo as it makes its Heliacal Rising"* which presents this same image but looking from the West. When viewed from the side (north or south) the image of the cosmic Akhet

54. Sphinx continue

Constellation Rw Ua-ti:
The Lion of the Zodiac
in conjunction with Ra, the Sun at the beginning
of the Great Year produces Her-m-akht
"Heru manifesting in the horizon."

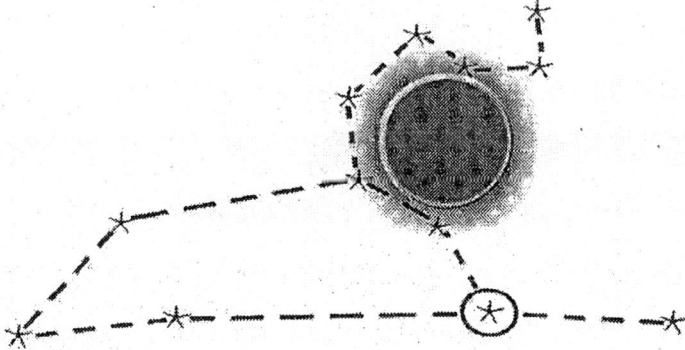

52. Constellation of the Lion Zodiac. Source The
African Origins by Muata Ashby

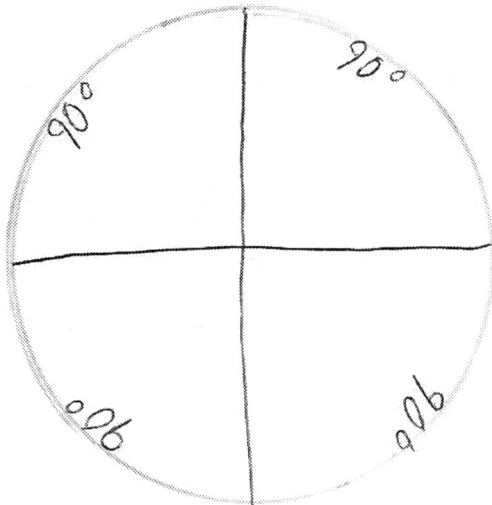

55. Circle of Perfection equals 90 x 4 = 360 which is a circle

Constellation Rw Ua-ti:
The Lion of the Zodiac
in conjunction with Ra, the Sun at the beginning
of the Great Year produces Her-m-akht
"Heru manifesting in the horizon."

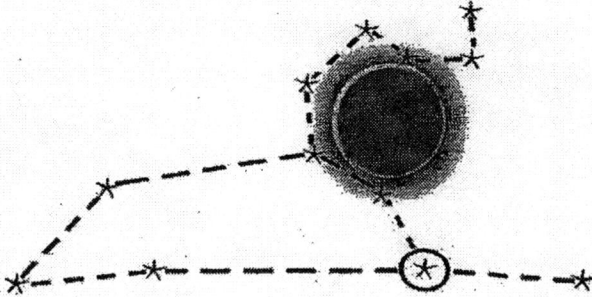

The Great Year is a system of time reckoning based on the precession of the equinoxes. Precession is the slow revolution of the Earth's axis of rotation (wobbling) about the poles of the ecliptic. It is caused by lunar and solar perturbations acting on the Earth's equatorial bulge and causes a westward motion of the stars that takes 25,800 years to complete. At the beginning of the Great Year, around 10,800-10,500 B.C.E. the constellation Leo rose up in the sky along the line of the ecliptic just as the sun dawned at the same time, marking the beginning of the current great year cycle which lasts 25,800 years.

The sphinx on earth as a counterpart to the sphinx in the heavens.

The sphinx on earth as a counterpart to the sphinx in the heavens (Astral Plane), i.e. the horizon of the earth plane and the horizon of the astral plane. In this view, the sphinx on earth and the sphinx in heaven complement each other and form two halves of the akher-akhet symbol but turned facing each other, looking at the sun which is between them, i.e. turning away from the earth plane and towards the transcendental spirit.

49. Sphinx

56. Pyramid Diagram

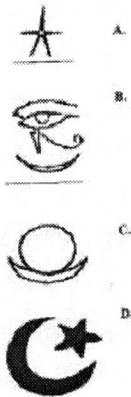

From top to bottom:
The Egyptian symbol of
A. The star, always five
pointed, B. The eye of
Thoth (Tehuti) and
Horus representing a
star and the moon
(united opposites,
completeness, Supreme
Being), C. Sun and
Moon (same as
previous). D. Symbol of
Islam.

57. The Original foundation of Islam. A. The star is a symbol of man and his relation to the heavens B. The eye represents Allah watching over are actions. C. the sun and moon further represents the pagan moon god/goddess Allah the beginning of the foundation of Islam D. the ultimate symbol of unity between god and man. Existed long before it was adopted by the Islamic faith.

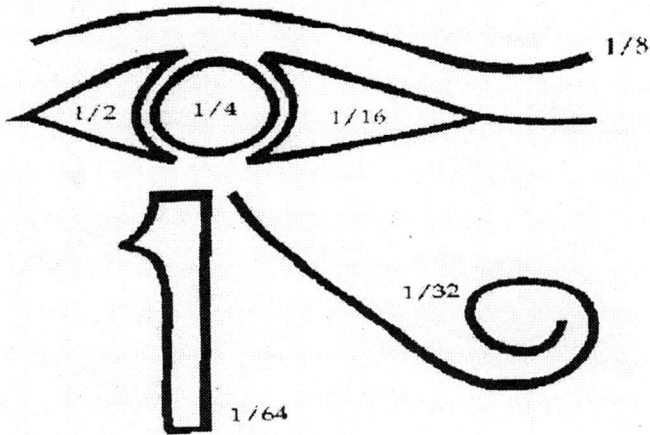

$$= \triangleleft + \bigcirc \dotplus \sim + \triangleright + \backsim + \text{\char"0031}$$

$$= \tfrac{1}{2} + \tfrac{1}{4} + \tfrac{1}{8} + \tfrac{1}{16} + \tfrac{1}{32} + \tfrac{1}{64}$$

58. Eye of Horus sometime called the udjat eye according to mythology Horus's eye had been torn out Seth but was put back together by Thoth. According to legend Horus transformed himself into a sphinx to guard over Egypt from the wrath of Seth. the pieces of this eye are used for the following fractions in Egyptian mathematics. This is the same eye that is represented on top of the pyramid.

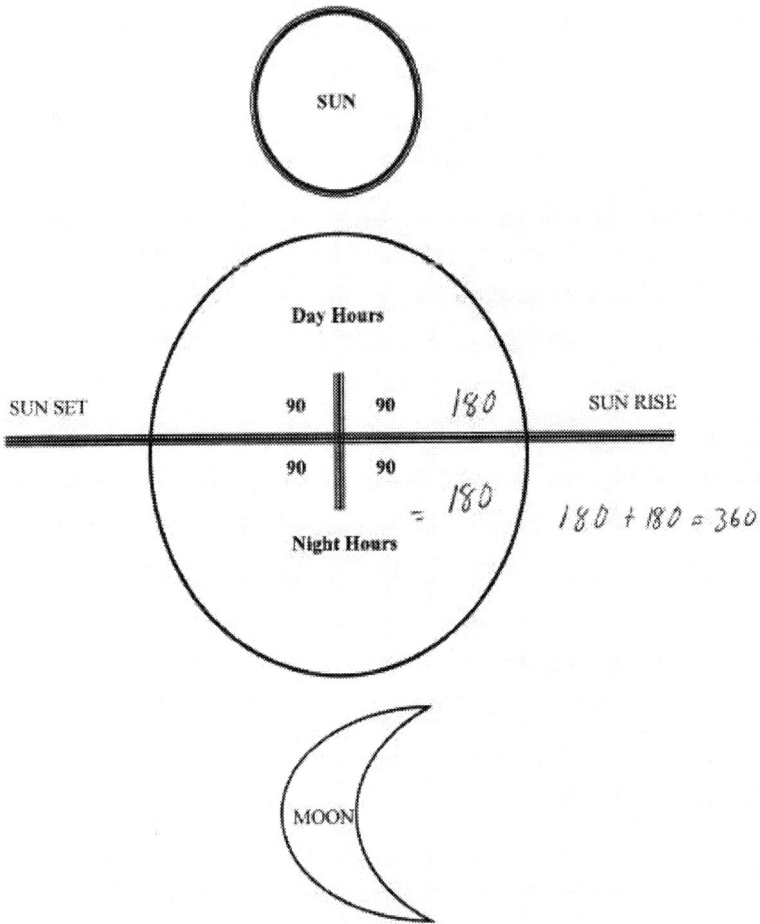

SUN

Day Hours

SUN SET   90   90   *180*   SUN RISE

90   90

= 180   *180 + 180 = 360*

Night Hours

MOON

60. *The Division of Time division of 24 hours in a day 8*8*8=24 originally there were 360 days in a year instead of 365 days. Remember the biblical prophet Enoch was 365 years old when god took him. 24hr * 15 = 360*

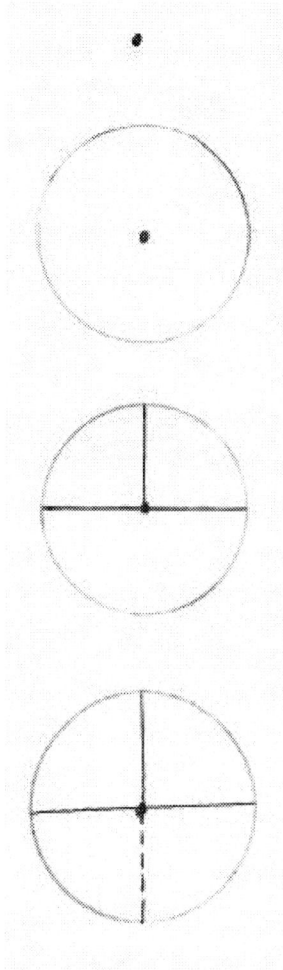

61. The Circle of Four The central point or one is the symbol of god as the absolute unmanifest. He taking the first step towards manifestation affirms his consciousness of his own being. This is depicted by placing of a circle around the point it is that which Jacob boehme calls the mirror or motherness in which god beholds his own glory thereby passing from the absolute unmanifest and becoming the supreme procreative being. Within the symbol of this duality the point within the circle then appears the creative trinity. The father begats the son, and from them proceeds the Holy Ghost. And in order that balance may complete itself, the triune creator must then be depicted in association with his creation. So arises the four within the circle and this glyph becomes the token of the archetypal idea of manifestation held in the everlasting circle of the manifestor and in the point source of the all. It is the sign of the first four seats of the round table in the making.

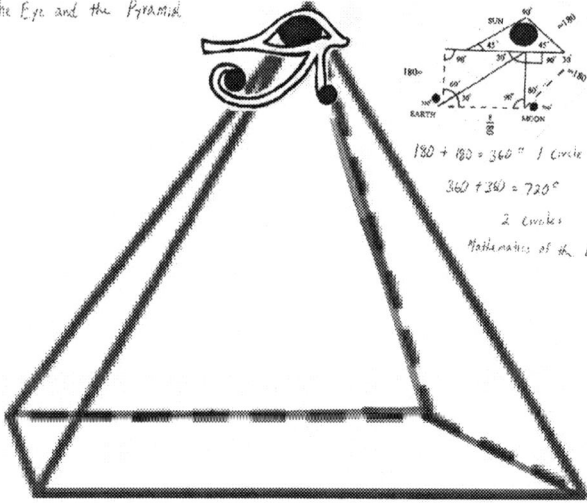

The Eye and the Pyramid

180 + 180 = 360° 1 circle

360 + 360 = 720°

2 circles

Mathematics of the e

62. *The Eye and the Pyramid 180 + 180 =360 I circle*
360+360 =720 2 circles the mathematics of the eye

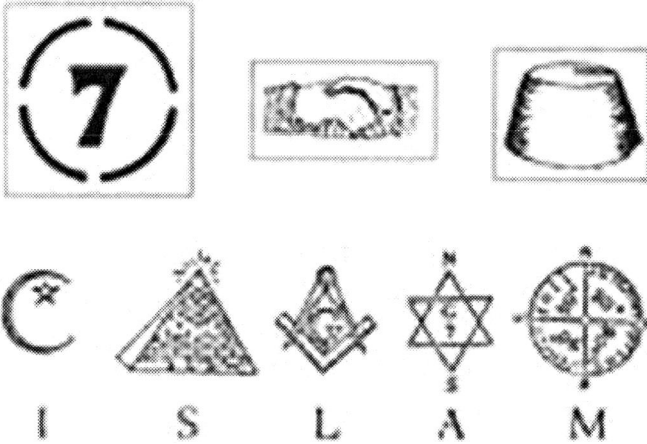

I   S   L   A   M

63. *Moorish science symbols. Here are more Moorish Science symbols.*
Noble Drew Ali, founder of The Moorish Science Temple, also wrote
the "Circle 7 Koran." The 7 in the circle symbolizes the seven angels,
or Eiohim, and appeared in that book. Eiohim is one of god's names
in the Jewish Torah and also means god in Hebrew. These Moorish
Science symbols indicate a strong connection to freemasonrv.

Chapter 13

Conclusion: Moorish Science Enlightenment

Dr. Muata Ashby, in his book, The African Origins, writes "The purpose of religion is to bring a human being closer to the Divine, which accomplishes the goal of leading. The practitioner comes closer to the Divine is a form of religious movement. Religion is an organized process of accomplishing that goal. Every human being has an innate desire to discover the ultimate, the infinite, the transcendental and immortal aspect of life. This is called mysticism. Therefore, authentic religion consists of three levels: myth, ritual and mystical experience. if the first two levels are misunderstood or accepted literally, the spiritual movement will fail to proceed to the higher level. In order for a religious experience to lead one to have a mystical experience all three levels of religion must be completed. Therefore, religion and its purpose must be well understood in order that the purpose be fulfilled."

There are various levels of religious understanding, each being a bridge to higher learning. In Moorish science, I would say that it is composed of two of the three levels; ritual and mystical experience. It is ritual because Noble Drew Ali defined his teachings as a science to be studied by all Asiatics in order to learn of their heritage. It is a mystical experience because once you have embraced its teachings, the person takes on an enlightened conscious. By embracing this science, man has been given certain powers or an inner strength and knowledge. Throughout this book, I have attempted to explore the various topics of the Moorish Science temple of America. Now I hope the reader has gained an understanding of the Moorish American doctrines. Its entire history and doctrines are designed to teach the arrival of new ideas and new philosophies. Noble

Drew Ali was a man, who out of the clear blue sky, decided to preach a doctrine that was designed to uplift blacks whom he referred to as Asiatics. he used a series of teachings that he prepared for anyone yearning for a different set of ideas.

In retrospect, the identity of the prophets' religion has been obvious for 90 years. To have named his movement, the Moorish science Temple of America, it clearly is linked to all the studies of new age thought. Studies such as Gnostic, Islam, far east religions, and finally the mysteries of freemasonry. Combine this with the nationalist and political views of the prophet, and there are a series of lessons aimed at, not only the mind, but more importantly, the soul. The soul which is that part of man which is that part of God connected from this material world of matter to a spirit realm inhabited by the great god Allah. It is this connection that brings us closer to ourselves and it establishes us to have an intimate relationship with Allah. In the Holy Koran Circle 7, the prophet writes, "Man will be fully saved, redeemed, perfected by the things he suffers on the plane of the flesh, and on the plane of soul. When man has conquered carnal things his garb of flesh will then have served its purpose well and it will fall, will be no more, then he will stand untrammeled on the plane of soul where he must fully complete his victories. Unnumbered foes will stand before man upon the plane of his soul; there he must overcome, yea, overcome them everyone. Thus hope will ever be his beacon light; there is no failure for the human soul, for Allah, for Allah is leading on and victory is sure. Man cannot die; the spirit man is one with Allah and while Allah lives man cannot die."

The prophet continues by saying, "Man has conquered every foe upon the plane of soul, the seed will have full opened out, will have unfolded in the holy breath. The garb of soul will then have served its purpose well, and man will, attain unto the blessedness of perfectness and at one with Allah."

The Moorish science Temple is deeply rooted in spirituality and esoteric learning. It is obvious the prophet was in tune with his creator, his ideas, and his visions. All are displayed as he walked this world of darkness and hatred. Teaching all members of his movement to be themselves and learn to love instead of hate. The very foundation of Moorish Science lies in the words and sayings of Noble Drew Ali. I think the best description of the prophets works is the liberation of Asiatics worldwide. He could not just limit this movement to blacks in America. it had to expand in large proportions.

I reflect on the work of Dr. Na'im Akbar. Dr Akbar, in his book, Light from Ancient Africa, writes, "We, as people of African descent living in

America, must struggle to thrive in a world that works quite differently from the Africa which gave us birth. Africans, like other peoples around the world, live and work within a defined philosophical context and operate according to certain rules and principles. Their perspectives on time, space, God, man and nature were and are very different from European perspectives. This explains why most African scholars approach the study of African civilization without utilizing any form of European and eurocentric thought."

There is a major conflict in what should be perceived as intellectual thought in general. In most written books, every major subject is viewed from a European thought, even the study of African civilization. As people of color, regardless of what shade of color, we must learn to embrace, not just the history of our own individual race, but the history of humanity itself. We should never live in a world where every race is somehow judged by other races of men. Religion tells us that we come from the same creator, and science tells us that we came from the same earth. In my dreams, I imagine a world with no hatred or separation of the races. We are different races because of the climate that our ancestors were from, and yet as members of the human race, we all have the same blood color. It is up to the future generations to determine whether we can rid ourselves of racism. It was my choice to discuss this issue because it shows some aspects of this research book. Throughout this book, I have attempted to explore every aspect of this science. I have explored its origins and examined its literature. I can only approach it with admiration. I will conclude this book with a review of the chapters.

Chapter 1: An exploration of the various Asiatics of diverse backgrounds. I divided this chapter into four sections. Section 1 explores the history and the origins of the black Dravidians and traces their origins to the ancient nubians of Africa. It covers the establishment of Dravidian cultures ranging from their great kingdoms to the foundations of religion. Hinduism was founded on Dravidian literary works namely the rig vedas. Then it explores the true origins of racism, which lie in the Aryan culture and how the Aryans took control of the black Dravidians and introduced the Hindu caste system. It also compares the Hindu god Lord Krishna to the Lord Jesus Christ and describes their similarities. Noble Drew Ali acknowledges Jesus and one of the divine prophets in his Moorish doctrines. Section 2 explores the origins of the Moorish science adept chamber and the cultural relations between India and Egypt. The knowledge of an adept was created in the Egyptian mystery religion. There is a theory that Drew Ali received his knowledge of the adept from two places. The first is the Shriners order where he was said to have received the degree of

Egyptian adept and next in Egypt where he was said to have received his knowledge from an Egyptian priest. Section 3 explores the life and racial background of the Buddha. The Buddha was a black Dravidian who received his knowledge from the Hindu religion. He began preaching his doctrines to a select few. Now the religion has a following of 300 million people worldwide. In Moorish science the Buddha is acknowledged as one of the divine prophets. I must also note that in the Aquarian Gospels, Jesus was said to have studied the Buddha's teachings during the missing eighteen years of the bible.

"One of the world's most prolific philosophical and religious leaders was the great sage called the Buddha. At different stages of his development he was referred to as Prince Siddartha. The Buddha's origin is traced back to India, yet his philosophical doctrines spread throughout Southeast Asia, Tibet, China and Japan. India had an indigenous black population which found its way into the subcontinent about 50,000 years ago from Ethiopia, ultimately establishing a great empire known as the Indus Valley civilization. There were two Ethiopias, one to the east of the Red Sea, and the other to the west of it, and a very great nation of blacks from India, did rule over almost all Asia in a very remote area. In fact, beyond the reach of history or any of our records." -- An unknown author.

Author Godfrey Higgins, in his book, Anaclypsis writes, "In 1500 B.C. this great empire was invaded by a tribe of barbarians from the north of India igniting a series of wars upon the Indian subcontinent which lasted nearly a thousand years. The conclusion of these classic battles ushered in India's first historical golden age, the age in which the Buddha was born, 563 B.C. Through cultural and racial assimilation the face of India and the face of Buddha began to change. Yet the Buddha in his most original appearance with flattened nose, powerful lips, and the curling hair in locks, can still be found."

Section 4 covers the rise of Islam beginning with the origins of prophet Muhammad and his revelations. Next it covers the true racial background of the prophet; that he was of dark color. Throughout the chapter, it explores the various other founding fathers of the religion, Abu bakr, Ali, and Bilal Ibn rabah. All of these men possess negro blood in their veins. Next it explores the history of pre-Islamic Arabia prior to the establishment of Islam. It traces the origins of Arabians to the biblical patriarch Abraham and his son Ishmael. All can be traced to the negro establishments in ancient Egypt, Nubia-Ethiopia and Yemen.

Chapter II explores the history of the Native American Moor. These indigenous people were originally Asiatics travelling extensively along a narrow strait body of land, settled in America only to establish vast civilizations which compared to the Egyptian civilizations of old. These indigenous people existed for thousands of years only to be invaded by the European exploration. Prior to coming to America, the indigenous people traded with early muslim sailors and perhaps inter-married, establishing a small number of muslims in America. Next African slavery was brought along with muslim beliefs with the combination of Europeans, African slaves, and sailors from the European exploration. These were the various ethnic groups of North and South America. All of whom Noble Drew Ali acknowledges as muslims.

Chapter III covers the rise of Islam among blacks in America and its masonic origins. It traces the theory that the founders of the black muslim movements were exposed to the knowledge of Islam from the Shriners order. It has been acknowledged that Noble Drew Ali was in fact a mason and various other founding members of the black muslim movements were exposed to his teachings. Next in chronological order it describes the arrival of Islam in America through the various stages from the arrival of muslim sailors to the black muslim movements of the 1920's.

Additional chapters introduce the reader to Moorish science history from its beginnings to its collapse in 1929. They explore its teachings, its doctrines and the origin of these teachings. More importantly, it explores the hidden side of Ali's teachings, digging deeper into the esoteric teachings of various religious and fraternal societies. Yet Ali continued to remind the followers of his religion of the glorious history of the Moors of North africa. Reading from a section of Moorish science literature, it states, "The Moors, or Mohammedans, added to the beauty and grandeur of Spain. For centuries art, science, literature and chivalry flourished among them while the rest of Europe was still sunk in the gloom of the dark ages. The Moors were the most ingenious and industrious of the subjects of Spain. Their expulsion from Spain in 1610 was one of the chief causes of decadence of that country. For both agriculture and industry fell into decay after their departure.

Throughout the remaining chapters, I selected various facts the prophet Noble Drew Ali used in his writings. I define them as landmarks of Moorish science teachings. They are: 1. The inhabitants of Africa are descendants of the ancient Canaanites from the land of Canaan. 2. Old man Cush and his family were the first inhabitants of Africa who came from the land of Canaan. 3. The dominion of Cush was Northeast and Southeast Africa while Northwest and Southwest Africa was his father's domain. In later years, many of their brethren from Asia and the holy lands joined them. 4. The Moabites form the land of Moab, who received permission from the pharaohs of Egypt to settle and inhabit Northwest Africa, were the founders and are the true possessors of the present day Moroccan empire, with their Canaanite, Hittite, and Amorite brethren, who sojourned from the land of Canaan seeking new homes. Their dominion and inhabitation extended from Northeast and Southwest Africa, across the great Atlantic even unto the present North, South and Central America, also much of Mexico and the Atlantic islands, before the great earthquake, which caused the great Atlantic Ocean. 5. The Niger River was deluged by the great pharaoh of Egypt. In those ancient days for trade with surrounding kingdoms. Also, the Niger River was deluged by the great pharaohs of Egypt in those ancient days for trade, and it extends eastward from the River Nile, westward across the great Atlantic. It was used for trade and transportation. According to all true and divine records of the human race there is no negro, black or colored race attached to the human family because all inhabitants of Africa are of the human race; descendants of the ancient Canaanite nation from the holy land of Canaan. What your ancient forefathers were, you are today without a doubt of contradiction. 6. There is no one who is able to change man from the descendant nature of his forefathers, unless his power extends beyond the great universal creator, Allah himself. These holy and divine laws are from the prophet Noble Drew Ali, the father of the uniting of the Moorish holy temple of science in North America. The laws are to be strictly preserved by the members of all the temples of the Moorish holy temple of science. That they will learn to open their meeting and guide it according to the principles of love, truth, peace, freedom and justice. 7. I, the prophet Noble Drew Ali, was sent by the great god, Allah, to warn all Asiatics of America to repent from their sinful ways before the great awful day which is sure to come. The time has come that every nation must worship under his own vine and fig tree, and every tongue must confess his own. Through sin and disobedience, every nation has suffered slavery due to the fact that they honored not the creed and principles of their forefathers. 8. That is why the nationality of the Moors was taken away from them in 1774 A.D. and the words negro, black and colored were given to Asiatics of America, who were of Moorish descent because they honored not the principles of their mother and father and strayed after the gods of Europe whom they knew nothing of.

These are what I would define as the 8 basic facts of Moorish science doctrines. They are a combination of biblical and historical facts brought together to discover the true historical origins of the Moors of North Africa and Spain. It was these facts that Noble Drew Ali used to re-establish the Moorish lineage to the blacks in America, and it was this establishment that was used to ask all black people in America to unite and reclaim your nationality, know the history of your forefathers, and become one with yourselves and your father god Allah, so that you may learn to love instead of hate. All this plays a vital role in the creation of this science. From its masonic origins to its Islamic influences, Moorish science gives it practitioner a series of philosophical ideas and hope for the future. Islam.

Table of Illustrations

1. Sultan Abdul Aziz Ibu Suad a descendant of Hagar and ruler of the holy city of Mecca. Source holy Koran circle 7
2. The Sultan of Zanzibar this is the man that Booker T Washington spoke of in his book up from slavery this man because of his nationality was granted special treatment Source
3. Moorish Map explains the connection between the united states and morocco
4. Moorish Nationality Card in English and Spanish
5. Civilization spreads throughout Asia explains the birth place of civilization was in Africa Source The African Origins by muata Ashby
6. The African family tree of cultural interaction Egypt is located in the North Eastern corner of the African continent. Source The African Origins by Muata Ashby
7. The Travels of Osiris in Ancient Times. Source The African Origins by Muata Ashby
8. Negroid Buddha and the Black Lord Krishna according to Hindu doctrines Krishna was known as the blackener.
9. The Eyes of Horus, Krishna and Buddha. Source The African Origins by Muata Ashby
10. Amunhotep and Buddha Source The African Origins by muata Ashby
11. Negroid Buddha
12. Genealogy of Prophet Muhammad Tribe the Koreysh this traces the African blood line of the prophet. Source African presence in early Asia by Ivan van sertima
13. King Mansa Kan Kan Musa African king who converted to Islam and perform the pilgrimage to Mecca in such fashion that it became legendary
14. Bilal the first muezzin or caller of prayer in Islam and a close friend of Muhammad
15. Allegorical Picture of the prophet Muhammad face is covered to hide his identity
16. Burial Shrine of Prophet Muhammad.
17. William J Florence and Dr Walter M Fleming founders of European shrinedom
18. John G Jones founder of Prince hall Negro shrinedom. Source history of the prince hall grand of Illinois from 1867 to 1983

51. Situations of the pyramid notice the two pyramids. Combine them together and you have the Star of David this is where the Hebrews adopted their symbol from. The pyramid it self is a symbol of perfection fours 90 degree squares equals 360 degrees.
52. Constellation of the Lion Zodiac. Source The African Origins by Muata Ashby
53. The Great Pyramid sky constellations. Source The African Origins by Muata Ashby
54. Sphinx continue
55. Circle of Perfection equals 90 x 4 = 360 which is a circle
56. Pyramid Diagram
57. The Original foundation of Islam. A. The star is a symbol of man and his relation to the heavens B. The eye represents Allah watching over are actions. C. the sun and moon further represents the pagan moon god/goddess Allah the beginning of the foundation of Islam D. the ultimate symbol of unity between god and man. Existed long before it was adopted by the Islamic faith.
58. Eye of Horus sometime called the udjat eye according to mythology Horus's eye had been torn out Seth but was put back together by Thoth. According to legend Horus transformed himself into a sphinx to guard over Egypt from the wrath of Seth. the pieces of this eye are used for the following fractions in Egyptian mathematics. This is the same eye that is represented on top of the pyramid.
59. The Circle 7 Theory seven is the number which centers around universal ideas it is a symbol of the totality of the universe (3the sky + 4the earth) it expresses the creation within which man evolves. The circle represents perfection which further represents the almighty god may it be most merciful.
60. The Division of Time division of 24 hours in a day 8*8*8=24 originally there were 360 days in a year instead of 365 days. Remember the biblical prophet Enoch was 365 years old when god took him. 24hr * 15 = 360
61. The Circle of Four The central point or one is the symbol of god as the absolute unmanifest. He taking the first step towards manifestation affirms his consciousness of his own being. This is depicted by placing of a circle around the point it is that which Jacob boehme calls the mirror or motherness in which god beholds his own glory thereby passing from the absolute unmanifest and becoming the supreme procreative being. Within the symbol of this duality the point within the circle then appears the creative

trinity. The father begats the son, and from them proceeds the Holy Ghost. And in order that balance may complete itself, the triune creator must then be depicted in association with his creation. So arises the four within the circle and this glyph becomes the token of the archetypal idea of manifestation held in the everlasting circle of the manifestor and in the point source of the all. It is the sign of the first four seats of the round table in the making.

62. The Eye and the Pyramid 180 + 180 =360 I circle 360+360 =720 2 circles the mathematics of the eye

63. Moorish science symbols. Here are more Moorish Science symbols. Noble Drew Ali, founder of The Moorish Science Temple, also wrote the "Circle 7 Koran." The 7 in the circle symbolizes the seven angels, or Eiohim, and appeared in that book. Eiohim is one of god's names in the Jewish Torah and also means god in Hebrew. These Moorish Science symbols indicate a strong connection to freemasonry.

Chicago Defender Newspaper Articles

Moorish Leader on Tour Chicago Defender Nov 24, 1928

Mrs. Drew Ali organizes young Moorish people Chicago Defender Dec 1, 1928

Moorish Head make plan for conclave Chicago Defender July 14, 1928

Hold Session of Moorish science body Chicago Defender Oct 20, 1928

Claude Green shot to Death in unity hall Chicago Defender Mar 23, 1929

Cult leader lured girls to his harem Chicago Defender Mar 23, 1929

Most Noble Drew Ali is laid to rest Chicago Defender Aug 3, 1929

Moors to celebrate Birthday of founder Chicago Defender January 8, 1928

Green heads Chicago Boosters Civic Club Defender 1925

Works Cited

Ashby Muata, The African Origins Books I, II, III Sema Institute of Yoga 1st Edition, Published 1995, Miami, Florida

Ashby Muata, Egyptian Yoga The Philosophy of Enlightenment Vol. 1 Sixth Edition Sema Institute of Yoga 1997, Miami, Florida

Brown, Robert Hewitt, Stellar Theology and Masonic Astronomy Published 1982, D Appleton and Co. New York

Churchward, Albert, Signs and Symbols of the Primordial Man A and B Publishers Group Brooklyn, New York 1993

Dixon, Lamont, The Geometrical Man Masonic Literature, 1986

El Amin, Mustafa, Freemasonry Ancient Egypt and the Islamic Destiny New Mind Production, 1988 Jersey City, NJ

Pimienta-Bey, Jose, Othello's Children in the New World 1st Books Library, 2002

Al Mahdi, Isa Al Haadi, Who Was Noble Drew Ali Copyright 1980

Shaikh Daoud vs. W.D. Fard Holy Tabernacle Ministries Eaton, Georgia 1981

York, Malachi Z., Let's Set the Record Straight All Eyes on Egypt, Eaton, Georgia, 2000

Latif, Sultan Abdul Latif, When Nations Gather Nadia's House of Publishing Chicago, IL

Bey, C.M., Clock of Destiny Copyright 1947

Pike, Albert, Morals and Dogma Scottish Rite, 1871

Articles

Black Gods of the Inner City, Prince A Cuba Fall 1992 / Gnosis Magazine, Pages 56-63

Moorish Peace Treaty of 1787 and 1836Ancient Kushite Empire of India Posted June 15, 2002

Ancient Kushite Empire of India Posted June 15, 2002

Mysteries of the Moorish Science Temple: Southern Black and American Alternative Spirituality in 1920Õs Chicago, Susan Nance, Religion and American Culture Journal, Volume 12, No. 2, pages 123-166.

Respectability and Representation: The Moorish Science Temple, Morocco, and Black Public Culture in 1920Õs Chicago, Susan Nance, American Quarterly, Vol. 54, No. 4 December 2002.

Light from Ancient Africa, NaÕim Akbar

Scripture, Text and other Moorish Literature

Holy Koran Circle 7, Noble Drew Ali

Koran Questions for Moorish Children, Noble Drew Ali

Shrinedom, Bishop H.Z. Plummer, Masonic Literature

The Holy Bible

The Holy Quran

Bhagarad-Gita as it is

Extra Sources

William H. Hardy, The Story of Prince Hall Masonry in Illinois from 1852-1992.

Expressions of Masonic Philosophy and Symbolism, unpublished manuscript by Keith Moore, 32nd degree.

Suns of God: Krishna, Buddha, and Christ unveiled by Achanya S. W Summer Davis foreword.

History of the shrine, ancient Egyptian Arabic order of the nobles of the mystic shrine.

Christopher Columbus and the African Holocaust: Slavery and the rise of European capitalism by John Henrik Clarke

Magazines and Articles

Magazine: The Black Scholar the Nation of Islam 1930-1996 vol. 26, No. 3-4 Religious and nationalist tradition the continuous evolution of the nation of Islam by Ernest Allen Jr.

Pagan Origins of the Christ Myth by John G. Jackson Published in 1941

Was Jesus Christ a Negro? by John G. Jackson Published in 1933

Nobles of the Mystic Shrine of Ali by Faison 19x moamin

The Masons and the Moors by Mehmet Sabeheddin

About the Author

Keith L Moore was born in 1973, and raised in the city of Chicago, Illinois. He received his B.S. in Education in 1999 from DePaul University, Il and his M.A. in Inner City Studies Education from Northeastern Illinois University in 2005. Currently he is working towards a second masters degree majoring in Education at the National College of Education. Since 1992, Mr. Moore's primary research interest has been the study of freemasonry and it's connection to what he defines as the African Moorish science experience. This exposure gave rise to formation of eastern religions and cultures among blacks in the western hemisphere namely North America. In 1994 he was initiated, passed, and raised to the degree of Master Mason and in 1999 to the 32nd degree of Freemasonry. Mr. Moore has always had a fascination with what he defines as the various studies into the esoteric sides of religions .Mr. Moore is a educator, researcher and member of several Masonic and afro centric research societies. Currently Mr. Moore is conducting research on the negro shriners order and their influences on the Islamic faith among blacks in America.

CPSIA information can be obtained at www.ICGtesting.com
Printed in the USA
BVOW071429231211

279054BV00003B/43/A